THE COMPLETE GUIDE TO

LIVING WILLS

THE SOCIETY FOR THE RIGHT TO DIE

THE COMPLETE GUIDE TO
LIVING WILLS

How to Safeguard Your Treatment Choices

Evan R. Collins, Jr.
with
Doron Weber

DEVELOPED BY THE PHILIP LIEF GROUP, INC.

BANTAM BOOKS
NEW YORK · TORONTO · LONDON · SYDNEY · AUCKLAND

*To Karen Ann Quinlan and
Nancy Cruzan*

The Complete Guide to Living Wills
A Bantam Book / November 1991

All rights reserved.
Copyright © 1991 by The Philip Lief Group, Inc.
& Society for the Right to Die.
Cover art copyright © 1991 by One Plus One Studio.

Developed by The Philip Lief Group, Inc.
6 West 20th Street
New York, N.Y. 10011

Library of Congress Cataloging-in-Publication Data:
Collins, Evan R.
*The complete guide to living wills : how to safeguard your
treatment choices / by Evan R. Collins, Jr. with Doron Weber :
developed by The Philip Lief Group, Inc.*
p.   cm.
ISBN 0-553-35435-3
*1. Right to die—Law and legislation—United States—Popular
works.   I. Philip Lief Group.   II. Title.*
KF3827.E87W4 1991
344.73'04197—dc20
[347.3044197]   91-25850   CIP

Published simultaneously in the United States and Canada

Printed in the United States of America

0 9 8 7 6 5 4 3 2 1

Acknowledgments

This book is dedicated to Karen Quinlan and Nancy Cruzan. The families of these two women, together with the countless other families who have fought to allow the deaths of people they love, have been the guardians of all our rights. We thank them for their courage and strength. Second, I thank the current directors of the Society for the Right to Die and those of our sister group Concern for Dying, for their tireless efforts in standing up for what is right. Thanks are also due to the Society's staff, in particular Fenella Rouse, our executive director, for their professionalism and commitment. Doron Weber has played an especially valuable role in the writing of this book. Alice Mehling introduced me to this issue and the organization. I owe her a great deal. Finally, my thanks to my family, particularly my wife Daisy, who provides me with both patience and understanding and has never complained when my commitment to this cause takes its toll in fewer hours at home.

—EVAN R. COLLINS, JR.

Many people contributed to this book. I would like to begin by acknowledging Fenella Rouse, executive director of the Society, who gave me the opportunity to work on this book and gave the book, in several drafts, a thorough and highly informed reading. Her wide knowledge of the field and sensitivity to its various constituencies has, I hope, worked its way into the text.

M. Rose Gasner, the Society's director of legal services, distinguished attorney and leading advocate for individual rights, helped with the manuscript at every stage along the way and discussed and debated many important legal issues with me. Her insight, wit, and humor made the entire process more enjoyable. Dr. Judith Ahronheim, outstanding geriatrician at Mt. Sinai Medical Center, gave generously of her time and supplied considerable medical expertise and guidance. As physician-consultant to the Society, Dr. Ahronheim worked with us on several projects and helped us to better understand the doctor's point of view in the patients' rights debate.

Dr. Charles Culver, professor of psychiatry and medical ethics at Dartmouth Medical School, shed light on many areas and shared his special perspective with me. In addition to his professional accomplishments, too numerous to mention here, Dr. Culver is distinguished for intellectual rigor that is allied to a persistently humanist point of view. He helped us in many ways.

Others experts who were consulted and who were helpful include Professor George Annas, Dr. Jeffrey Buckner, Professor Alexander Capron, Dr. Molly Cooke, Dr. Ronald Cranford, Carol Farkas, Marc Haddad, Dr. Joanne Lynn, Reverend Don McKinney, Dr. Diane Meier, Professor Mike Mulvihill, David Orentlicher, Dr. Conrad Rosenberg, Dr. O. J. Sahler, Marilynne Seguin, Dr. Peter Singer, and Professor William Winslade.

I am personally grateful to Joe and Joyce Cruzan for the time I spent with them.

I would also like to acknowledge Alice Mehling, former executive director of the Society, who devoted many years of passionate and productive service to the cause of patients' rights.

At the Society, William Prip, a gifted and promising paralegal, read the manuscript closely and questioned me on many important points. His strong analytic ability and direct, personal engagement with the issue stimulated many productive conversations. I am also grateful to Nicole Rousmaniere for her assistance in typing and preparing the manuscript.

My thanks also to Philip Lief, Lee Ann Chearneyi, Jack Maguire, Connie Jones, Candace Levy, and Rhea Braunstein for all their help.

At Bantam Books, Toni Burbank provided skillful editing and a sure, practiced hand throughout.

Finally I would like to salute my mother, Helga, who was out ahead on this issue, my father, Robert, and my sister, Anat. And always, of course, Shealagh, my wife and first, best reader, and Damon, my son.

—DORON WEBER

Contents

Introduction

At midday on June 25, 1990, the telephones began to ring at the Society for the Right to Die. At first the callers were predominantly press, looking for comments and interpretations of the Supreme Court's decision in the *Nancy Cruzan* case. Soon the calls from people concerned about protecting their rights began, thousands of them in the next six weeks, each spurred to ask for a living will or durable power of attorney so that he or she would not be maintained as Ms. Cruzan was, without hope of recovery, without any conscious awareness, but kept like that because not enough evidence of her own wishes could at that time be produced. Nothing in the Society's fifty-two-year history had equalled the demand provoked by the publicity the case received.

Missouri, the state in which Nancy Cruzan resided, has a demanding rule of law that asks for precise information to show that the incompetent person previously made his or her own wishes about not wanting life support known. The person's family is not able to choose for the patient by voicing their views of what the patient would want. Nancy Cruzan's parents were eventually able to find enough people who had spoken directly with their daughter for the Missouri court to be satisfied. Tube feeding was withdrawn and Nancy Cruzan died on December 26, after nearly eight years of unconscious existence.

Between June when the Supreme Court ruled and December when Ms. Cruzan died, the Society for the Right to Die and its sister organization, Concern for Dying, distributed more than 1 million advance directives to Americans concerned with protecting their rights. Such a degree of national awareness marked a major achievement since 1967, when the concept of a "living will" was first developed and when the Society and Concern began advocating for its acceptance in the legislatures and the courts of every state. Still, no one knows the exact number of completed advance directives. Estimates range but indicate that between 10 and 20 percent of adult Americans now have these documents. State law varies and some precision in thought and execution is required. The decisions being made are important, important for those of us who choose to use advance directives and for our families, friends, and those who provide us with medical care. Beginning December 1, 1991, federal law requires that each one of us, on entry to the medical system, be asked whether we have an advance directive. This book is designed to give you the information you need to make the kind of choices that will confront each one of us. Individual choice varies widely. We hope that we have given you help in thinking about these issues and the means to make your own wishes known.

—FENELLA ROUSE

PART ONE
Everything You Need to Know

CHAPTER ONE
Why Write a Living Will?

Would you please send me the Draft of Living Will Documents for the State of Iowa. I am seventy-two years old and I have not been well for quite some time. I want to die with dignity. I do not want to live on any life support of any kind. I do not want my children to see me suffer. I could not take that at all. Thank you.

—MRS. K. A. G.
Davenport, Iowa

I am thirty-four and not morbid at all but my brother-in-law's accident made me realize it could happen to me or any of my friends. Please send me a living will right away.

—MR. H. M.
Santa Barbara, Calif.

I would like to inform you that my mother filed her Right to Die document with her doctor and the hospital and, as it turned out, it became the deciding factor in the decision not to use life support equipment.

My mother passed away just as she wished, without any prolonged pain. Keep up your important work.

—MR. T. S. Z.
Libertyville, Ill.

What's the point of drawing up a property will if my entire estate goes to pay for my dying?

—MRS. T. B.
New York, N.Y.

I'm glad to find that you exist! I struggled with the M.D.'s and won when my mother was near death but I struggled alone and it was the hardest emotional struggle of my life. One should not have to fight with doctors at a time when one's spirit is so grieved. I worry about going through that struggle again with another parent or if my husband became terminally ill. There is such need for your work. Thank you for all that you do.

—DR. G. B. T.
Nashville, Tenn.

These excerpts are a small sampling of the many thousands of letters the Society for the Right to Die receives from individuals all over the country. People from every walk of life who are struggling daily to retain their dignity and their right of self-determination before a medical technology that has created dilemmas unprecedented in human history. People like this woman from Pleasant Hill, Tennessee, who wrote us:

LIFE is more than breathing by artificial means. LIFE is being able to think and feel and serve in some way, however small. When LIFE is gone there is no need to try to prolong living. DON'T INTERFERE WITH MY DYING!

If you have picked up this book, you have already shown two distinctive qualities: curiosity and the courage to learn more about a difficult subject many people find frightening or intimidating.

Yet this book is not about *dying* but about *living*—and how you can plan for it and integrate dying into your life's plans.

This book is about people, like you and me, and how we can take appropriate measures now to safeguard our bodies and our minds, and those of our loved ones, against a future when life-threatening illness or injury strikes and renders us mute.

It is about empowering the individual—you the reader—so that your instructions about your own health care will be followed even when you can no longer speak for yourself. You will learn about your rights and how to protect them.

It is about families and community—how each of us can best care for our loved ones and honor their wishes or relieve them of unnecessary burdens.

It is about the personal legacy, the image of ourselves, we wish to leave behind.

> The timing of death, once a matter of fate, is now
> a matter of human choice.
>
> —JUSTICE BRENNAN

As Americans we are keenly aware of our individual right to live in freedom, provided we do not interfere with the rights of others. But what about the right to die in freedom? How much do we think or care about this right? How many of us even know what this right entails? Or whether our status as Americans grants it to us?

Many of us think of dying—if we think of it at all—as an awful fate that lies totally outside our control. We tend to treat it as a subject to be avoided until the last possible moment. At that point, we are very likely to be in a hospital, where the precise manner of our dying can be determined by advanced medical technology. Technology has given us phenomenal new capabilities to fight illness and injury—many of its advances are truly miraculous—but when it becomes an end in itself, rather than a means to improve or save the lives of patients, it poses new problems. Patients today can be kept "alive" longer than ever before, even when their minds are gone and their bodies have stopped functioning naturally. This means someone must take the responsibility of deciding when exactly death will come—not now, but twenty-four hours from now? Some element of control, of human choice, now frequently determines when and how we die.

Eighty percent of U.S. deaths today occur in hospitals and long-term care institutions, and 70 percent of these deaths (about 1.4 million annually) are "negotiated" or somehow "timed." Nearly every death involves a decision whether to undertake, or not to undertake, some medical procedure that could prolong the process of dying.

But just how long should our dying be prolonged if there is no hope for recovery? The decision is often based on last-minute discussions among the patient, the patient's family, and the doctor about what forms of life support to use or not use. American medicine tends to treat patients aggressively— some claim we overtreat—as a matter of principle, as if it would be a personal defeat for us to let death come. These decisions, moreover, are often determined by institutional policies and state laws relating to life-sustaining measures that apply to every patient, regardless of his or her personal values and preferences.

In such a complex and highly charged emotional climate, choices are hard. If you become incompetent before discussions take place and if you have left no legal, written instructions on how you want to die (true at this moment for at least 80 percent of the U.S. population), then, ultimately, you may have no say in the manner of your death. Furthermore, the wishes of your loved ones, *even if they reflect wishes you yourself have stated repeatedly,* may not prevail. Even when health care providers are fully sympathetic, there may be honest disagreements.

Should an eighty-five-year-old man dying of cancer undergo the rigors of dialysis when it can, at best, prolong his existence for a few weeks?

Should the young woman in coma with no hope of recovery be forced to receive tube feeding indefinitely?

Should an incompetent patient in the final stages of a terminal disease receive cardiac resuscitation if his heart should stop suddenly?

Should a nursing home resident in a state of severe mental deterioration receive antibiotics if she develops an acute infection?

These and similar decisions are reached every few minutes, of every day, of every week, of every month in hospitals and nursing homes all across America. *You and I will eventually have to make them also.* If we are lucky enough not be among the three out of four confronted with the decision for ourselves, then we will almost certainly be involved in deciding for our loved ones: our parents, spouses, distant relatives, or close friends—even our children.

Making deliberate decisions about withholding or withdrawing life support is a new, inerasable fact of life. For better or worse, this is how we die in the United States today. We cannot turn back the clock on these technological options any more than we can return to a preindustrial age without automobiles—and without automobile accidents. But we can plan and prepare ourselves.

Who Decides?

As long as you are fully conscious in the hospital and *competent*—the legal term for having capacity to make your own decisions—then you can always speak directly for yourself. Your doctors and nurses must listen to you. You can oversee your own medical treatment and make your own decisions simply by declaring your wishes in person.

Even technical competence can be problematic, because you may be able to say "It hurts" or "I'm hungry" but not so able to grasp all the delicate nuances and percentages involved in making the best treatment choices during a complex illness. The combined effects of your illness, various life support systems, and painkilling drugs may render you only partially competent or temporarily incompetent. Because decisions will frequently have to be made when your condition is unstable, advance planning and forethought are helpful.

When you are clearly "incompetent" and lack decision-making capacity, *you may lose the opportunity to make your own treatment decisions.* It is worth noting that we tend increasingly to die of chronic illnesses today; modern medicine is better at reversing acute illness—and chronic illness often leads to incompetence. The two leading killers in the United States—heart disease and cancer—as well as degenerative diseases—multiple sclerosis and Alzheimer's—and any of the immune disorders—such as AIDS—are all chronic illnesses that frequently lead to a terminal period of incompetence. As a result, someone else will have to make major life decisions for you. And they may not be the decisions you want, the ones you would have made for yourself.

This loss of decision-making ability is the most worrisome part for many of us. We fear having such personal, intimate decisions taken out of our own hands. We dread losing control of our minds and then, humiliatingly, of our bodies. If a machine can take over our breathing and a surgically implanted tube supply us with nourishment, our body may be artificially sustained for an indefinite period even though we are mentally and emotionally "gone," with no hope of recovery. Would you want to be suspended in this kind of limbo? I do not.

I know I want to chart my own course of treatment, insofar as possible, when my time comes. Although I will always seek the best medical advice and information, no physician can make such a decision for me. I certainly don't want a lawyer or a judge or a hospital administrator to decide for me. Nor do I want any person that *I haven't selected* to be involved in my final act of autonomy, my dying.

I want to die in freedom, in accord with my own values and choices, just as I have lived. Whose death is it anyway? Mine.

Safeguarding Your Decision

That is why I have written out a living will, a simple one-page legal document spelling out my treatment wishes in advance, in the event I am hopelessly ill and incapacitated. This living will—a "will" because it expresses my wishes, "living" because it goes into effect while I am still alive—is legally enforceable. Mine conforms to New York State case law, because that is where I live and New York is one of eight states that does not yet have statutory living will legislation. As long as my living will is present at my bedside, it should be consulted and its instructions honored. This living will document is my mouthpiece, the voice that speaks when I cannot, and it says exactly what I want it to say in my own words.

As an additional safeguard, I have also appointed my wife health-care proxy through the New York statute for that purpose. With my living will, health-care proxy, and our intimate talks on this subject as guides, she is now legally empowered to speak for me and make any and all health-care decisions on my behalf if I become incompetent. My doctors and nurses at the hospital will have to listen to her. She is my health-care agent, an appointed spokesperson for me. Her word is mine.

I am in excellent health. But as a competitive race car driver, I have had several—and seen countless—bad accidents in the last twenty years. I want to be prepared. I am acquiring extra protection for myself, much as one buys life insurance. Unlike life insurance, however, my living will and health-care proxy are costing me nothing. Not one cent.

Of course, I've had to think long and hard about possible medical outcomes and what my treatment choices would be. I have discussed my wishes with my wife and family. If I am rendered unconscious, and temporarily slip into a coma, I will continue to receive full and proper care. I've indicated that I want everything possible done for me as long as there is a reasonable chance I can fully recover.

However, I also know my chances of emerging from certain, prolonged types of coma are virtually nil. Serious burns would be even worse. In my living will I've indicated that once I pass the point of medically reasonable recovery—I trust that my doctors, with my wife's oversight, will diagnose my condition accurately and reach a consensus—then I want all life-sustaining measures withdrawn. I do not look forward to a totally inert, vegetative existence. The truth is, I'd rather be dead.

My family is another important consideration. Why should I impose on them the burden of shutting off my life support, a decision that is mine to make? With all the grief and stress they'd be undergoing, why should they have to feel guilty, too? And what if my medical insurance ran out? Should my wife and family be responsible for the enormous financial cost of my care—life-prolonging care that can do me no good and would be administered against my wishes? The answer, for me, is an emphatic no!

I hope you will follow my lead and begin thinking, and acting, on these decisions now. *Remember:* Deliberate decisions about withholding or withdrawing life support are being made every few minutes in health-care institutions all across the United States. The fundamental question remains "Who is making these decisions and who will continue to make them?" Medically, legally, and ethically, we have the right to make our own treatment decisions, including the right to refuse unwanted life-sustaining treatment. But like any right, this one remains theoretical unless we activate and exercise it.

The Patient Self-Determination Act

In December 1991 a new federal bill goes into effect that informs us in a dramatic new way of our legal options for refusing or accepting treatment. The bill is called the Patient Self-Determination Act (PSDA) and it affects all health-care facilities that receive federal funding: hospitals, nursing homes, hospices, home health-care services, and health maintenance organizations (HMO).

The next time you check into a hospital for whatever reason—a sprained ankle, a standard test—you will be handed a sheet of paper explaining your state's law about refusing treatment and your hospital's policy about it. You will be asked whether you have written a living will or appointed a health-care proxy. Your response will be entered in your chart and become a permanent part of your medical record.

In the words of Senator John C. Danforth, a Republican from Missouri who cosponsored this legislation, the Patient Self-Determination Act is an historic measure "providing people with information so that they can have the dignity of deciding what they want and what they don't want, of deciding their own fate."

We at the Society for the Right to Die, along with many other groups, expect the Patient Self-Determination Act to have a dramatic and positive impact on how Americans approach their right to influence treatment decisions. This right will be called to the attention of millions of Americans every time they or their loved ones enter a hospital or sign up with an HMO or move into a nursing home.

Patients can protect their rights by completing a legislatively approved living will in forty-two states and the District of Columbia. at the time this book is being written. (Part Two contains information about your specific state.) Most of the eight remaining states have court decisions ("case law") that authorize the use of living wills. In the few states with neither statute nor court decision, the relevant law is the law of informed consent, which prohibits giving medical treatment without the patient's consent. In its landmark 1990 decision in *Cruzan,* the U.S. Supreme Court confirmed that individuals have a constitutional liberty interest protecting them from unwanted medical treatment.

In thirty-four states at the time this book is being written, patients can legally appoint a health-care proxy through a durable power of attorney for health care. All fifty states have statutes providing for some form of durable power, and according to a growing number of legal authorities, the ordinary durable power appointment, with some exceptions, can be adapted to include medical decisions where there is no specific DPAHC.

In other words, there is now legal authority (through the legislature, the courts, or the constitution) in virtually every state in the United States to write a living will or appoint a health care proxy. Even where this authority is less than definitive, these documents are highly persuasive in any decision-making environment affecting your health care. Advance directives carry not only legal weight but provide important medical and ethical guidelines as well. No American of adult years should be without such protection.

So the law already exists to protect your treatment rights—but this law is of little benefit unless people know about it and have access to what it offers. The Patient Self-Determination Act means that many more of us will now be given the information we need—both on arrival at health-care institutions and through the public education activities the act requires.

The PSDA also encourages a more collaborative relationship between care givers and patients, with a new emphasis on institutional responsibility. Health-care facilities and providers will have to be more responsive and accountable to the people they serve. These institutions must honor the individual needs and treatment wishes of patients, as expressed personally or through advance directives, as a condition for receiving Medicare and Medicaid funding. Hospitals that choose not to honor living wills for religious or moral reasons must give patients advance written notice.

The Patient Self-Determination Act, an historic victory for patients' rights, is firmly grounded in individual choice. It rises strongly from the development of the law in the last fifteen years, from *Quinlan* to *Cruzan,* all of which emphasizes individual choice as the central value to be protected, and thus compels an acknowledgment of diversity. By making information about the possibility of individual choice in medical treatment an essential part of health-care institutions' everyday activities, Congress has firmly asserted the centrality of our rights in this area and ushered in a new era of awareness.

A Brief History of the Right to Die: From Quinlan to Cruzan

Although the freedom to die as one chooses has always been assumed to be the legal right of every U.S. citizen, the courts were never called on to articulate that right until roughly two decades ago. It was then that technological advances in medical care first made it possible to sustain biological life long past the time when a patient would otherwise have died and, in many instances, long past the time when he or she had ceased to exhibit any signs of a mental or emotional life.

The first legal case to attract national attention to a patient's right to die was brought by the parents of Karen Ann Quinlan. In April 1975, Quinlan, a twenty-one-year-old New Jersey resident, was at a party with friends when she ceased breathing for two fifteen-minute periods, causing her to suffer severe brain damage. The circumstances leading to her respiratory arrests were never clarified, although she is believed to have consumed a dangerous mixture of alcohol and barbituates. As a result of this tragedy, she was reduced to what her doctors identified as a "persistent vegetative state" (PVS), a state of permanent unconsciousness where the patient has no cognitive functions and no reasonable hope of ever recovering them. To keep her body alive, doctors connected Ms. Quinlan to a mechanical respirator and to a nasogastric feeding tube (a tube inserted through the nose that supplies artificial nutrition and water to the stomach).

Quinlan's parents were convinced that she would not have wanted to live in this condition, but the hospital refused to withdraw her life support, so the Quinlans sought permission from a New Jersey court to disconnect their daughter's respirator. When the court refused the request, arguing that such a decision should be left in the hands of the medical profession, her parents appealed to the New Jersey Supreme Court. In a landmark decision handed down on March 31, 1976, the New Jersey Supreme Court reversed the lower court ruling and granted the Quinlans permission.

Explaining their decision, the justices of the New Jersey Supreme Court referred to Karen Ann Quinlan's "constitutional right of privacy" and, citing her dim prognosis, added,

> We think that the States' interest [in preservation of life] weakens and the individual's right to privacy grows as the degree of bodily invasion increases and the prognosis dims. Ultimately, there comes a point at which the individual's rights overcome the State's interest.

The court further concluded that "Karen's right of privacy may be asserted on her behalf by her guardian under the peculiar circumstances here present."

The *Quinlan* case did a great deal to support an individual's right to die with dignity. It produced the first judicial decision enunciating the constitutional right of privacy as the basis for withholding or withdrawing life support from a terminally ill patient. It also established the principle that any decision making about the health care of a patient who is mentally incapacitated should be left to the patient's guardian, family, and physician, with review by the hospital's ethics committee. In other words, the decision making should not have to be referred automatically to the court system. (It is ironic that the Quinlan's had to go to court to allow their daughter to die and have since been followed by many other families despite this early, and very sound, admonition to avoid the courtroom.)

The Karen Ann Quinlan case also marked the first time Americans became aware, on a mass level, of a new kind of modern nightmare: the possibility that, due to tragic illness or injury, an unconscious victim might be sustained by technology against his or her own wishes and those of his or her family. In other words, that there might be a fate worse than death.

The *Quinlan* case captured the public imagination in a stark and dramatic way. Several books, films, and television movies on the subject were produced. The massive publicity also helped California to pass the first piece of living will legislation in 1976, known as the California Natural Death Act.

But the *Quinlan* case did *not* establish several important points. One was whether artificial feeding systems can be classified as life support mechanisms that can be withdrawn. Ironically, Quinlan began breathing on her own after her respirator was removed, and she continued living in a persistent vegetative state for nine years longer, sustained at a seventy-pound weight by her nasogastric feedings. She died in June 1985. Meanwhile, the debate over whether feeding tubes could be considered "withdrawable" life support mechanisms raged from courtroom to courtroom across the United States. Finally, in June 1990, it reached the Supreme Court in the case of Nancy Cruzan who, like Karen Ann Quinlan, was young, vital, and doomed to live for an indefinite period of time in a persistent vegetative state, if she remained connected to her artificial feeding system.

Nancy Cruzan's story is especially poignant and illustrates the kind of dilemma that could overtake anyone of us—or someone we love—as long as the right to die remains so ambiguously defined and as long as we give it so little forethought. In the early morning hours of January 11, 1983, Nancy Beth Cruzan, twenty-five years old, was driving home from her night-shift job at a cheese factory in Carthage, Missouri, when her old Nash Rambler apparently spun out of control on an ice-covered country road and overturned, flinging her body face down in a ditch thirty-five feet away. By the time paramedics found her and resuscitated her, Nancy Cruzan's brain had been permanently damaged from oxygen deprivation, and she had slipped into a state of unconsciousness from which she would never recover. In one terrible act, a vibrant young woman had become a spastic quadriplegic with severe and irreversible brain damage, a lacerated liver and contractures of all four limbs. A few weeks after the accident, she was diagnosed with PVS, and it became necessary to surgically implant a feeding tube into her stomach to keep her alive.

Cruzan's parents, Lester ("Joe") and Joyce Cruzan, did everything they could to try to bring their daughter back. They visited her daily and consulted every medical expert. Ms. Cruzan received regular rehabilitation treatment but to no avail. Her parents even moved her back to the house where she had grown up and surrounded her with favorite old toys, singing her the songs and lullabyes she had loved as a child. Nancy Cruzan did not react or show any improvement. Occasionally there would be violent contortions an uninformed stranger might mistake for signs of wakening but her parents and doctors were all too aware that they were only reflexive symptoms of her brain-damaged condition.

Three years passed before the Cruzans accepted that their daughter would never recover. The turning point came when Lester Cruzan read a description of the persistent vegetative state in a medical textbook and recognized the symptoms as Nancy's.

On September 11, 1986, Lester Cruzan wrote the following letter to Fenella Rouse, executive director of the Society for the Right to Die who was then legal counsel:

In January, 1983, my daughter, then 25 years old, was injured in an automobile accident. She arrested at the scene, was examined twice by a highway patrolman who was first on the scene. He stated he could find no sign of life and felt she was dead. However, with high-tech ability, she was resuscitated by ambulance attendants when they arrived. Since the time of the accident, she has never had what we felt was a thought-produced response to anything.

We feel that she is in a persistent vegetative state. This has been substantiated, we believe, by CAT scans and EEG evaluations. She was on a ventilator for about four weeks after the accident. Because of our love for her, after this period of time in which she has shown no improvement, we feel the most humane and kind thing we can do is to help her escape this "limbo" between life and death that she is caught in by terminating her life. I would like to emphasize that she would not have wanted to live like this and that our feelings are for her sake and not for ours. While I am not sure we could go through with removing nourishment, I feel very strongly that society must come to terms with this problem. I believe this option must be available if one should choose to use it.

To my knowledge, it is presently illegal to remove hydration and nutrition from a person in the state of Missouri. This belief comes from a book I purchased from the Society for the Right to Die entitled *The Physician and the Hopelessly Ill Patient*. We would like to begin a process to change this law.

Do you know of any advocacy groups or legal aid available that might help us in this endeavor? We have discussed this at length with our attorney and he suggested possibly legal briefs from other cases where this law has been challenged.

The Society for the Right to Die put the Cruzans in touch with the American Civil Liberties Union, which led them to attorney William Colby. Thereafter, the Society stood by them as they conducted their torturous campaign to stop the artificial feeding of their daughter's body. It was a struggle made all the more horrendous by the intense, ongoing media coverage on a local and national level and the strenuous opposition of "right-to-life" groups.

In 1987, after the hospital refused to end their daughter's gastrostomy feedings, the Cruzans went to the Jasper (Missouri) County Court. They presented medical evidence that their daughter was permanently and irreversibly brain damaged with no hope of recovery. A former housemate testified that Nancy Cruzan told her that if she ever became seriously ill or injured, she would not want to continue her life unless she could live at least halfway normally and not "like a vegetable."

The trial court ruled the Cruzans could remove their daughter's feeding tube because evidence strongly suggested Ms. Cruzan "would not wish to continue with nutrition and hydration." Ms. Cruzan had a "right to liberty." To deny her parents, as co-guardians, the right to act on her behalf, would deprive her of equal protection under the law. The Judge also stated that he was impressed and moved by the Cruzan's love for their daughter and their closeness to her at the time of her accident.

But Nancy's court-appointed guardian and the state attorney general appealed, and in a four-to-three decision, the Missouri Supreme Court reversed the ruling, stating that Missouri has an "unqualified interest in preserving life at all costs" and there was, in fact, no "clear and convincing evidence" Nancy felt any differently. (Missouri and New York are the only two states that prohibit the removal of feeding tubes, or any other life support mechanism, from an incapacitated patient without "clear and convincing evidence" the patient would not have wanted these medical treatments under the circumstances. In legal terms, "clear and convincing evidence" is the highest and strictest standard of evidence that can be demanded.)

The Missouri Supreme Court decision was unusual; most other courts were protective of individual and family rights. Unlike the State of New Jersey in the *Quinlan* case, Missouri was saying it had a better sense of Nancy Cruzan and her interests than the parents who had raised her and known her when she had been a functioning person. It was also demanding a higher standard of evidence for Nancy Cruzan's wishes. In addition, Missouri claimed artificial nutrition and hydration—the provision of nutrients and water through a tube—was not medical treatment and thus could not be withdrawn; this position put Missouri at odds with the medical and ethical consensus and such respected national groups as the American Medical Association and the Hastings Center. The Cruzans appealed to the U.S. Supreme Court, and it agreed to hear their appeal. It was the first right-to-die case to make it there; the Court rejected the *Karen Ann Quinlan* case fourteen years before.

The *Cruzan* decision drew intense nationwide attention. C. Everett Koop, then U.S. surgeon general, summed up the high sense of expectation when he said, "This is a decision that will affect virtually every member of our society." Not least affected were the Supreme Court justices themselves, three of whom were older than eighty and another of whom had undergone major cancer surgery. As Linda Greenhouse, the *New York Times* legal correspondent who covered the *Nancy Cruzan* case, wrote, "Perhaps the reason her Supreme Court Case is compelling on such a personal level is that the Justices, no less than the rest of the public, look at Nancy Cruzan and see themselves."

Only a little more than a year ago, on June 25, 1990, the U.S. Supreme Court, by a five-to-four vote, upheld the Missouri Supreme Court's decision. It ruled that Missouri can require, if it chooses, clear and convincing evidence Nancy Cruzan would have decided to forgo life support before allowing the exercise of her constitutionally protected right to refuse unwanted medical treatment. In other words, Nancy Cruzan had the right to refuse tube feeding but Missouri could demand that she make her wishes about refusing treatment more clearly known.

In so ruling, the Supreme Court stated for the first time that a person's right to refuse treatment is guaranteed by the liberty clause in the U.S. Constitution: "The principle that a competent person has a constitutionally protected liberty interest in refusing unwanted medical treatment may be inferred from our prior decisions."

Liberty means the right to be let alone. Any limitation on the competent individual's right to refuse treatment would thus run the risk of violating the constitution. Furthermore, the Court drew no distinction between providing food and water by tube and providing other forms of treatment like surgical intervention or mechanical assistance with breathing. Providing tube feeding alone against a patient's wishes could be an invasion of a liberty interest and constitutionally impermissible.

The Court also suggested another person or surrogate selected by a competent patient would have the same right to refuse treatment as the patient him or herself. This strongly implies it would be unconstitutional to ignore the treatment instructions of a health-care agent or proxy.

From the court's ruling, it is likely that both living wills and DPAHC documents would be constitutionally protected; if a person has either of them, a state could *not* refuse to recognize them.

While giving the right to refuse treatment a constitutional dimension for the first time, the Supreme Court also acknowledged that states have *a general interest in preserving the life of their citizens;* states may thus, as Missouri did in the *Cruzan* case, legitimately seek to ensure that the patient would have chosen to refuse treatment by imposing the highest standard of proof: clear and convincing evidence. Each state is free to set its own standard of evidence where matters of life and death are concerned. As Chief Justice William H. Rehnquist, writing for the majority, said, "While a state need not apply such a rigorous evidentiary standard, we cannot say that the Supreme Court of Missouri committed a constitutional error in reaching the conclusion it did."

Sadly, the Supreme Court ruling was not a victory for the Cruzans. In upholding the individual's right to refuse treatment, the court also upheld the state's authority to deny that right to people who have not claimed it in clear and convincing terms. The Cruzans were forced to renew their appeal at the same county court that had originally ruled in their favor three years earlier.

This time, three more friends told of specific conversations in which Nancy confided she would never want to be kept alive "like a vegetable" with medical technology. Their testimony was buttressed by Dr. James Davis, Nancy's personal physician. Acknowledging he had been opposed to removing Nancy's feeding tube during the first hearing in 1987, Dr. Davis painted a harrowing picture of Nancy's deteriorating physical state since then: the decomposing skin, incontinence, alternating constipation and diarrhea, the bleeding gums, the contorted limbs, the recurring seizures. Asked by Nancy's court-appointed guardian if it was in Nancy's best interests to continue like this, Dr. Davis admitted, "No, sir, I think it would be personally a living hell."

On December 14, 1990, the county court again authorized the discontinuance of Nancy Cruzan's feedings. This time there were no objections, as the state attorney general had already withdrawn from the case, arguing his sole interest had been to establish the law in this area. Two hours later, Dr. Davis removed Nancy Cruzan's feeding tube, and on December 26, she died. Lester Cruzan, referring to Nancy as "our bright flaming star who flew through the heaven of our lives," reiterated his and his wife Joyce's belief that their daughter had been "gone from the world" since that cold January night in 1983. He paid her the most eloquent tribute of all:

Because of Nancy, I suspect hundreds of thousands of people can rest free, knowing that when death beckons, they can meet it face to face with dignity, free from the fear of unwanted and useless medical treatment. I think this is quite an accomplishment for a twenty-five-year-old kid and I'm damn proud of her.

Taking Personal Responsibility

Perhaps the most important conclusion we can draw from both the June 25, 1990, United States Supreme Court decision and from the profoundly disturbing fate of Nancy Cruzan is that to protect our right to die as we choose, we must plan ahead and leave a record of our treatment choices. A living will accompanied by a durable power of attorney for health care represents the best possible insurance that our wishes will be honored even if we become incapacitated, a fact acknowledged by several of the United States Supreme Court justices in their written opinions regarding the *Cruzan* case.

There have been significant social and demographic changes in our experience of death. Where once we used to die at home, surrounded by family, today we die in "homes," impersonal institutions where we are surrounded by technology and anonymous technicians. Meanwhile family members, when they are allowed to visit, stand awkwardly in the background, intruders in this foreign landscape, the modern health-care setting. Death is far less private, and less personal. We don't have the experience or memory of grandfather on his deathbed at home; and we don't know what death looks and smells like.

None of us likes to contemplate his or her own death or the death of a loved one. It's a dreaded event that makes us feel helpless and desperate and our society discourages us from acknowledging such feelings. It's as if we are afraid that "thinking makes it so" or as if we unconsciously hope that not thinking might make it not so.

Combine fear and ignorance with our natural reluctance about death, and it's little wonder so few of us have formulated clear guidelines on how far we wish to continue treatment when we are dying. Only 30 percent of us even bother to fill out a property will. A 1988 nationwide survey conducted by the American Medical Association (AMA) revealed that 56 percent of the respondents had discussed "extraordinary" medical treatment preferences with family members, but only 15 percent had filled out a living will. A 1991 Gallup poll found an even larger discrepancy between those who approved of living wills and intended to fill them out (75 percent) as opposed to those who had actually done so (20 percent).

A mere quarter century ago, people could afford to take the classic "patient" role and leave matters involving their end-of-life medical care in the hands of doctors. Death was simple: You ceased breathing, your heart stopped. But there has been a revolution in medical science's ability to postpone death by supporting one organ system after another. As Dr. Charles Culver, professor of psychiatry and medical ethics at Dartmouth Medical School writes:

> It was once true that when the dying process began, a person died all at once, within a relatively brief time. As soon as one major organ system became seriously dysfunctional, the effects of its dysfunction affected other organ systems and soon the organism as a whole ceased to function. (The definition of death is the permanent cessation of function of the organism as a whole.) But modern technology allows the support of one seriously dysfunctional organ system after another, such as the heart, the lungs, the bone marrow and the kidneys. By supporting these organ systems one after another as they fail, death can be forestalled—often for a very long period of time. As system after system fails it becomes increasingly unlikely, though sometimes not impossible, that the chain of failures can be reversed: but death is still not present.

Through the use of cardiopulmonary resuscitation (CPR), mechanical ventilation, dialysis, surgical techniques, antibiotic drugs, and artificially supplied nutrition and hydration (tube feeding), our technological ability to prolong life has greatly expanded. This revolution has given us enormous benefits—the wonderful ability to sustain life while patients are cured of serious diseases—but also new possibilities for pointlessly, even cruelly, prolonging dying.

The line between life and death has now been blurred, and the potential gap between what you personally define as death and what your doctors—or your state—define as death can be considerable. Each new year brings with it new and unforseen medical treatment possibilities. For example, several medical research-and-development facilities are working now on an artificial liver machine. It is urgent for each American to determine and declare where to draw the line between life and death for him or herself.

Decision-making does not mean becoming a medical expert. Instead, it bids you to anticipate possible end-of-life situations (from accident or illness), to consider the various life-prolonging measures that exist, and, finally, to make commonsense decisions based on your own beliefs about when medical technology withdraws so nature can take its course. Clearly it's best to go through this decision-making process while you're enjoying life in reasonably good mental and physical health.

This book has been created to help you translate your wishes into an effective living will and durable power of attorney for health care. It will guide you, step by step, through the tangle of legal, medical, and ethical issues surrounding advance directives and the right to die.

In Chapter 2, the most frequently asked questions are answered about the content, format, and function of a living will and a durable power of attorney for health care and about the major types of medical treatment now considered life sustaining: "How can I know in advance what medical care I'll want or not want?" "Will my living will be honored?" "Whom should I appoint as my durable power of attorney for health care?"

Chapter 3 is devoted to the practical task of filling out the documents, taking you through the forms, line by line, explaining the terminology and elucidating key concepts and ambiguous langauge. "What does terminal condition mean?" "Would it apply if I had Alzheimer's disease?" "What if I change my mind?"

Once you have composed your living will and durable power of attorney for health care, Chapter 4 examines how these documents function in reality. "How can I make sure the physician and the hospital (or nursing home or hospice) will follow my wishes?" You will be guided through the layers of bureaucracy as well as the distinctive philosophy of each health-care institution.

Chapter 5 examines important social and ethical considerations that pertain not only to a living will and a durable power of attorney for health care, but go beyond them to the right-to-die issue and health-care decision making in general. Subjects such as physician-assisted suicide, rationing of health care, and alternatives to the living will, including the values history and the medical directive, are discussed.

Part Two provides an invaluable resource for helping you keep your documents legal and up to date and ensuring that they are enforced according to your wishes. For the first time in one book, this part presents, state by state, every living will and every durable power of attorney form that has been passed in the United States. Living wills from Canada are also included. These documents can be photocopied and used. A detailed set of guidelines for each state provides useful information for filling out the particular forms.

A glossary of common terms and a resource list appear in the Appendix.

Taken together, Parts One and Two of *The Complete Guide to Living*

Wills offer you a truly complete, thoughtful, and pragmatic guide to the living will and the durable power of attorney for health care. You should have all the information you need to protect yourself and your family with these two vital documents and to secure the peace of mind that comes with planning wisely and concretely for the future.

CHAPTER TWO
Tough Questions

Death and the sun are not to be looked at steadily.
—LA ROCHEFOUCAULD, *Maxims*

Here are thirty-five of the most common, and difficult, questions people ask the Society for the Right to Die about the living will, the durable power of attorney for health care, and the process of dying as we know it.

1. What can and can't a living will do for me? A living will is a written document that allows you to express your wishes in advance regarding what life support systems you want or do not want in the event you develop an incurable or irreversible condition and will never regain what you consider to be a meaningful life. It tells your family and your doctor what your choices are about life-prolonging medical procedures so that they will be able to follow your instructions when you are unable to make your own decisions. Your treatment wishes become a matter of record, no matter what happens to you.

A general living will is a personal document that may say anything you wish about your treatment, whereas most statutory living wills—those passed by state legislatures into law—require that the patient be in a "terminal condition" or "permanently unconscious" before life support can be withdrawn. These terms are defined differently in each statute, and the precise medical conditions covered vary from state to state. State living wills do not normally address situations that are not terminal and do not involve permanent unconsciousness or the loss of your decision-making capability; independent choices about life support would be made by you (if possible) and your family or guardian, in consultation with a doctor and in accord with institutional policies and state law.

Although you may request specific forms of life support through a living will, the documents are most commonly used to refuse further life-sustaining treatment when you are in an incurable or irreversible condition and permanently unable to make decisions.

In end-of-life medical situations, it is understood that any and all applicable life support systems will be offered by the attending doctor: It is his or her professional obligation to offer them as long as they are not medically futile. Therefore, a living will is more commonly used to refuse individual forms of treatment than to ask for them.

A living will *can* be used to emphasize that you want maximum pain relief, or specify certain life support systems if applicable to your condition, and the length of time you desire to remain attached to them—say a month, a year, or for as long as you remain alive.

Although it is hard to use a living will to describe a complete program of medical treatment in advance, it is important to be as specific as possible. Ideally you should specify what kinds of life-sustaining treatment you would or would not want and what the medical conditions are in which you would or would not want further treatment. Most state documents are only one-page long, but you are free to add additional pages containing your personal instructions.

The bottom line is mercifully simple. A living will ensures that you as a human being will retain your power to answer yes or no to some very important life support and pain-management questions even after your mind has lost that power. I know of no better way to underscore the value of this insurance to you and your loved ones than to tell you about the *O'Connor* case.

Mary O'Connor was a seventy-five-year-old retired hospital employee living in upstate New York when she suffered a series of strokes over a two-month period, leaving her conscious but confined to her bed and dependent on spoon feeding for nourishment. Three doctors diagnosed her as having severe, irreversible dementia. Mrs. O'Connor's condition worsened and she was transferred to a hospital for care. She lost the ability to swallow.

In June 1988, the hospital sought consent from her two daughters to insert a feeding tube through Mrs. O'Connor's nose, and they refused. In July, the hospital went to court seeking permission to insert the nasogastric tube in Mary O'Connor despite her daughters' objections. Both practical nurses themselves, her daughters pleaded that the tube not be inserted. They swore that although their mother had not detailed her wishes in a living will or spoken to them specifically about tube feeding, she had repeatedly said she did not want her life prolonged solely by artificial means. They noted she was well qualified to have made such statements: Mary O'Connor had been a hospital employee for twenty years, had attended her husband and brothers during long final illnesses, and had been previously hospitalized for a heart attack. Furthermore, one of her long-time friends and coworkers testified Mary O'Connor had told him, based on her own workplace observations, it was "monstrous to keep people alive with machinery when they were not going to get better."

While Mary O'Connor remained alive on intravenous feeding, her fate became a legal football. The trial court, the Supreme Court in Westchester County, New York, refused to allow the nasogastric tube to be inserted. The Westchester County Medical Center appealed the decision. When the appellate division affirmed the lower court's decision, the medical center appealed again.

On October 14, 1988, New York's highest state court, the Court of Appeals—not Mary O'Connor or her daughters—rendered the final judgment on the matter: Mary O'Connor had not left behind "clear and convincing evidence of her wishes," as required by New York State law; the nasogastric tube could not be withheld. (As stated previously, New York is the only other state besides Missouri with such a strict standard of evidence). In a decision with far-reaching consequences, the court further stated that the "ideal situation is one in which the patient's wishes are expressed in some form of writing, perhaps a 'living will,' while he or she is still competent."

Mary O'Connor died on August 26, 1989, with her nasogastric tube in place. She may not have died the natural death she would have preferred, but her dying saga—well publicized as it was—alerted thousands of people to the important service a living will can perform for a powerless individual and the loved ones he or she leaves behind.

2. What specific medical life support technologies do I need to be concerned about in my living will? A living will is only applicable when you are dying or in an incurable condition and unable to communicate. At such times you may wish to refuse medical treatments that might have been previously desirable, but now can only prolong the dying process and offer no hope of improvement. The life support technologies most often administered in end-of-life situations and most appropriate to address in a living will are discussed below. (These treatments and why they are most likely to cause conflicts between patients and health-care providers are discussed in more detail in Chapter 3 and most are also listed in the glossary.)

Cardiopulmonary Resuscitation (CPR) refers to a variety of measures used to restart a patient's heart when it stops beating (cardiac arrest) and to provide artificial respiration when breathing stops (respiratory arrest), including mouth-to-mouth resuscitation, the application of manual pressure, or electric shocks with paddles to the chest. Intravenous drugs to restart the heart and return blood pressure to normal may also be administered.

Mechanical Respiration connects a patient to a machine (known as a respirator or a ventilator) that pumps air into and out of the lungs and thereby assists or takes over the patient's breathing function.

Tube Feeding, also called "artificial feeding" or "nutrition and hydration by tube," involves the provision by tube of prepared nutrients and fluids to patients who are not able to swallow enough food to maintain proper nutrition. It can deliver either all necessary nutrients and fluids or just nutrients and fluids necessary to supplement normal food intake. Depending on the patient's condition, a tube is inserted into a vein (intravenous feeding, which is usually not total feeding), into the stomach through the nose (nasogastric feeding), or into the stomach directly via a surgical incision (gastrostomy feeding).

Antibiotics are drugs administered by mouth, through a feeding tube, or by injection, to fight infections that commonly attend and hasten death in the course of a long-term debilitating disease or a steadily deteriorating physical condition. Often it is not the primary disease that results in death but another (intercurrent) infection. Serious infection in dying patients can lead to sleep or coma and may be the body's way of producing a peaceful death. By curing the infection, an antibiotic may make the hopelessly ill patient more conscious of his or her discomfort.

Dialysis uses a machine that cleanses blood when the kidneys do not function adequately. Blood can be cleansed directly, through tubes placed into blood vessels (hemodialysis), or indirectly, through tubes placed into the abdomen (peritoneal dialysis). Dialysis is usually performed two or three times a week. The procedure takes three hours or longer.

Surgical Procedures such as amputation can be used to restrict the spread of life-threatening infection. Surgery is also often performed to relieve pain.

The following treatments are less likely to be the subject of dispute between patients and physicians but they do come up occasionally.

Diagnostic Tests or procedures that are safe and simple to perform include blood tests, X rays, examination of the urine, and sophisticated scans such as computerized axial tomography (CAT) and magnetic resonance imaging (MRI) (for examining the brain or other parts of the body). More complicated or invasive procedures may produce discomfort and sometimes serious side effects.

Intravenous (IV) Line is a tube placed into a vein for the purpose of administering fluids, blood or medication. Veins in the arm are usually used, but sometimes the IV line is inserted into a vein in the neck area. Although inflammation, clotting, or damage to the vein can sometimes cause pain, an intravenous line is not necessarily uncomfortable once it is in place.

Chemotherapy and Radiation are treatments for cancer. Chemotherapy administers drugs that frequently cause nausea, vomiting, or serious complications, although in many cases it is well tolerated. Chemotherapy temporarily reduces the discomfort of a cancer, even if it does not cure it. Radiation therapy uses high levels of radiation to shrink or eliminate a tumor. Although it may sometimes produce side effects, radiation therapy is generally better tolerated than chemotherapy and is sometimes given as comfort care. With some forms of cancer, recurrence after a series of anti-cancer treatments, such as chemotherapy or radiation, means the cancer is most likely incurable. Further treatment may, at most, prolong life for a few months.

Comfort Care is any kind of treatment that increases a person's physical or emotional ease. It generally does not require advanced technology. It can include oxygen; food and fluids by mouth; moistening of the lips; cleaning, turning, and touching a person; or simply sitting with someone who is bedridden.

3. In addition to life-sustaining technologies, what are the medical conditions I should know about for my living will? It is just as important to know under what medical conditions you would want, or not want, treatment as it is to know what kinds of treatment you might choose. In fact the two are intimately connected. A particular type of treatment, say renal dialysis, might be extraordinary in one kind of clinical situation—an unconscious person with terminal cancer who has, at best, another month to live—but might make more sense for someone recovering from a stroke who has even a 50 percent chance of recovery. You cannot make decisions about life-sustaining care in a vacuum but must always consider the context, or precise medical condition, in which you find yourself.

Following are four general kinds of conditions, with some examples, that you might wish to consider. While it is not possible to predict every outcome, your instructions about how you wish to be treated under these scenarios may give your health-care providers important guidance, direct or indirect, about your treatment preferences. You may wish to update these instructions as your age and medical circumstances change.

1. The most clear-cut condition is one where you are terminally ill and incompetent with no chance of ever regaining decision-making capacity. A person in the final stages of an incurable cancer who has a cardiac arrest and lapses into a coma is obviously in a very hopeless situation. To initiate a whole battery of life support treatments for such a patient can only delay the dying process, but this may happen unless you fill out a living will or durable power of attorney for health care. There are, of course, patients who might want treatment even in this condition.

2. Patients in a persistent vegetative state (PVS) are permanently unconscious and have suffered such total or near-total destruction of the cerebral cortex that they have virtually no chance of ever recovering consciousness. Yet such patients, like Nancy Cruzan (for eight years) and Karen Ann Quinlan (for ten years), are often kept alive for a very long time. PVS is an extremely complex neurological dysfunction in which the patient's eyes may be open despite a total lack of cognitive function. Family members and other observers often find it difficult to accept that, in the words of the American Academy of Neurology, "at no time is the patient aware of himself or his environment." PVS does not result only from traumatic injury but it may also occur in the most advanced stages of progressive brain diseases—Alzheimer's or Parkinson's diseases—or in severe strokes and brain hemorrhages. It is helpful to declare in advance whether you would—or would not—wish your body kept alive if you suffered an irreversible loss of consciousness and found yourself in a persistent vegetative state.

3. You are unconscious and in a prolonged coma that is not PVS. You would have a very small statistical chance of regaining consciousness—and would almost certainly be brain damaged if you did—yet the possibility of recovery exists. Prolonged unconsciousness after a massive stroke, severe head trauma, or a cardiac arrest, may require that your life be artificially sustained for many months before ruling out the chance of some recovery. While relatives usually agonize over terminating treatment for a loved one when there is even a one percent chance of hope, many competent patients, especially the elderly, say they would not want further aggressive treatment when the odds are so poor. Others, however, may choose to buck the odds and try every available treatment option. It is a very personal decision and should be made by every individual for himself or herself. Consider such factors as age, your current general health, and how long you would wish to remain in coma when determining your treatment decisions.

4. Some patients experience dementia from Alzheimer's and related disorders. Alzheimer's disease, which afflicts about 4 million Americans, causes a progressive and unrelenting malfunction of the brain affecting memory and reasoning. Patients with advanced (but not end-stage) Alzheimer's may lack decision-making capacity yet still have some higher functions left. They might be demented with occasional periods of lucidity; they might be incontinent and unable to eat adequately but still able to move their limbs and have an awareness of their surroundings. However, if such a patient developed pneumonia and slipped into a coma, he or she might choose against treatment; the patient would be at the end of a spectrum of decreasing mental capacity with severe and irreversible dementia.

4. What is brain death and what is its relation to advance directives? This term refers to the permanent, irreversible loss of all functions of the entire brain. It is a legal definition of death. Brain death means that neither the "higher" portion of the brain—the cortex, which controls thinking and awareness—nor the "lower" portion—the brain stem, which controls reflexes and breathing—show any activity whatsoever. It is sometimes called "whole brain death." Nancy Cruzan was not brain dead following her accident because only the higher portion of her brain was destroyed; she still had some lower brain stem function.

Despite objections from certain strict religious groups, there is a widespread consensus that a patient who is brain dead is dead; there is no cause to worry about receiving unwanted treatment. Therefore, you do *not* need to mention brain death in your living will or DPAHC.

5. Is it possible to protect myself in advance from medical life support technologies that don't even exist yet? A living will includes a general statement that you do not want to receive any technology that serves only to prolong the process of your dying without increasing comfort or chances for recovery. You can reinforce this statement with your own, personalized directives. In addition, you can—and should—update your living will on a regular basis to include any recent developments in medical technology; a doctor can advise you.

6. To what extent are my living will requests likely to be honored? At the time this book is being written, forty-two states and the District of Columbia have passed living will legislation. The eight states that do not yet have this kind of legislation are Massachusetts, Michigan, Nebraska, New Jersey, New York, Ohio, Pennsylvania, and Rhode Island. Assuming that you live in a state that has a living will law, and that you complete the form correctly, your requests are protected by law and must be honored.

Some of these forty-two states have very restrictive statutes. The Society for the Right to Die supplies a generic living will form (see Chapter 3), in addition to state documents, that allows you to add any instructions not permitted by your state form. In the eight states without living will statutes, many court judgments indicate that a generic living will would be legally enforceable.

There has tended to be a fairly wide variation in how different medical facilities and physicians honor living wills: Some are sensitive and highly responsive to the patient's wishes, whereas others have shown more resistance and even a flagrant disregard for the patient's rights and the law. Now, however, with the passage of the Patient Self-Determination Act, all health-care facilities that receive Medicare or Medicaid will have to inform patients on admission of their policies toward living wills and other advance directives. Any institution that does not honor living wills must publicly declare its position and agree to transfer the patient to another facility that will abide by the patient's written instructions.

Remember, an individual has the right in *every* state to refuse any type of medical treatment. The issue addressed in this book is how to refuse life support treatment in advance, in case you end up in a situation where you are not competent to state your own wishes. A living will and a durable power of attorney for health care (see question 18), properly signed and witnessed, are the best instruments for protecting your treatment wishes in every state. I discuss the legal differences among individual states as well as other legal issues pertaining to advance directives in Part Two.

7. What happens if I have a living will for one state but am suddenly injured or struck by illness in a different state. Will my living will be honored? The answer is almost certainly yes. Once you have put your wishes in writing, there is clear and convincing evidence of how you want to be treated. For any state to disregard your wishes would then be a violation of the law of informed consent and your constitutional right to liberty, which includes the right to be free from unwanted medical treatment. In practice, no one can guarantee how health-care providers or institutions in one state will react to a living will or durable power of attorney from another, but as a matter of law they are obligated to honor your clearly expressed wishes. The story of Anna Zodin is a case in point.

Anna Zodin was a chronically vegetative patient maintained by a feeding tube in the Americana Healthcare Center of Cobb County, Georgia. She had filled out a living will but it was from the state of Texas. When her nasogastric tube fell out, Anna Zodin's daughter asked the Georgia health center that it not be reinserted, in accordance with her mother's Texas living will. The Superior Court of Cobb County, Georgia, ruled that Anna Zodin's wishes should be honored. Even though she had recorded her treatment choices in an out-of-state document, there was clear evidence of Anna Zodin's preferences, which the Georgia court recognized and upheld.

8. Will my family have to go to court to enforce my living will? Matters involving the implementation of living wills seldom go to court. Difficulties most often arise when there is no living will or other advance directive. The most important point to remember is that you need some record, preferably in writing, of your treatment wishes. It is doubtful whether most of the better-known right-to-die cases would ever have gone to court had the plaintiffs been able to produce a living will.

9. Can't I just leave these decisions for my family to make? As we saw in the tragic case of Nancy Cruzan and Missouri, when there is no clear and convincing evidence of your wishes, your family may not be allowed to make decisions for you. Had Ms. Cruzan been fatally injured in neighboring Arkansas, her case should not have reached the lower court, let alone the U.S. Supreme Court. Arkansas is one of thirteen states with a surrogate decision-making statute that would automatically have allowed Nancy Cruzan's family to make medical decisions for her when she could no longer make them herself (assuming there was no evidence her family was acting in bad faith). The other states are Connecticut, Florida, Hawaii, Iowa, Louisiana, Maine, New Mexico, North Carolina, Oregon, Texas, Utah, Virginia, and the District of Columbia.

Surrogate decision-making provisions delineate the individuals who are empowered to make decisions on behalf of an incompetent patient who has not executed a living will or DPAHC. In this stated order of priority, these people have decision-making authority in the event you become incapacitated and have not executed any document:

Your legal guardian
Your spouse
Adult children
Parents

Siblings

Your physician

The statutes usually require that you be in a terminal condition before anyone can authorize the removal of life support.

Surrogate decision making is the area where fewest legislatures have acted, yet these provisions are very important. They give providers and families acting in good faith the legal security to make medical decisions without undue worry. The Society for the Right to Die, along with many other national groups, believe every state should pass surrogate decision-making statutes. We feel this is one more way of ensuring that personal treatment decisions remain within the patient-family-doctor relationship.

However, even if you live in one of the thirteen states that has this protection, you might not agree with the individuals chosen to represent you and might wish to pick your own surrogate. For example, people who live in nontraditional relationships, such as gay or unmarried couples, might prefer to have a lover rather than a parent make these decisions for them. Some nuns prefer that decisions be made for them by the members of their community rather than blood relatives. Yet under surrogate decision-making statutes, the decision would automatically fall on the next of kin. Similarly, if you had a falling out with your relatives, or simply didn't see eye to eye with them on this issue for personal, political, or religious reasons, you would need to specify your own wishes through a living will or select your own health care proxy.

10. Why aren't decisions about my end-of-life medical care best left to my doctors? The first and most obvious reason: The majority of people today do not have personal physicians—and so they have never discussed their private feelings about end-of-life treatment with a doctor. Another reason is that our society has traditionally taught doctors to preserve life at all costs. While many physicians temper this belief with the need to relieve suffering, others view death as the eternal enemy, to be fought with every means available in the arsenal of medical technology. It is their duty, after all, to heal. Often doctors may privately agree with your treatment wishes but are constrained by their public role or by hospital policy. They must avoid the impression of influencing your decision beyond presenting all available medical options. Unless a physician has clear and convincing proof that you feel otherwise, he or she may feel duty-bound to give you the maximum, most aggressive treatment.

Although many doctors are reluctant to bring up the subject of death and dying, almost all find it useful to have specific guidance from their patients about end-of-life treatment. In a 1989 survey called "Physicians' Attitudes Toward Advance Directives," published in the *Journal of American Medical Association,* 88 percent of physicians polled said they found living wills to be a helpful and effective way for patients to influence their medical treatment if they became incompetent, 91 percent said they believed living wills facilitate physician-family agreement on treatment options, and 83 percent of physicians said their attitude toward the benefits of these documents had become more positive as a result of direct, personal experience using them. An overwhelming number of physicians endorsed the use of living wills and praised them for providing improved communication and trust, easier and more confident treatment decision, less stress and guilt, and the promotion of patient autonomy.

Having a living will, however, no matter what it may say, does not deprive you of a doctor's counsel. Living will or no living will, if you're a patient in a hospital, a doctor will fight to do everything possible to preserve your life until the condition you specified in your living will occurs, including helping you to understand, for as long as you're capable of reasoning, all the options you have. A living will simply gives you the power to draw limits you know you want to draw. Thus you remain autonomous in any decision making having to do with a long-term degenerative illness or a crippling accident, and your physician remains a costrategist regarding your care, instead of a final authority.

11. What if my living will requests are not considered to be in my best interests by my doctor or my family? Legally speaking, your right to decide what's in your own best interest—as expressed in your living will—remains paramount. Patients who are capable of understanding the consequences of their decisions are not required to do what their families or physicians advise. The fact that a person's living will request seems unusual is not in itself grounds for doubting his or her competence to make medical decisions at the time the living will was written, even if he or she later does become incompetent.

The best way to avoid any conflicts of this nature is to forestall them by making sure all parties involved, or potentially involved, know exactly what your living will states so there are no surprises, misunderstandings, or hurt feelings. It would be very difficult for any medical team to ignore your family if they opposed your wishes so you should speak to family members (and to your physician) ahead of time about your living will.

12. What if my doctor doesn't believe in living wills? If after all your efforts to express your feelings on this subject, your doctor still has a problem with living wills, you may wish to change doctors.

13. Don't doctors risk prosecution if they honor someone's living will request to withhold life support? No doctor has ever been successfully prosecuted for withholding or withdrawing life support technology in accordance with a patient's or a family's wishes. Indeed, there is only one case on record of a doctor prosecuted for withdrawing life support technology from a terminal patient—the case was thrown out before trial in California and became a ringing endorsement of the patient's right to refuse treatment.

More to the point, a living will legally absolves a doctor from any civil or criminal liability in honoring a request to withhold or withdraw treatment. Your doctor cannot refuse to honor your living will requests on the grounds that he or she would otherwise face prosecution. *A living will protects both the doctor and the patient.* Doctors face a greater risk of liability for *not* honoring your living will—or not transfering you to another physician who would—than for following your legally valid instructions. If a doctor has a conscientious (e.g., moral or religious) objection to living wills, he or she is under an ethical and legal obligation to transfer care of the patient rather than ignore the written instructions and continue treatment.

14. Is there any situation in which the state might intervene to block one of my living will requests, even if the state has a living will statute?

In the Browning *case in Florida (see Chapter 3), a woman wrote in the state's living will that she would not want tube feeding if she were in a terminal condition. However, Florida law did not allow for the refusal of tube feeding and, after suffering a stroke, Mrs. Browning was in a permanently unconscious, as opposed to terminal, condition so her request was ignored. Doctors argued that Mrs. Browning must be fed by tube because her death was not "imminent." She died with the tube in place but three years later the Florida Supreme Court ruled that Mrs. Browning did have the right to refuse all life-sustaining treatment, including tube feeding, whatever her condition, in keeping with the Florida state constitutional right of self-determination. Taking its cue from* Cruzan, *the* Browning *decision made it clear that a patient's clearly expressed wishes must always be honored.*

The only situation when a patient's explicit wishes might be ignored is when a pregnant woman is permanently comatose. Even if her living will requests that she be given no artificial life support, support may nonetheless be provided if the fetus is viable and could mature to a point at which it could be delivered. Although this situation is exceedingly rare, some state statutes prohibit pregnant women from filling out living wills. The courts have not authoritatively addressed the effectiveness of advance directives during pregnancy.

15. How does a living will affect organ donation: Can a living will in any way prevent a patient from becoming an organ donor? Can a living will in any way make a patient more likely to be used as an organ donor? People concerned that a living will may prevent them from donating organs are worried that the withholding of certain kinds of life support may render their bodily organs unsuitable. This rarely happens. The withholding of life support technologies would not have any deleterious effect on such donatable body parts as the cornea or skin. It could cause damage to the so-called vital organs—the heart, liver, and kidneys—which, for donation purposes, must be protected from any trauma until they are removed from the body; but in most cases involving life support, these organs have already been rendered unsuitable by the underlying illness and/or by the age of the patient. Vital organs are often donated by young, healthy accident victims who have sustained immediate and fatal brain trauma. Living wills are irrelevant because the donor is already dead.

Although you may address the issue of organ donation in your living will, it will not necessarily be respected. If you want to become an organ donor, arrangements should be made with an appropriate institution, and an organ donor card carried (see *Resources,* p. 311, for more information).

As for whether you become a prime candidate for organ donation if you have a living will, this is a groundless fear. Organ donation can never be considered until the donor is legally dead, that is, until the entire brain has ceased to function or the heart has stopped permanently. In no case can a patient's treatment be terminated for the purpose of hastening death so that he or she can become an organ donor. There is absolutely no conflict between having a living will and being an organ donor.

Your underlying medical condition and age at the time of your death are virtually certain to determine your eligibility as an organ donor. Your living will has no bearing on these factors.

16. What is a DNR? Once you are admitted to a health facility, such as a hospital or a nursing home, you can, if you so desire, requires a "do not resuscitate" order (commonly referred to as a DNR).

A DNR is attached to your medical chart and instructs medical staff not to try to revive you if your breathing or heartbeat has stopped. This means physicians, nurses, and others will not initiate emergency procedures such as mouth-to-mouth resuscitation, external chest compression, electric shock, insertion of a tube to open your air passage, or any other intervention to restart your breathing or heartbeat.

DNR practices vary from state to state (and from hospital to hospital) and only a couple of states (New York, Montana, and Tennessee) have DNR statutes, but any adult patient can request a DNR order. If you are sick and incapable of deciding about resuscitation, a family member or someone close to you is allowed to decide on your behalf. If you want more control over who makes this decision you may appoint a person orally with two witnesses present or indicate your wishes in writing through a living will, a durable power of attorney for health care, or a separate statement signed by two witnesses.

Remember that a DNR applies to only one medical procedure—resuscitation after breathing or heartbeat has stopped—whereas a living will covers a much broader spectrum of treatments and scenarios. DNR orders may be included in your living will as one important treatment option but they can never be a substitute for a living will.

17. Will my living will be honored in an emergency? Will emergency medical services (EMS) resuscitate me? In an emergency outside the hospital it is usually impossible to determine the patient's chances of survival. Therefore, all possible efforts are made to preserve life and the patient's consent is presumed. When the patient's condition has stabilized to the degree where a better prognosis can be made, the living will can be implemented to withdraw or withhold unwanted treatment. DNR orders are sometimes written for patients—for example, in a hospice program—who plan to die at home. A number of emergency medical services have systems for honoring such requests.

18. What can and can't a durable power of attorney for health care (DPAHC) do for me? A durable power of attorney for health care is a legal document that lets you authorize another person (variously called an attorney-in-fact, a health-care agent, or a health-care proxy, depending on the state where you reside) to make health-care decisions for you when you lose capacity to make decisions for yourself. Situations involving lack of capacity, or incompetence, include unconsciousness (even temporary), coma, brain damage where you have lost your decision-making capability, or just being too sick to make reasoned medical choices. Someone you trust is legally empowered to represent and serve your best interests if you can't do so yourself.

The DPAHC has several advantages. It confers broader powers than a living will because it can allow your agent to make all health-care decisions for you, not just those involving terminal conditions. Your DPAHC spokesperson may be more assertive and insistent than a written document. He or she may, ideally, make a more convincing case at the bedside and be a more forceful advocate for your wishes. In addition, a personal agent who is familiar with your feelings and attitudes can be more flexible and adapt this thinking to new and unforeseen medical circumstances not included in your living will. Depending on your state, the specific responsibilities a health-care proxy assumes may include any combination, or all, of the following:

1. Giving, withholding, or withdrawing consent to specific medical or surgical measures with reference to your condition, prognosis, and known wishes and authorizing appropriate end-of-life care, including pain-relieving procedures.
2. Communicating your previous treatment decisions and, if necessary, interpreting your living will.
3. Granting releases to medical personnel.
4. Employing and discharging medical personnel.
5. Access to and disclosure of medical records.
6. Resorting to court action, if unavoidable, to obtain authorization regarding treatment decisions.
7. Expending (or withholding) funds needed to carry out medical treatment.

A durable power of attorney for health care is also only as effective as you allow it to be. You would be wise to discuss your treatment wishes thoroughly with your health-care agent, making sure he or she understands them and agrees to advocate for them if necessary.

19. Whom should I appoint as my health-care agent? The person you appoint could be your spouse, a relative, or close friend. Above all, it should be someone you trust and have confidence in. Make sure to choose someone who will respect your treatment decisions, is willing to take action on your behalf, and does not shrink from the burden of what may be a difficult and painful responsibility. All of this requires careful thought and full consultation with your agent.

20. Should I fill out both a durable power of attorney for health care and a living will? Ideally, yes—because executing both documents would provide you with the greatest amount of protection. However, the DPAHC is not an option for all patients. A great many people simply do not have anyone to appoint— either their spouse and other close relatives and friends have died, or else they have lost contact and are unavailable. This painful problem is frequently apparent when addressing audiences at hospitals and nursing homes. Slowly and politely, the hands raise and the questions emerge: "What if I don't know anybody to appoint?"

Sometimes, it is not a responsibility many feel a loved one can handle or their preferred agent is reluctant to undertake this duty. Moreover, not every patient is willing to give up what's left of their dwindling powers to another person. Some elderly or frail patients feel as if their lives have become a series of losses and surrenders; they are loathe to give up yet one more right to someone else.

For those who have no agent to appoint, a living will is absolutely essential.

Completing a living will as well as a DPAHC forces you to go through a detailed and systematic process of self-questioning: Would I want tube feeding if I were in PVS? or a prolonged coma? Living wills uncover and articulate your own most deeply held convictions, and motivate you to discuss attitudes about dying with family members and doctors. Ideally, DPAHCs should demand the same process. But there is a tendency among some people to simply hand over responsibility: "I appoint Jill as my agent and Jill will take care of everything. . . ." Your agent will have full legal authority to decide, but won't know what decisions to make on your behalf.

It is wise to fill out both a living will and a durable power of attorney for health care; the two documents complement and reinforce one another.

21. What guarantee do I have that my durable power of attorney for health care will be honored? A DPAHC has a high likelihood of being honored. The Patient Self-Determination Act will require increasing familiarity with both forms of advance directive, making its legitimacy even stronger.

All fifty states and the District of Columbia have statutes providing for some form of durable power. While an ordinary power of attorney lapses if you, the "principal," become incompetent, the durable power of attorney remains effective (or, in some states, takes effect) when and if you do become incompetent. It is "durable" because it endures or survives past the point of your incapacity.

Although durable powers of attorney have been used traditionally in connection with money or property, there is virtually no statute or court decision that restricts the use of durable power to such matters alone (Oklahoma is one exception). Many states (twenty-eight) have DPA statutes that permit agents to make medical decisions—including to withhold or withdraw treatment; still others (six) have statutes that through court decisions, attorneys general's opinions, or other statutes have been interpreted to give agents these rights. The six states are: Arizona, Colorado, Hawaii, Maryland, New Jersey, and Virginia.

In states that do not have statutes, the ordinary durable power of attorney appointment offers a potentially useful legal instrument. There is a general presumption in the legal community that if challenged, courts would allow such usage. Consult a local lawyer to draw up a durable power of attorney that addresses health-care issues in the most effective manner.

This does not mean you are giving your health-care proxy the right to make financial *and* health-care decisions for you. The two powers of attorney remain quite distinct unless you specifically request that one person be invested with *all* your decision-making powers. A durable power of attorney for health care is, as its name implies, a very specific instance of appointing another person to make health care, and only health care, decisions for you.

DPA statutes vary from state to state in terms of language, filing requirements, and restrictions imposed on use. Details and issues associated with completing and enforcing a DPAHC appear in Chapter 3 and Part Two.

22. Do I have to choose between my children for my durable power of attorney for health care or health-care agent? Yes. Ideally, you should *not* name them to equal power. Hospital personnel need one person they can depend on for a definitive decision. If you named all your children equally and one was unavailable, the others would not be able to proceed without him or her. And there is the chance for disagreement among your children regarding your real preferences. If you wish, you can name your children in a stated order of priority, for example, "If Jane is unavailable, then Mary."

23. What if I choose someone outside my family and my family doesn't like my health-care agent? Your family cannot void a DPA designation except through a court order. To do so, proof must exist that your health-care agent did not act according to your wishes or best interests, a difficult charge. People who live in unmarried relationships may prefer to name their companion as agent. Others who simply disagree with their families may also choose someone else. As a precaution, always talk to your friends and family members about your preferences. They should know why you have chosen your agent and what your wishes are.

24. Couldn't I just express my general wishes in writing, without having to fill out a form that forces them to fit specific issues? Naturally you are free to express your general wishes in writing, and such a document may, indeed, carry weight in any decisions made about your future medical treatment—

especially if that document is dated and signed by yourself and a witness. However, it is generally preferable to have a legally sanctioned and recognizable advance directive form. You can always attach additional thoughts to a living will or DPAHC (see Chapter 3).

25. Should minors (people under eighteen years old) have a living will and a durable power of attorney for health care? A living will and DPAHC have no legal validity unless the person who completes them is more than eighteen years of age. However, anything concerning his or her medical care that a minor cares about enough to put into writing may be influential in cases where difficult decisions need to be made.

26. Can parents fill out a living will for their children? Generally no, although in four states (Arkansas, Texas, Louisiana, and New Mexico) parents can fill out a living will for their child or make medical decisions through the living will act. As a matter of practice, parents have legal guardianship of their children until they are adults and exercise common law control over the child's health care. Parents can generally make decisions to end a child's life support if to do so would be in the child's best interest.

27. Can parents or guardians fill out a living will for a mentally retarded person? No. Only competent adults may execute living wills. A person need not be able to write his or her name (another person can usually do that) but must be able to understand what a living will is, its content, and function. As with children (see questions 25 and 26), parents and guardians generally (but not in all states) have medical decision-making authority for mentally retarded persons and may make treatment choices based on the best interest of the patient.

28. What about living wills and the physically handicapped? People who are physically handicapped have exactly the same rights as people who are not. The determining factor in composing a living will is whether an individual has decision-making capacity or mental competence, not what his or her physical condition might be.

29. What is the religious attitude toward treatment refusal? While I can't speak for all personal belief systems, I can say that within all the major organized religions in the United States there is strong moral authority for a person's right to refuse medical treatment in the types of extreme situations we've been examining. Some religious subgroups—for example, certain segments of the Catholic Church and some Orthodox Jewish groups—believe all life-sustaining treatment must be given. However, the mainstream of Catholic,

Jewish, and Protestant opinion holds that the individual's right to self-determination, and to freedom from undue pain and suffering, permits the refusal of life support. With their emphasis on spiritual values, these religions do not believe that the continuance of mere physical or molecular existence is morally defensible or socially desirable:

Pope John Paul II. "When inevitable death is imminent in spite of the means used, it is permitted in conscience to take the decision to refuse forms of treatment that would only secure a precarious and burdensome prolongation of life."

Central Conference of American Rabbis. "The conclusion from the spirit of Jewish law is that while you may not do anything to hasten death you may, under special circumstances of suffering and helplessness, allow death to come."

United Methodist Church. "We assert the right of every person to die in dignity without efforts to prolong terminal illness merely because the technology is available to do so."

No decision regarding medical treatment at the end of life is free from moral or ethical concerns. Whatever the particular situation, there's always the difficult issue of determining what treatment program will simultaneously benefit the patient physically, honor the patient's specific moral and ethical belief system, and harmonize with prevailing cultural attitudes toward the primacy of life. Ultimately, your own personal religious views are paramount, whether or not you subscribe to the official position. It may be a good idea to discuss your feelings and convictions with your priest, rabbi, minister, or any other religious or spiritual adviser whom you respect.

30. How does the general public feel about treatment refusal? The overwhelming majority of Americans believe individuals may refuse life support when there is little or no hope for recovery. A 1991 Gallup poll found that "adults in the U.S. strongly feel death is preferable to living in permanent pain or on life-support systems." When asked directly, a dramatic 84 percent said they would want treatment withheld. Only 9 percent said they would want to be left on life support systems.

An extensive nationwide poll conducted by the National Law Journal at the time of the U.S. Supreme Court decision on Nancy Cruzan (June 1990) posed two questions:

1. Suppose a patient is in a coma, doctors say there is no chance of recovery, and the patient is getting food and water through a feeding tube. Should a close member of the family have the right to tell the doctor to remove the feeding tube and let the patient die, or not?
2. Suppose you were in a coma with no chance of recovery and were being kept alive by a feeding tube. Would you want the doctor to remove the feeding tube and let you die, or not?

81 percent of the respondents answered yes to question one; 85 percent said yes to question two. There is a strong consensus in favor of a person's natural death as opposed to sustaining life solely by artificial means.

31. What is the difference between the right to die, euthanasia, and suicide?
Many people confuse these terms. Here are a few quick definitions that make some important distinctions.

Euthanasia. This means the bringing about of a gentle death (the Greek root *euthanatos* literally translates as "good death") for someone else who would otherwise not have it.

Passive Euthansia. This means the right to refuse life support systems if they are all that's keeping you alive. Almost every state in the United States has recognized a common law and constitutional right to passive euthanasia and most have passed legislation protecting it. Living wills and durable powers of attorney for health care are legal forms allowing individuals to safeguard this right and avoid unwanted medical treatment. As defined by the Society for the Right to Die, the right to die involves passive euthanasia, because death is allowed to come naturally, without intervention. We do not support active euthanasia (i.e., hastening death by lethal injection or what most people commonly refer to as "euthanasia") which is illegal.

Active Euthanasia. Also known as "mercy killing," active euthanasia directly causes death by some active means, such as administration of a lethal injection. Holland is the only country in the world where active euthanasia is openly tolerated, although it is technically against the law. However, if certain specified criteria are met (patients are hopelessly ill, in great pain, have repeatedly requested to die, and have been examined by several physicians who agree they are rational and have no chance for recovery), then Holland legally permits this practice. In the United States there is no legal mechanism for permitting active euthanasia.

Suicide. Suicide is the willful (i.e., conscious and decisive) taking of one's life by some sort of active means, such as swallowing poison or throwing oneself in front of a moving automobile. The Hemlock Society advocates the choice of suicide as an option for terminally ill patients. Although suicide has been decriminalized in the United States, people do not have a legal "right" to commit suicide. The Society for the Right to Die acknowledges that many people wish to have this kind of control over the timing of their death.

Assisted Suicide. This refers to enlisting someone else's help in taking your life by some active means. Physician-assisted suicide is a specialized case where physicians are sought to help bring on death by patients who are still capable of making decisions. It is an issue of conscious self-determination rather than incompetency. Physician-assisted suicide may include the *Kevorkian* case, where an otherwise healthy middle-aged woman suffering from Alzheimer's disease enlisted the aid of a doctor she had never met before, and used his highly publicized suicide machine to terminate her life, and the *Quill* case, where a doctor prescribed sleeping pills so a woman with severe leukemia, a patient whom he had treated for many years, could kill herself. About half the states have laws forbidding assisted suicide; in the other half, the law on this issue is unclear. There is no legal mechanism allowing an individual to request assistance in taking his or her own life.

If you are concerned about moral and ethical issues as they pertain to a living will or to dying in general, by all means discuss this issue with people who share your belief system, especially those with experience in counseling and in attending deaths, such as religious advisers or mental health professionals.

32. Will my life insurance be affected if I have a living will? No. Your living will has no effect on your life insurance. Many living will laws explicitly state that new insurance applications cannot be turned down or existing policies affected by the signing of a living will.

Signing a living will, terminating life-prolonging treatment, or not starting treatment at all is *not* considered suicide.

33. Should I videotape my living will? This is an option for those who want it, but it is not essential. Cost is one factor, because some groups charge as much as $300 for a living will videotape "package." You would also need to take special precautions to make sure the tape could not be tampered with. A videotape is not especially practical in health-care settings, where videocassette recorders (VCRs) are not available by most bedsides. However, a living will videotape would probably constitute clear and convincing evidence of your wishes. You might want to take this additional step and record your treatment preferences on tape in the event your case went to court. A living will videotape may be a useful supplement, but it can never be a substitute for the written living will form.

34. What is the status of living wills and DPAs in Canada? Any Canadian has the right to refuse life-sustaining medical treatment or to have such treatment terminated. Many hospitals and physicians, including the Canadian Medical Association, accept advance directives in principle and one organization, Dying With Dignity, has distributed more than 200,000 in the past decade. Nevertheless, Canada has lagged behind the United States in securing legislative approval for living wills and durable powers of attorney for health care.

In 1988, Nova Scotia authorized appointment of delegated decision-makers for health care but stipulated that specific government forms must be used. To date, no such forms have been developed.

In Quebec, a law called the Mandat allows patients to grant their regular power of attorney the right to make health care decisions. However, this provision is included as part of the testamentary will, which is not usually addressed until *after* the principle has died. Giving the same person control over your property and health care decisions may also create conflicts of interest.

Two bills now before the legislature could make Ontario the first province to legalize living wills and DPAHCs. One, a broad living will bill called the "Consent to Treatment Act," would grant patients the legal right to refuse unwanted treatment give and health care providers civil immunity from liability for following such instructions. The second, a DPAHC bill called "Substitute Decisions Act," would allow patients to appoint a health-care agent. The two bills, which have broad, multi-party support, are being closely watched by other provinces, such as Manitoba and Alberta, both considering similar initiatives.

A generic Canadian living will and DPAHC form are currently available from Dying With Dignity. Consult the appendix and resource list for more information. Because there are as yet no legislatively-approved forms in Canada, you may also use generic forms from the Society for the Right to Die and other American groups.

35. Wouldn't it be better to wait until I face a particular life-and-death situation before making out my living will and durable power of attorney for health care? Under no circumstances is it better to wait before making out a living will or a durable power of attorney. At any time, you can suddenly be physically and mentally incapacitated by an accident or even a stroke or heart attack, in which case you may well need the protection.

Let's assume you escape such a sudden catastrophe and don't make out a living will and DPAHC until a deteriorating medical situation hospitalizes you and there becomes a palpable need to do so. Odds are overwhelmingly in your favor that these documents will be effective even though completed at the last minute. Nevertheless, you're betting on a bureaucracy and gambling with your life. And as your condition further deteriorates, you may not be able to give the advance directive your full mental powers. The time to make out your living will and durable power of attorney for health care is now.

CHAPTER THREE

Composing Your Living Will and Durable Power of Attorney for Heath Care

It is just as neurotic in old age not to focus upon the goal of death as it is in youth to repress fantasies which have to do with the future.

—C. J. JUNG, *"The Soul and Death"*

This chapter would be much easier to write if there were one uniform living will and one durable power of attorney for health care accepted by every state. Unfortunately, there aren't, and probably won't be for some time. In its landmark 1990 *Cruzan* decision, the U.S. Supreme Court, while acknowledging that competent individuals have a constitutional liberty right to be free of unwanted medical treatment, pointedly left the issue of how to regulate this right for incompetent patients to the states. As Justice Sandra Day O'Connor wrote, "Today we decide only that one state's practice does not violate the Constitution; the more challenging task of crafting appropriate procedures for safeguarding incompetents' liberty interests is entrusted to the 'laboratory' of the states."

One of the biggest difficulties confronting the laboratory of the states—a challenge faced by any individual who wishes to safeguard his or her own interests through an advance directive—is the problem of defining terms. Some states speak of not using "heroic measures" to sustain a life that is obviously ending. Other states call such measures "life-prolonging." Still others refer to them as "death-prolonging." Each of these phrases invites a slightly different interpretation of what specific measures can and can't be withdrawn in a particular end-of-life situation, and all of these phrases are so vague that a great deal is left to the doctor's or the court's discretion.

The variety of phrases used to describe relevant end-of-life situations is even more confusing. At what stage in an incompetent patient's illness does a living will become applicable: When the patient has "no reasonable expectation of improvement"? When the patient is "terminally ill"? When "death is imminent"? Or only when two—or all three—of these descriptions apply? Frequently, statutes include very precise definitions of these words but they are in the law books, not the document itself.

After suffering through the deaths of numerous friends hooked up to feeding tubes, eighty-five-year-old Estelle Browning, a life-long resident of Dunedin, Florida, had the foresight to make out a living will in 1985. Unfortunately, her Florida living will instructions were more limited than she intended. In her living will, Browning stated she did not want to be fed by tube if she were in a condition where death was "imminent." A year later, a stroke left her totally and irreversibly paralyzed, unable to communicate or swallow. Doctors at her nursing home, obeying a state requirement that nursing homes must feed all patients, inserted a feeding tube into her stomach. When her guardian tried to honor her wishes by petitioning for removal of the feeding tube, doctors refused on the grounds that Browning's death was not "imminent." Assuming she remained connected to the feeding tube, they argued, she could remain alive indefinitely.

The Browning case eventually went to court. The trial court upheld the doctors' position. When an appellate court reversed it, the state attorney appealed to the Supreme Court. Browning died at age eighty-nine with her nasogastric tube in place, while the case was still pending in the Supreme Court, having existed for more than two years in precisely the situation her guardian knew she had wished to avoid.

At least Browning's dilemma was not in vain. In a unanimous decision in 1990, the Florida State Supreme Court emphasized the patient's desire as the controlling factor. Basing its ruling on the right to privacy found in the Florida state constitution, the court held that the right to die is a "fundamental right of self-determination" and that food and water can be refused by patients or by surrogates acting in their behalf in any situation of the patient's permanent incompetence, providing there is written or oral evidence the patient would have desired such a refusal.

Whether or not your state has its own specific living will document, it's a good idea to record your wishes as clearly and thoroughly as possible in a less restricted "generic" living will. If you live in a state that already has a legal form, you should fill it out. But you should also fill out the generic living will to amplify and expand your wishes, giving you broader powers than most state documents. For example, Missouri's living will prohibits the refusal of tube feeding. If you live in Missouri and want to refuse tube feeding, you can do so by filling out a generic living will and there is a good chance your wishes will be constitutionally protected. By defining exactly what your wishes are, you can avoid becoming a victim—like Estelle Browning—of the limitations, vagueness, and built-in problems of the official state form. If you live in a state without any living will legislation, the generic living will can serve as the clearest and most convincing evidence of your wishes. Courts in any state are capable of recognizing a patient's or a surrogate's legal right to reject life support measures under certain conditions even when there is no specific state statute. Even more important, detailed instructions regarding what you do and do not want—regardless of whether these wishes are legally protected by your state—will help your family and doctors implement your decisions.

In this chapter, I will assist you, step by step, as you complete the generic living will designed by the Society for the Right to Die. It covers a wider range of medical situations and treatments than most living will forms authorized by state law. I will also give you advice on making out a durable power of attorney for health care form, using the statutory Health Care Proxy form of New York State. Unlike the society's generic living will form, which you should fill out regardless of your state law, the New York Health Care Proxy form is valid only for New York. Nevertheless, it will give you a good overview of the key issues and questions that arise with regard to specific state DPAHC forms. More information about the legal differences among states is offered in Part Two.

You can get copies of the generic living will form by photocopying the page from this book or writing to the Society for the Right to Die, 250 W. Fifty-seventh Street, New York, NY 10107. Your state's living will (if such a document exists) and durable power of attorney for health care forms are available from its department of health or other relevant state agency, as well as from the Society for the Right to Die. Part Two has the appropriate documents for each state, and the appendix provides a list of resources.

The Generic Living Will

In the discussion that follows, I will be taking you line by line through the Society for the Right to Die's generic living will or "Living Will Declaration." A copy of the entire living will form appears on the opposite page. Passages from the will are followed by explanatory commentary.

Society for the Right to Die

50 West 57th Street/New York, NY 10107

Living Will Declaration

To My Family, Doctors, and All Those Concerned with My Care

I, _____, being of sound mind, make this statement as a directive to be followed if I become unable to participate in decisions regarding my medical care.

This declaration sets forth your directions regarding medical treatment.

If I should be in an incurable or irreversible mental or physical condition with no reasonable expectation of recovery, I direct my attending physician to withhold or withdraw treatment that merely prolongs my dying. I further direct that treatment be limited to measures to keep me comfortable and to relieve pain.

You have the right to refuse treatment you do not want, and you may request the care you do want.

These directions express my legal right to refuse treatment. Therefore I expect my family, doctors, and everyone concerned with my care to regard themselves as legally and morally bound to act in accord with my wishes, and in so doing to be free of any legal liability for having followed my directions.

You may list specific treatment you do not want. For example:

Cardiac resuscitation
Mechanical respiration
Artificial feeding/fluids by tube

Otherwise, your general statement, top right, will stand for your wishes.

I especially do not want: _____

_____

_____

_____

_____

You may want to add instructions or care you do want—for example, pain medication; or that you prefer to die at home if possible.

Other instructions/comments: _____

_____

_____

Proxy Designation Clause: Should I become unable to communicate my instructions as stated above, I designate the following person to act in my behalf:

Name _____

Address _____

If you want, you can name someone to see that your wishes are carried out, but you do not have to do this.

If the person I have named above is unable to act on my behalf, I authorize the following person to do so:

Name _____

Address _____

This Living Will Declaration expresses my personal treatment preferences. The fact that I may have also executed a document in the form recommended by state law should not be construed to limit or contradict this Living Will Declaration, which is an expression of my common-law and constitutional rights.

Signed: _____ Date: _____

Witness: _____ Witness: _____

Address: _____ Address: _____

_____ _____

Sign and date here in the presence of two adult witnesses, who should also sign.

Keep the signed original with your personal papers at home. Give signed copies to doctors, family, and proxy. Review your Declaration from time to time; initial and date it to show it still expresses your intent.

(1) LIVING WILL DECLARATION
   To My Family, Doctors, and All Those Concerned with My Care

This document is called a Living Will Declaration and is addressed to anyone who might be involved with your care. It is a personal statement, almost in the form of a letter, in which you formally set down your wishes as a matter of record.

(2) I, _____, being of sound mind, make this statement as a directive to be followed if I become permanently unable to participate in decisions regarding my medical care.

The living will does not go into effect until you have *irrevocably* lost either your mental capacity to make decisions about medical care or your ability to communicate or both. As long as you retain such decision-making and communicating capabilities, you can refuse or permit any form of medical treatment in person, as it is offered. As long as you can speak for yourself, you are always in charge of your health care. The living will is thus a contingency (just-in-case) document: It is a form of insurance against some eventuality you hope will never arise—but if it does, you are now prepared to deal with it.

   Even if patients are still able to communicate, they can lose their ability to make medical decisions when they are no longer able to understand information about their medical condition and its implications. The ability to understand other, unrelated concepts is not relevant. Determination of capacity is not generally a strictly legal or a medical matter; what is at issue is a commonsense evaluation of whether the patient does or does not have decision-making capacity about the particular decision at hand. In the words of the 1983 President's Commission for the Study of Ethical Problems in Medicine and Biomedical and Behavioral Research, whether a patient is competent or incompetent is a "judgment of the type an informed layperson can make," a determination of whether a patient has the ability to "understand" a situation and to make a choice "in light of that understanding."

Courts have specifically ruled on what capacity means and does not mean in the context of refusing treatment. These rulings often function as guidelines for physicians who must make capacity judgments. For example, courts have found a patient may not be deemed incompetent solely because his or her refusal of treatment seems irrational to the physician. In a case involving a woman who refused life-sustaining treatment on religious grounds, a court ruled:

> Even though we may consider appellant's beliefs unwise, foolish, or ridiculous, in the absence of overriding danger to society we may not permit interference therewith for the sole purpose of compelling her to accept medical treatment forbidden by her religious principles, and previously refused by her with full knowledge of the probable consequences.

Also, a patient cannot be deemed incompetent because he or she is generally inclined to be forgetful or confused. In the words of one court, referring to a patient of this type, what must be determined is whether the "areas of forgetfulness and confusion cause, or relate in any way to, impairment of ability to understand that in rejecting the [treatment] the patient is, in effect, choosing death over life." A patient in the very early stages of Alzheimer's disease, for example, who is forgetful but can still hold intelligent conversations cannot be regarded as incompetent.

Even a diagnosed mental illness does not necessarily imply legal incompetence for decision-making purposes. A patient suffering from chronic undifferentiated schizophrenia who had been committed to a Pennsylvania state hospital was not found to be legally incompetent for the purpose of making a medical decision. The court found the "mere commitment" for treatment of a mental illness does not destroy competency. Although the court accepted that the patient was later, and at the time of the hearing, delusional, her original refusal to consent to a surgical biopsy was, in the opinion of the court, "informed and conscious of the consequences."

There are, however, cases where patients are not able to make a competent decision. In Tennessee, a patient was found to be incompetent to make a decision about amputation of her feet because she could not, or would not, accept the fact that her feet were infected. This delusion was central to the medical decision to be made, and therefore, it rendered her incapable of making it. Untreated, the infection would lead to her death.

Almost always, capacity is obvious to all observers, whether or not they have a medical background. In rare cases of real dispute between the family and the doctor, competency judgments may be referred to the court. The court will then hear testimony from the patient, various medical personnel, family members, and friends of the patient. If the court is unable to hear firsthand testimony from the patient, a court delegate may be appointed to go and observe the patient at the bedside. Finally, the judge will decide whether the patient is able to make decisions that adequately protect his or her interests.

---

(3) If I should be in an incurable or irreversible mental or physical condition with no reasonable expectation of recovery, I direct my attending physician to withhold or withdraw treatment that merely prolongs my dying.

The circumstances described in these lines cover the extreme situations when permanently incompetent patients are likely to be candidates for medical treatments that can prolong their lives indefinitely without any reasonable hope of improving their condition. The decision-making capability of the patient is presumed to be lost forever, and the only medical possibilities in the patient's future—with or without life support treatments—are presumed to be physical decline and death.

The term *incurable* covers many terminal conditions and suggests a steady, inevitable deterioration, as in metastatic cancer, whereas *irreversible* includes certain neurologic conditions, such as a persistent vegetative state (PVS), that will never be reversed but will not necessarily deteriorate further. It usually takes time to determine whether a condition is irreversible. For example, the extent of damage as a result of stroke cannot and should not be decided too hastily. Once it is clear that there is no possibility of reversing an injury or illness and the patient is incompetent, the living will comes into play.

No reasonable expectation of recovery indicates we are within the bounds of reasonable medical certainty. No one can ever totally rule out the possibility of a "miraculous" recovery but a living will addresses the most likely or scientifically predictable outcomes.

Hope and recovery are crucial. Most people would be willing to put up with a great deal of burdensome treatment for a realistic chance of recovery. But when there is no hope, or virtually none, many patients do not want life sustaining technology that "merely prolongs my [their] dying."

Nowhere in the passage does it say death must be *imminent,* the term that caused so much trouble in the *Browning* case. Usually in incurable or irreversible conditions, however, death is expected to occur relatively soon if no life support measures are employed. Death is perceived as a natural process, the body's way of closing down when it has been permanently impaired and overwhelmed by illness or injury. The physician is thus directed to "withhold" (refrain from initiating) or "withdraw" (discontinue) medical interventions that can have no effect on the underlying condition but only postpone the moment of death.

---

(4) I further direct that treatment be limited to measures to keep me comfortable and to relieve pain.

It is not by accident that comfort measures follow so closely on withholding or withdrawing treatment. Patients who wish to assert their right to refuse life sustaining care in terminal situations also have the right to demand they receive adequate comfort care. This would include relief from any pain that might be caused by the withholding or withdrawing of treatment.

Some life support treatments are painful and discomforting—withholding or withdrawing them may actually increase comfort. There are also certain sophisticated modalities for providing pain relief including analgesic pumps, nerve blocks, and palliative radiation, that can be administered independently.

Some people object to the removal of tube feeding because they fear the discomfort it might cause. Yet death after withdrawing tube feeding usually occurs peacefully within two to fourteen days. Unconscious patients are believed to be completely unaware of the process. Conscious patients who are neurologically impaired quickly slip into a coma and become equally unaware. Throughout the interim before death, the overwhelming preponderance of medical evidence and observation indicates these patients experience neither hunger, thirst, nor pain. As an extra precaution, adequate sedation is provided prior to removing the feeding tube. Lester Cruzan confirmed this about his daughter Nancy's death following the removal of her feeding tube, when he said "Her final days of dying were very peaceful."

---

(5) These directions express my legal right to refuse treatment. Therefore, I expect my family, doctors, and everyone concerned with my care to regard

themselves as legally and morally bound to act in accord with my wishes, and in so doing to be free of any legal liability for having followed my directions.

You have the legal right to refuse treatment you do not want, and you may request the treatment you do want. Regardless of your specific state's living will, or lack of one, every American has a common law right to bodily integrity—the possession and control of your own person, free from all restraint or interference. Even the touching of one person by another without consent or without legal justification is a battery. Bodily integrity translates into a requirement of informed consent for medical treatment; you must fully understand and agree to any medical procedure before it can be undertaken on you. The doctrine of informed consent also means, conversely, that you possess the right *not* to consent, that is, to refuse treatment.

In this section you are not only asserting your legal right to refuse treatment—and the legal and moral obligation of others to honor your wishes—you are also absolving them of any legal liability for following your instructions. This immunity clause is very important to physicians and others who might be concerned about lawsuits, or the threat of lawsuits. You are making it crystal clear that the decision to refuse treatment is yours, and yours alone; others are merely acting on your direction.

---

(6) I especially do not want:

This section allows you to list specific treatments you do not want. You are under no obligation to write in anything. This living will is designed to stand on its own as a broad document. Your general statement earlier (3) can represent your wish to withhold or withdraw treatment that only prolongs your dying.

If you *do* have particularly strong feelings about certain kinds of treatment you wish to refuse, you may state them here by customizing the living will to fit your specific needs. Treatments most commonly included are cardiac resuscitation, mechanical respiration, artificial feeding and administration of fluids by tube, antibiotics, dialysis, surgical procedures, invasive diagnostic tests, intravenous line, chemotherapy, radiation, and blood transfusions.

Life support treatments that you *do* want administered in such extreme situations are not listed because these requests are generally unnecessary. Your doctor will always provide medically appropriate care as long as there is any chance of recovery. Nevertheless, if you want to emphasize your wish to be provided with specific life support treatments, or if you want to set any conditions affecting the administration of those life support treatments, you can do so later in passage (7).

Be specific about tube feeding, a subject of disagreement among some groups. Despite the fact the Supreme Court ruled in *Cruzan* that it could discern no difference between tube feeding and other forms of life support patients may refuse—and as a result, any state statute restricting artificial feeding is now constitutionally suspect—it is still prudent to make a specific statement concerning your feelings about this form of treatment.

For the sake of clarity, I have divided passage (6) into separate categories so that we can discuss individual treatments you may wish to refuse. Each new treatment is italicized.

(6a) I especially do not want *cardiac resuscitation.*

If cardiac (and cardiopulmonary) resuscitation is started promptly, it is possible the patient can be restored to his or her previous level of health. If not, the brain and other vital organs can be permanently damaged. Following such resuscitation, further medical intervention in an intensive care unit is often instituted, even if it cannot alter the overall prognosis.

In hopeless illness, cardiopulmonary arrest allows death to occur peacefully. For this reason, you may wish to state you would not want CPR to be administered if your condition were incurable.

In Chapter 2, I discussed how to initiate do not resuscitate (DNR) orders when you enter a hospital. But for maximum protection against unwanted cardiac resuscitation, you need to specify this in your living will. Indeed, if you're incapacitated by an accident or an unexpected stroke or heart attack before you get to a hospital, you may never be able to initiate a DNR, in which case a living will directive becomes all-important.

Edward Winter, an eighty-two-year-old retired furniture refinisher from Cincinnati, Ohio, suffered a heart attack that would have killed him had he not been revived through electric shock treatment to the heart. Winter had recently watched the slow, upsetting death of his wife—she suffered brain damage after being resuscitated from a heart attack of her own—and resolved nothing like that would happen to him. When his time came, he told his children they should simply let him die. He told his doctor the same thing. But the instructions were not recorded on the monitor by Winter's hospital bed and, when he began to die, an attending nurse applied electrodes to his chest and revived him. Two days later, he suffered a debilitating stroke that left him partly paralyzed and largely confined to bed in a nursing home. According to newspaper reports at the time, the totally dependent Winter could "utter only a few words before he begins to cry, in despair."

Depressed and angry that he had not been left alone and allowed to die in peace and dignity, Winter filed a "wrongful life" suit against the hospital, charging them with negligence for failing to follow his instructions and with battery for giving him a jolt of electricity without his authorization. His medical bills had climbed over $100,000, depleting the life savings he had wished to leave his children and saddling him with debt for treatment he had specifically rejected. According to his lawyer, "Mr. Winter did not believe in cardiac resuscitation. When he went into the hospital he told everyone who would listen, 'If it's my time, it's my time.'" After his worst fears were realized and he was revived, Winter's doctors agreed he would remain bedridden and dependent for the rest of his life. Two years later, in June 1990, Edward Winter died. His family is continuing a suit to recover his nursing home costs and damages for emotional suffering.

The Winter case illustrates the strong feelings of many patients, particularly the elderly, about not being resuscitated once their prognosis becomes poor. In the types of situation covered by a living will, cardiac resuscitation (known in the hospital world as "a code") most often takes the aggressive form of chest pressure or stimulation of the heart with an electric paddle. While CPR can be a tremendous lifesaving measure in cases of sudden, unexpected cardiopulmonary failure, it is not always desirable for terminal, irreversibly ill patients. Still many may opt for this treatment.

(6b) I especially do not want *mechanical respiration.*

Patients are connected to mechanical respirators (or "ventilators") for one of two reasons: they are still capable of breathing on their own, but need mechanical assistance to achieve adequate levels of oxygen and to expel carbon dioxide or they have ceased breathing on their own altogether. The ability to breathe is regulated by the brain stem or "lower brain," meaning that even a person who has lost all cerebral function but maintains brain stem activity and exists in PVS may still not need a respirator.

The respirator itself is a machine that alternates between pumping oxygen into a patient's lungs and drawing carbon dioxide out. The patient is usually connected by a tube inserted into the patient's trachea (windpipe) through the nose or through the mouth and throat. The tube can cause a significant amount of discomfort as well as damage to the trachea. Some conscious patients who need long-term mechanical respiration may be more comfortable or better off with a tracheostomy, a surgical procedure that leaves a small hole though the neck and trachea into which the respirator tube can be inserted.

Assuming your underlying physical condition is fairly stabilized and tolerable, you may want to rely on mechanical respiration temporarily if it means surviving a bout of pneumonia—or even permanently, via a portable respirator, if it means living an acceptable life with emphysema or amytrophic lateral sclerosis (Lou Gehrig's disease). Conversely, you may not want to be hooked up to a respirator to overcome pneumonia if your underlying physical condition is terminal and intolerable, and you may dread the prospect of permanent dependence on a respirator no matter what the circumstances.

You may wish to refuse mechanical respiration if it only prolongs the dying process, but would want all other measures to preserve comfort, including oxygen or sedation, as needed. If you would like to make any further qualifications regarding mechanical respiration you can do so later in passage (7).

(6c) I especially do not want *artificial feeding/fluids by tube.*

Tube feeding is administered when a patient loses the ability to swallow. This almost always happens when a patient is unconscious, and commonly occurs when a conscious patient suffers massive brain damage or a neurological disorder such as severe dementia, Parkinson's disease, or a stroke. Patients with serious burns or bedsores are also given tube feeding if they are not able to take in enough nutrients by mouth to make up for those lost through their damaged skin. All patients connected to respirators must also be tube fed because people who are intubated (hooked up to a respirator tube) cannot take food by mouth.

Intravenous feeding, in which a tube is inserted into a vein, is the most basic form of tube feeding, but it does not always satisfy the patient's complete nutritional needs. It may provide calories and some minerals, as well as fluids to maintain metabolism for the short term. But in most cases of serious illness where long-term maintenance is indicated, doctors rely on nasogastric or gastrostomy feeding.

Nasogastric tubes are inserted through the nostril into the stomach. They come in two sizes: "large bore" (about the diameter of a pencil) and "small bore" (about half that diameter). For the conscious patient, insertion of a large-bore tube can be an uncomfortable, if not painful, process, and the tube may continue to cause discomfort while it's in place. The small-bore tube is better tolerated, and although it may still be uncomfortable, it is vastly preferable for feeding purposes.

There are other patient-related complications associated with nasogastric tubes. A conscious but uncooperative patient may try to remove it, necessitating the use of hand restraints. If a conscious patient is aware of the tube but does not understand its purpose (e.g., someone with Alzheimer's disease), he or she may experience fear, agitation, and depression. Also, a nasogastric tube makes it difficult to swallow, worsening the risk that saliva or food from the stomach can be inhaled and increasing the chances the patient might develop "aspiration pneumonia."

In cases of long-term artificial feeding, an alternative to the nasogastric tube is a gastrostomy, or G-tube, placed directly into the stomach by way of a surgical incision through the abdominal wall. Although placement of a gastrostomy tube requires a surgical procedure, once in place, it is far more comfortable for the conscious patient, and because it is less noticeable to the patient and, therefore, less likely to be pulled out, hand restraints are not often required.

Permanently unconscious and severely brain-damaged people can often be maintained for many years on tube feeding if other medical problems are treated. Without liquids, death occurs in approximately two days to two weeks, as a result of dehydration or infection. Most evidence indicates people who are unconscious or who have severe brain damage do not experience discomfort from this process. In seriously ill or dying patients, the process of dehydration generally produces sleepiness and coma, making the person unaware of the dying process. Narcotics and sedatives can be used if there is any question about pain. However, there is no evidence that this kind of death is painful. But forced feeding by tube can be an extremely unpleasant way to spend the last months of life.

Many people regard tube feeding for hopelessly ill patients as an artificial disruption and prolongation of the dying process, just like other life sustaining medical treatments. The techniques used to pass artificial nutrients and fluid into the patient's alimentary canal all involve some degree of intrusion and constraint. As Justice O'Connor wrote in *Cruzan*, "Artificial feeding cannot readily be distinguished from other forms of medical treatment. . . . Accordingly, the liberty guaranteed by the Due Process Clause must protect, if it protects anything, an individual's deeply personal decision to reject medical treatment, including the artificial delivery of food and water."

If you would like to make any further qualifications regarding feeding tubes (i.e., specifying a maximum length of time to be kept alive by a feeding tube), you can do so later in passage (7).

(6d) I especially do not want *antibiotics.*

During the natural process of dying, especially when that process involves a chronic disease or a long-term degenerative disease like cancer, diabetes, multiple sclerosis, Huntington's chorea, chronic renal failure, Alzheimer's disease, or Lou Gehrig's disease, the body often develops specific infections that can ultimately cause death. The most familiar of these is pneumonia. If you are at the end of life or chronically ill or progressively deteriorating, you may prefer not to have such infections treated with antibiotics, because your recovery would not improve your underlying health.

It is important to remember that serious infection in dying and brain-damaged people can lead to sleep or coma even before other symptoms occur. This may be the body's way of producing a peaceful death. By curing the infection, an antibiotic may make the hopelessly ill patient more fully conscious of his or her discomfort. You may wish to state that you would not want antibiotics if they merely prolonged the dying process.

In some situations, it can be difficult to determine whether or not curing a given infection would be in the patient's best interest. In these situations, a more specific living will instruction can make a big difference. If you find yourself facing a particular illness, you should gather all the information you can about the types of infection you may encounter with that illness and then express your wishes for or against antibiotic treatment relevant to each of those infectious situations in an attachment to your living will.

Tom Wirth, a forty-seven-year-old New Yorker, paid a heavy price for not doing this. Wirth had been diagnosed as having AIDS related complex (ARC) before he was hospitalized on July 6, 1987. On April 13, 1987, he had executed a living will and a medical power of attorney appointing his friend of twenty-two years, John Evans, as his attorney-in-fact. The living will stated:

> *I direct that life-sustaining procedures should be withheld or withdrawn if I have illness, disease or injury or experience extreme mental deterioration, such that there is no reasonable expectation of recovering or regaining a meaningful quality of life. These life-sustaining procedures that may be withheld or withdrawn include, but are not limited to: Surgery, Antibiotics, Cardiac Resuscitation, Respiratory Support, Artificially Administered Feeding and Fluid.*

On arrival at the hospital, Wirth was stuporous and unable to communicate. Medical tests showed he had multiple brain lesions probably attributable to toxoplasmosis, a parasitic infection found in many patients with ARC. Toxoplasmosis often responds favorably to treatment with antibiotics. All parties agreed Wirth was not able to make his own medical decisions, and Evans insisted he would not have wanted antibiotic treatment in this situation. Nevertheless, while acknowledging that a living will was a valid instrument to express a patient's wishes, the hospital contended Wirth's will did not clearly apply to the facts of the case. The hospital felt justified in acting on its own opinion that Wirth could "recover" from the toxoplasmosis to enjoy a "meaningful quality of life."

The hospital began antibiotic treatment on July 10, 1987. On the same day, Evans petitioned the court to stop it. After Wirth had been receiving antibiotics for two weeks and had still not improved, the court issued its decision: treatment could not be withheld.

In making its ruling, the court pointed out Wirth's living will made no specific reference to toxoplasmosis or ARC, and called the will "ambiguous" with respect to "recovering or regaining a meaningful quality of life." Because people can recover from toxoplasmosis and return to the condition they were in prior to its onset, treatment must continue. The court did not accept Evans's position that Wirth meant he would not want antibiotic treatment if he would not recover from ARC. Evans also contended that even before Wirth developed toxoplasmosis, he had decided his medical condition did not constitute, for him, a "meaningful quality of life" and he "wanted to get off this AIDS train."

Although denying Wirth what his agent (Evans) claimed he wanted, the court did emphasize that a living will was a proper method for a person to express his or her wishes about medical care. Because of the ambiguity it found in the "amorphous expression" of Wirth's living will, it urged that "great pains be taken by the drafters of living wills to dispel the ambiguities which necessitated this preceding."

Meanwhile, Wirth's condition worsened. After more than a month of futile antibiotic treatments and unbroken stupor, life-sustaining procedures (including antibiotics) were finally stopped in accordance with his living will. He died a week later.

Of course, it is not always possible to anticipate the circumstances likely to surround one's death. Until then, we must content ourselves with relatively general directions. When, however, like Wirth, we do know what we may be facing, we can and should amend our living wills to cover more specific scenarios. If possible, we should also use a DPAHC or proxy form to appoint a health-care agent who can adapt our general wishes and philosophy to new and specific circumstances. (In 1987, in New York, Evans was not allowed to interpret Wirth's living will; today, New York has a health care proxy form that would have allowed Wirth to give Evans full authority to make all health-care decisions for him.)

(6e) I especially do not want *dialysis.*

Dialysis involves a machine taking over the blood-purifying function of the kidneys when they fail. It can be very uncomfortable, though many people with kidney failure undergo regular dialysis for many years and tolerate the procedure very well, leading relatively normal lives. Dialysis may be used temporarily, while patients are awaiting kidney transplants, or if the kidneys are expected to recover, or to relieve lung congestion from fluid overload or nausea caused by a build-up of toxic substances.

Total kidney failure eventually produces cardiac arrest or coma, allowing death to come peacefully. When kidney failure is combined with another hopeless illness, dialysis would only prolong the dying process. It cannot cure the underlying condition. If you had chronic kidney failure and became hopelessly ill, or if you were hopelessly ill and then developed kidney failure, you might wish to refuse dialysis.

(6f) I especially do not want *surgical procedures.*

Surgical procedures such as amputation can be used to restrict the spread of life-threatening infection. Surgery can also relieve pain, as in the case of a bowel obstruction, where it would merely be palliative. There *are* times when adequate relief may be obtained by pain medication. You may wish to state that you would prefer to receive doses of pain medication adequate to relieve suffering, rather than undergo surgical procedures.

(6g) I especially do not want *invasive diagnostic tests.*

Invasive monitoring techniques involve the insertion of catheters (snakelike tubes) through channels in your body to keep track of its functions. A Foley catheter, for example, may be inserted through your urethra up into your bladder to measure minute-by-minute urine flow. A Swan Ganz catheter may be inserted through a large vein in your neck down into the right side of your heart to measure pressures there. Monitoring of this type is often an important component of proper hospital care. However, you may wish to state that if you were hopelessly ill, you would want to forgo all but the simplest tests and monitoring devices, or any testing or monitoring that would not change your comfort treatment.

(6h) I especially do not want an *intravenous (IV) line.*

An intravenous line is a tube placed into a vein to administer fluids, blood, or medication. People who are conscious but confused sometimes dislodge or pull out the intravenous line and are placed in preventive restraints. Some individuals may wish to state they would refuse an intravenous line if its burdens were greater than its benefits.

(6i) I especially do not want *chemotherapy and/or radiation.*

With some forms of cancer, recurrence after a series of anticancer treatments such as chemotherapy and radiation means the cancer is probably incurable, and further treatment may, at most, prolong life for a few months. Some late-stage cancer patients may wish to state they would not want further chemotherapy or radiation except as a means of pain control.

(6j) I especially do not want any *blood transfusions.*

The most common reason for refusing a transfusion among gravely ill patients (apart from religious reasons) is that receiving blood requires an intravenous line and yet may bring no benefit. A transfusion is thus seen as an invasive procedure, particularly among patients whose veins, after repeated puncturings, have been traumatized. Acute hepatitis can result from a transfusion after as early as four weeks and may be extremely unpleasant. There is also the possibility of a transfusion reaction, usually mild, such as a fever, but occasionally severe. It should be pointed out that blood transfusions sometimes make patients feel better and thus have some therapeutic value as comfort care. With a doctor's advice, one needs to weigh the burdens of a blood transfusion against the benefits in each individual case.

In passages (6a) through (6j), this living will form expresses the artificial life support technologies in extreme, end-of-life situations that people most often wish to refuse. Your specific instructions help to ensure your basic desires regarding currently used life support technologies will be respected.

Nevertheless, you may want to qualify these directions or add other directions, especially in the event that you gain more specific knowledge regarding health situations you're likely to face in the future, or in the event new life support technologies emerge. You can do so on an extra sheet of paper that you attach to the living will form, provided it is signed and witnessed separately. One note of caution, however; your goal is to be as clear as possible regarding your wishes about future medical care. If you are overly elaborate in expressing those wishes, or if you offer too many hypothetical scenarios, you may defeat the goal of clarity. Remember, be as specific as possible about what you know you *don't* want or *do* want in an extreme end-of-life situation.

_____

(7) Other instructions/comments:

_____

You may want to add instructions for treatment or care you do want in this section, for example, pain medication or that you prefer to die at home. As with passage (6), you may attach an additional sheet of paper, signed and witnessed, to more fully express your wishes. Remember, a living will is a personal document and it should say anything you want it to say, in your own words. Generally speaking, the more that is known about your treatment wishes and values, the easier it will be for your family and health care providers to make decisions for you. But the same caveat applies: Be as clear and precise as possible.

In regard to requesting maximum pain relief in an end-of-life situation, it is always possible that health-care institutions or health-care institutional personnel will not utilize their full capacity to control your pain. Sometimes a painkilling drug will be withheld because the doctor or nurse (or even the patient) thinks it will produce addiction. An exaggerated fear of addiction has long been a serious hindrance to adequate pain relief, even for dying patients.

Yet, it is extremely rare for true addiction to develop in patients treated for pain with narcotics and it is a largely theoretical fear for dying patients. Sometimes adequate sedation won't be offered for fear it may depress the respiratory function and hasten death. Sometimes it's simply a matter of a conservative attitude toward pain medication that prevails unless it is disputed.

You may also wish to qualify treatments that you refused in the previous section or specifically request to have certain forms of treatment. For example, you could say:

> If I am in a persistent vegetative state or any kind of permanent coma, I do want mechanical respiration, tube feeding, or any other relevant form of life support for three months. If after that time there is still no sign of improvement and my diagnosis remains unchanged. I direct that all forms of life support be withdrawn except treatment whose sole aim is to relieve pain and make me more comfortable.

The purpose of this direction—or any similar qualification you might wish to make—is only to allow for a "miracle" recovery. Most experts believe you can make a diagnosis of PVS after three months, and it is almost impossible to recover after a longer period of complete unconsciousness. If you did recover, you would almost certainly be severely brain damaged. If you believe in miracles or if you want to try and buck the odds, you can do so here.

You may also indicate here your wish to receive certain forms of life support *without any qualification.* If you have a religious or personal objection to refusing tube feeding, you may specifically request that treatment here. Or you may wish to receive all treatment available.

> I do want my life to be prolonged to the extent medically possible by [name the technology or technologies: cardiac resuscitation, mechanical respiration, tube feeding, antibiotics etc.].

The purpose of this direction would be to emphasize that you *do* want certain life support measures to be employed for as long as they sustain your life. Most people do not use a living will for this purpose but it is important for you to understand that you have the option to request, or refuse, anything you want.

Another important issue is the question of home or hospice care. On the whole, hospice provides a comprehensive home care program for the management of a terminal illness. An interdisciplinary team provides palliative care and support services to both patient and family. The emphasis is on symptom management and pain relief. Sometimes, toward the end of a terminal illness, inpatient care at a hospice institution is required.

Once it is clear a condition is incurable, as in terminal cancer, many patients prefer to spend their last weeks or days in a familiar environment surrounded by loved ones. They often find greater privacy and dignity, as well as emotional and physical comfort, at home. Personnel from hospice units, including physicians, nurses and home health aides, may visit to help provide necessary care.

While home hospice care can be ideal, it often requires that someone be at home to take care of you. Furthermore, to be reimbursable under most insurance plans, your condition must be one from which you are expected to die within six months. Your family or loved ones must also be instructed about dealing with possible problems, and they must receive outside assistance and support, because home care often becomes too difficult for the family to handle alone. Hospice programs include support and bereavement counseling for families.

Once you have considered these factors, you might write:

> If at all possible, and if the medical costs are not unduly burdensome, I declare that I want to die at home (or at least remain at home as much as possible) with appropriate medical, nursing, social, and emotional support and any necessary medical equipment or treatment needed to keep me comfortable.

The purpose of this directive would be to minimize the personal, emotional, and social discomfort, as well as the expense, of remaining in a hospital unnecessarily until death.

Some people use this passage to specify certain medical conditions under which they would not wish to sustain life. In Chapter 2 I discussed some of these conditions—minimal consciousness following a stroke or late-stage Alzheimer's disease. You might say, "If I am diagnosed as having advanced Alzheimer's disease and I develop pneumonia, I do not wish to be treated with antibiotics or a respirator but would like to be allowed to die naturally." Some people might wish to say, "I do not want to be resuscitated if, after the full course of treatment, the quality of my life would be drastically impaired, tantamount to 'social death,' or if I would be so severely disabled I couldn't function independently and would require continuing nursing care."

If you have any strong religious or philosophical views, or if you would want your priest, rabbi, or minister consulted about your end-of-life care, you should indicate your feelings here.

Record any other thought or relevant personal instruction.

At the bottom of each separate sheet you attach to your living will form, be sure to include a section for your signature, the signature of two witnesses, and the date, identical to the section described for passage (10).

---

(8) Proxy Designation Clause: Should I become unable to communicate my instructions as stated above, I designate the following person to act on my behalf:

Name _____

Address _____

If the person I have named above is unable to act on my behalf, I authorize the following person to do so:

Name _____

Address _____

This section allows you to name someone else who can make sure your wishes are carried out and interpret any ambiguities or uncertainties. It is similar to a DPAHC appointing a spokesperson authorized to speak for you in regard to medical decisions when you are no longer able to speak for yourself. However, the living will proxy designation clause is more narrow than a durable power of attorney for health care, because its power is limited by the same terms as the living will. For example, if you are in an accident and temporarily incapacitated—but your recovery is expected—a proxy designated through your living will would not be able to make decisions for you because your condition is not "incurable or irreversible." Nevertheless, insofar as end-of-life situations are concerned, it is a good idea to name a proxy through your living will if you know someone who understands your feelings and who can be trusted to actively intervene on your behalf. It is also advisable to name a second, or back-up, proxy, if you have someone who can step in if your proxy is not available.

You are under no obligation to name a proxy and can leave this blank. It is better not to name anyone than to choose someone you are unsure of. Designating a proxy involves a great deal of trust and responsibility. You need someone reliable.

(9) This Living Will Declaration expresses my personal treatment preferences. The fact that I may have also executed a document in the form recommended by state law should not be construed to limit or contradict this Living Will Declaration, which is an expression of my common-law and constitutional rights.

In the event there is some conflict between your state living will and this general living will declaration, this statement ensures that the wishes expressed here cannot be ignored. Even if your state sets a restriction on your right to refuse certain forms of life support, this general declaration asserts your broader powers, under both common law and the Constitution, to be protected from unwanted medical treatment.

(10) Signed: _____ Date: _____
     Witness: _____ Witness: _____
     Address: _____ Address: _____

Sign and date your living will in the presence of two adult witnesses, who also sign. The witnesses should be adults who will *not* benefit from your estate, that is, who cannot be charged with having a vested interest in your death. The person you appoint as your proxy cannot also be a witness. In some states, the statutory living will cannot be witnessed by specific relatives and needs to be notarized (see Part Two, for the states that require notarization).

(11) *Keep the signed original with your papers at home. Give signed copies to doctors, family, and proxy. Review your Declaration from time to time and initial and date it to show it still expresses your intent.*

Talk with your family and your doctor about what kind of medical care you want in end-of-life situations. Use your generic living will and, if applicable, your state-approved living will as a basis for discussion. This way, you can be sure everyone understands your wishes and the personal thinking and philosophy behind them, and accepts your right to have those wishes enforced. Give a photocopy of your signed generic living will and, if applicable, your signed state-approved living will, to your family, your doctor, and anyone else who may someday have to produce such a document.

Keep the original documents among your important personal papers, in a place known to your family and close associates, to be easily located in an emergency. It is *not* advisable to use a safety deposit box for this purpose, as your living will would not be readily accessible there. It's also a good idea to keep a card in your wallet saying that you have a living will, where it is located, and a contact for information.

For a nominal fee, the Society for the Right to Die will keep an up-to-date copy of your living will—and any other advance directive such as a durable power of attorney for health care—in its Living Will Registration Service where it will be permanently available to any health-care institution or professional that needs it. Once your will is entered into the registry, you'll receive a card to carry in your wallet stating that you do have a living will and giving the address and phone number of the registry. For more information, write to the Living Will Registration Service, Society for the Right to Die, 250 West Fifty-Seventh Street, New York, NY 10107.

The Durable Power of Attorney for Health Care

It bears repeating: You are better off with both a durable power of attorney for health care *and* a living will. The two documents can reinforce each other, thereby making your intent as clear as possible. Although most doctors are likely to respect a living will, even in states with no living will statute, a living will may not cover every clinical circumstance or available treatment option that ultimately confronts you. Or you may wind up with a doctor who feels so hesitant about complying with your wishes that he or she denies their relevance.

You and your loved ones can be spared such a fate with a DPAHC that legally empowers a surrogate to make medical decisions for you if you are too sick to make them yourself. Because there is no general common law right to have an agent or proxy speak for you, as there is to have your own treatment preferences honored through some form such as a living will, I can't offer you an effective generic DPAHC form. You must work with the form that's approved for your particular state. In states that only have a general DPA statute that doesn't mention health care, consult a lawyer. I discuss this issue more specifically in Part Two. At this point, however, let me offer several guidelines that will be helpful no matter what form you use and then, for the sake of example, I will take you through the New York form, known as the Health Care Proxy.

1. The person you appoint to be your surrogate or attorney-in-fact could be your spouse, a relative, or a close friend. Whoever it is, it should be someone in whom you have total confidence, someone who understands what kind of medical care you want, and someone who would be likely to make the same decisions you would make for yourself. This person must be willing and able to take action on your behalf, in case you face the threat—or reality—of not getting the medical care you want. All of this requires careful thought and full consultation with your surrogate. Remember, durable powers of attorney for health care are not usually restricted to end-of-life medical decisions. Discuss your convictions regarding all medical treatment, not just terminal care.

If you select a doctor as your agent, he or she will have to choose between acting as your agent or as your attending doctor: A physician cannot do both. If you are a patient or resident of a hospital, nursing home, or mental hygiene facility, there may be special restrictions about naming someone who works for that facility as your agent. Ask the appropriate staff member at the facility to explain these restrictions.

Also consider appointing more than one agent—the second to act in the event that the first one dies or is unavailable, and so on. However, if you do appoint one or more back-up agents, specify that the back-up is only qualified to act if and when the agent named is unavailable. Also make sure to discuss your medical care wishes in detail with each back-up agent.

2. On some DPAHC forms, you can give written directions about what kind of medical care you do and/or do not want, either on the form itself or on an attached sheet. These directions would be like the directions included in your living will. You might use any one—or any composite—of the following openers:

- If I become terminally ill, I do/don't want to receive the following treatments: . . .
- If I am in a coma or unconscious, with no hope of recovery, I do/don't want the following treatments: . . .
- If I have brain damage or a brain disease that makes me unable to recognize people or speak and there is no hope that my condition will improve, I do/don't want the following treatments: . . .

Among the treatments to consider are cardiac resuscitation, mechanical respiration, tube feeding, antibiotics, dialysis, surgical procedures, invasive diagnostic tests, intravenous lines, chemotherapy and radiation, and blood transfusions (see "The Generic Living Will," for fuller explanation).

Discuss this form with a doctor or another health-care professional, such as a nurse or social worker, before you sign it to make sure you understand the types of decision that may be made for you. Give your doctor a signed copy. In most states you do not have to give specific instructions in writing as long as your health-care agent or surrogate knows what your preferences are.

3. Most DPAHC forms give the person you choose as your agent authority to make *all* health-care decisions for you (although, as Part Two points out, some states impose restrictions on an agent's power, for example, not being able to refuse life support technology unless you have already done so in writing). If you wish, you can limit the authority of your agent by specifying the limitations in writing on the form itself. Otherwise, your agent will be allowed to make all health-care decisions you could have made. (*Health care* generally means any treatment, service, or procedure to diagnose or treat your mental or physical condition).

4. Your living will serves as a companion document to your durable power of attorney for health care to ensure that your specific medical care wishes are a matter of record for your agent, family, and doctor. All agents you appoint should receive a copy of your signed DPAHC form and your signed living will(s), and all agents should be apprised of any changes you make in these documents as soon as you make them.

5. Your durable power of attorney for health care should be signed by two adults other than the agent or any back-up agents.

6. Keep a copy of the DPAHC form wherever you keep a copy of your living will (see "Generic Living Will," passage (10)). Also, note on a card in your wallet the name of your attorney-in-fact for health care matters and all appropriate contact information.

I will now guide you briefly through the New York State Health Care Proxy, a DPAHC form that came into effect in January 1991. It was the first statute in the country passed after the U.S. Supreme Court decision in *Cruzan*. While the New York document is an excellent one, and we are proud of our efforts as part of the coalition that helped it to pass, it is valid only for New York State. Consult Part Two for the appropriate DPA form for your state, if one exists, or for more information.

You can see the New York form in its entirety on the opposite page. Actual passages from the health care proxy form are followed by explanatory commentary. Because each section is numbered in the form itself, you may simply follow the numerical sequence.

HEALTH CARE PROXY

(1) I, _____

    hereby appoint _____

               (name, home address and telephone number)

_____

as my health care agent to make any and all health care decisions for me, except to the extent that I state otherwise. This proxy shall take effect when and if I become unable to make my own health care decisions.

Write your name and the name, home address, and telephone number of the person you are selecting as your agent here. Selecting an agent requires a great deal of discussion and forethought. Do not make your decision lightly.

Tell the person you choose that he or she will be your health-care agent. Fully discuss your health-care wishes, and be sure to give him or her a signed copy of the form. Your agent cannot be sued for health-care decisions made in good faith. Also, he or she cannot be held liable for costs of your care, just because he or she is your agent.

Your agent will start making decisions for you when doctors decide you are unable to make health-care decisions for yourself.

Health Care Proxy

(1) I, _____

hereby appoint _____

(name, home address and telephone number)

_____

as my health care agent to make any and all health care decisions for me, except to the extent that I state otherwise. This proxy shall take effect when and if I become unable to make my own health care decisions.

(2) Optional instructions: I direct my proxy to make health care decisions in accord with my wishes and limitations as stated below, or as he or she otherwise knows. (Attach additional pages if necessary).

_____

_____

(Unless your agent knows your wishes about artificial nutrition and hydration [feeding tubes], your agent will not be allowed to make decisions about artificial nutrition and hydration. See the preceding instructions for samples of language you could use.)

(3) Name of substitute or fill-in proxy if the person I appoint above is unable, unwilling or unavailable to act as my health care agent.

_____

(name, home address and telephone number)

_____

(4) Unless I revoke it, this proxy shall remain in effect indefinitely, or until the date or condition stated below. This proxy shall expire (specific date or conditions, if desired):

_____

(5) Signature _____

Address _____

Date _____

Statement by Witnesses (must be 18 or older)

I declare that the person who signed this document is personally known to me and appears to be of sound mind and acting of his or her own free will. He or she signed (or asked another to sign for him or her) this document in my presence.

Witness 1_____

Address _____

Witness 2_____

Address _____

New York State Department of Health

(2) Optional instructions: I direct my proxy to make health care decisions in accord with my wishes and limitations as stated below, or as he or she otherwise knows. (Attach additional pages if necessary).

_____

_____

_____

(Unless your agent knows your wishes about artificial nutrition and hydration [feeding tubes], your agent will not be allowed to make decisions about artificial nutrition and hydration.

See the preceeding instructions for samples of language you could use.)

If you have special instructions for your agent, write them here (see guideline 2 for examples). If you wish to limit your agent's authority in any way, state specific restrictions. If you do not state any limitation, your agent will be allowed to make all health-care decisions you could have made, including the decision to consent or refuse life-sustaining treatment. Your agent must follow your oral and written instructions, as well as your moral and religious beliefs. If your agent does not know your wishes or beliefs, he or she is legally required to act in your best interests.

Note: It is advisable that you state your wishes about tube feeding in writing. As a practical matter most health care providers still look for a specific statement about tube feeding (However, even if you have not left explicit instructions, according to New York law as long as your agent knows how you feel on this subject, he or she will be allowed to make the decision you would have made).

(3) Name of substitute or fill-in proxy if the person I appoint above is unable, unwilling or unavailable to act as my health care agent.

_____

(name, home address and telephone number)

_____

_____

You may write the name, home address, and telephone number of an alternate agent who can act for you if your health-care agent is not available or able to act when decisions must be made. Make sure the second agent understands he or she is strictly a backup. You must choose *one* proxy. In virtually every state, if you try to appoint two people to act at the same time, you run the risk of invalidating your document. You do not want more than one person at a time controlling events. You may, however, instruct your first agent to consult with the others.

_____

(4) Unless I revoke it, this proxy shall remain in effect indefinitely, or until the date or condition stated below. This proxy shall expire (specific date or conditions, if desired):

_____

_____

This form will remain valid indefinitely unless you set a date or condition for its expiration. This section is optional; fill it in only if you want the health-care proxy to expire. It is easy to cancel the proxy, to change the person you have chosen as your health-care agent, or to change any treatment instructions you have written on your health-care proxy form. Just fill out a new form. If you choose your spouse as your health-care agent and you get divorced or legally separated, the proxy is automatically canceled.

(5) Signature _____

Address _____

Date _____

Statement by Witness (must be 18 or older)

I declare that the person who signed this document is personally known to me and appears to be of sound mind and acting of his or her own free will. He or she signed (or asked another to sign for him or her) this document in my presence.

Witness 1 _____

Address _____

Witness 2 _____

Address _____

New York State Department of Health

Sign and date the proxy. If you are unable to sign yourself, you may direct someone else to sign in your presence. Be sure to include your address. Two witnesses, at least eighteen years of age, must also sign. The person who is appointed agent or alternate agent cannot sign as a witness.

Even after you have signed this form, you have the right to make health-care decisions for yourself as long as you are able to do so, and treatment cannot be given to you or stopped if you object. You can cancel the control given to your agent by informing him or her or your health-care provider orally or in writing.

Now that you have composed both your living will and your durable power of attorney for health care, I will show you how to put them into action in the health-care setting and how to make them as effective as possible.

CHAPTER FOUR

What Happens in the Health Care Institution

> In 1965, when Elisabeth Kübler-Ross was looking
> for dying persons to interview, the heads of the
> hospitals and clinics to whom she addressed herself
> protested, "Dying? But there are no dying here!"
> There could be no dying in a well-organized and
> respectable institution. They were mortally of-
> fended.
>
> —PHILIPPE ARIES, *The Hour of Our Death*

The nineteenth-century German philosopher Friedrich Nietzsche insisted, "However much we may live with others, we all die alone." True, no one can relieve us of a dying process that is uniquely and inevitably ours, share it with us, or even know what it's really like. Nevertheless, as we near the end of the twentieth century, there is one important respect in which Nietzsche was wrong. Eighty percent of us now die in hospitals or nursing homes; our deaths are more public.

Besides family members and friends (who often have greater access to a dying person in a hospital room than they would if that person were at home), medical supervisors can include primary physicians, consulting physicians, physicians' assistants, nurses, orderlies, hospital administrators and staff, clergy, social workers, community service group personnel, advocacy group personnel, hospital patient's representatives, hospital ethics committee members, guardians (personal and court appointed), health-care agents or proxies, personal lawyers, hospital lawyers, and judges.

In such a people-intensive situation, the possibilities for mistakes, confusions, misunderstandings, differing opinions, and outright conflicts are very high. Your living will and DPAHC can help cut down and even eliminate these frightening possibilities, but they can't do so simply by virtue of their existence. Put the documents into action: (1) discuss them as far in advance as possible with any person who may become an important player in the process of your dying, (2) make the documents' existence known and have copies of them easily accessible, and (3) reinforce, amend, and/or defend them whenever circumstances arise that warrant these measures.

The Impact of Institutions

Even those people who die at home have usually spent time in a health-care facility—the nature and structure of these institutions have important implications for decision making.

In its seminal report, *Deciding to Forgo Life-Sustaining Treatment,* the President's Commission for the Study of Ethical Problems in Medicine and Biomedical and Behavioral Research described the impact of institutional care and how it affects a patient's decision-making ability. They pointed out that "patients forfeit control over what to wear, when to eat and when to take medicines" and that "they almost inevitably lose substantial privacy—intimate body parts are examined, highly personal facts are written down and someone they have never seen before may occupy the next bed." Patients are compelled to place their trust in "strangers selected by the institution," professional experts who are often interchangeable and shifted around. The Commission concluded

> All these factors serve to isolate patients, rob them of their individuality, foster dependence, and diminish self-respect and self-confidence, even when illness, medication and surgery have not already had these effects. The situation can seriously impair patients' power to exercise self-determination and thus to be active participants in decision making.

In light of these built-in institutional encroachments on your individuality as a patient, a personal statement of your own wishes, such as a living will or a durable power of attorney, is especially relevant. These advance directives act as a counterweight to the impersonality and anonymity of a vast bureaucracy. They call attention to your rights and demand that personal attention be paid to you—medical, legal, and ethical attention. The hospital or nursing home must take account of your written instructions, which is another way of saying that they must take account of *you* as an individual with a set of personal preferences, values, and beliefs. As you become increasingly isolated, you may find yourself grateful for the existence of these documents which assert—loudly and clearly and legally—your fundamental right to be involved in decisions about how you live and die.

Living wills and durable powers of attorney for health care are an essential form of protection, but you need to be aware of how they function in the context of health-care institutions. Keep in mind that health-care facilities, however good they are, have other goals besides serving your needs. They are public or private entities in their own right, which must balance budgets and pay salaries, maintain internal efficiency, conduct research and education, and preserve a public reputation and accreditation. They are also affected by national and local regulations, laws, and in particular, financial incentives such as reimbursement methods.

Although health-care institutions share many attributes, there are also significant differences among them that affect how your living will and DPAHC will be received. Hospices (and hospice home care) are dedicated to the idea of making you as comfortable and symptom free as possible as you face your final days and accept your dying; nursing homes (or long-term care facilities) will try to extend life but may not be quite as aggressive as hospitals, where they may transfer you for acute care; and hospitals (or acute-care hospitals) will generally use every available means of high technology to prolong your life.

Hospice and Hospice Home Care

Strictly speaking, a hospice is not a building, like a hospital or nursing home, but a concept of care. Most hospice care is delivered to people in their homes where they can receive medical and support services for terminal illness. However, inpatient care at a hospice institution is sometimes required. Patients may receive respite care: the hospice takes the patient in to give temporary relief to the care giver at home. Families and others who provide home care often have a hard time coping with a patient's last days and may turn to an institution for assistance. There are about 1,700 hospice programs in the United States and the number continues to grow. Hospices and hospice home care would be among the most responsive institutions to your living will or durable power of attorney for health care. Unlike patients who enter a hospital with the hope of being cured, those who go to a hospice have already accepted that they will die in a relatively short time. Many hospices, for example, ask a patient to sign a do not resuscitate order before being admitted. Entry to a hospice program means a choice not to receive aggressive treatment, even though it might be considered routine by a hospital. The hospice patient receives treatment for pain control and symptom management—but not life-sustaining technology—to help make the remaining days, weeks, or months as comfortable and normal as possible.

Hospice care is also more sensitive to the patient's family and its care and counseling needs. There is a greater emphasis on emotional and spiritual, not just physical care. A hospice is very likely to respect the wishes of a health-care agent or proxy.

Hospice care is available under Medicare and covers a wide range of home services including physician's services, nursing care, medical appliances and supplies (including outpatient drugs for symptom management and pain relief), home health aide and homemaker services, therapies, medical social services, and counseling. Short-term inpatient care is also covered, especially if it is a Medicare-certified hospice. To qualify, the patient must meet certain requirements which vary from state to state. Contact your nearest Social Security office or local hospice program to obtain further information.

NURSING HOMES

One in four Americans who reaches the age of sixty-five today will spend at least one year in a nursing home or other long-term care facility. The vast majority of the 1.6 million residents are older than eighty. As medical advances have increased the number of the elderly in the population, and as the traditional three-generational family breaks up, the role of care giver for the elderly has shifted from the family to health-care professionals.

Although nursing homes are dedicated to providing the best care available, they are, by definition, less aggressive than acute-care hospitals in providing life-sustaining treatment. Nursing homes are generally not equipped with the technology hospitals have. In some nursing homes, if a resident suffers a cardiac arrest, the staff may call an ambulance to transport the patient to a hospital emergency room. Most nursing homes do not have respirators, dialysis machines, or other expensive forms of life support. If a patient needed a feeding tube surgically implanted, he or she would have to go to a hospital for the procedure. On the other hand, nursing home patients are often fed through various kinds of feeding tubes, sometimes because it is more economical than being spoon fed by staff.

While their relatively unaggressive approach to treatment might seem to make nursing homes more responsive to advance directives, this is not always the case. Due to some examples of abuse, many nursing homes go out of their way to reassure the public that they deliver proper care and are not places where people go to die. They are sometimes reluctant to withdraw life-sustaining care because they do not wish to be perceived as places where patients die due to lack of treatment.

In July 1986, Mrs. Jean Elbaum, at the age of sixty, suffered a brain hemorrhage and was diagnosed by North Shore University Hospital in New York as being in PVS with no hope of recovery. Her husband and two adult children were informed that Elbaum, who was being fed through a nasogastric tube, would need long-term nursing care, and must have gastrostomy tube feeding. The family, who knew Mrs. Elbaum had repeatedly and expressly said she would not want to be kept alive by artificial means such as a feeding tube if she were in a "vegetativelike" state, was told no nursing home would accept her unless the gastrostomy was performed. Threatened by the hospital with legal proceedings that would force their consent, the Elbaums agreed. In September, gastrostomy tube in place, Mrs. Elbaum was transferred to Grace Plaza Nursing Home.

Mr. Elbaum and his daughter met with the nursing home director on the eve of her transfer and reiterated that Mrs. Elbaum did not want any life support. Some weeks later Mr. Elbaum wrote to the nursing home to authorize a do not resuscitate (DNR) order and also to request that no antibiotics or drugs be used if Mrs. Elbaum should develop an infection. Nevertheless she received antibiotics on at least half a dozen occasions. The nursing home director asserted treatment was necessary to prevent the spread of infection to other patients.

In October Mr. Elbaum wrote to Grace Plaza Nursing Home and requested his wife's gastrostomy tube be removed, in keeping with her expressed wishes. The nursing home director wrote back that withdrawal of the tube was contrary to the "dedication to the law and to the policies and philosophy of Grace Plaza." Mr. Elbaum stopped making payment for his wife's care.

In June 1988, Mr. Elbaum began a legal action to prevent the nursing home from providing any life-sustaining treatment, including tube feeding, to his wife. At the trial court hearing, he testified that his wife had begun to express her views against life support in response to the Karen Ann Quinlan *case. Later she had expressed similar feelings in reference to a friend's stroke as well as the* Sunny Von Bulow *case, saying, "I do not want to be sustained as a vegetable, I want to die with some dignity." Mrs. Elbaum's sister testified to similar conversations and stated that when their mother, terminally ill with cancer, had been fed through a nasogastric tube, Jean Elbaum had made her "pledge" that similar measures would not be administered to her if she were ill with no hope of recovery. The pledge had been reiterated after their mother's death and most recently when their mother's tombstone was unveiled, only two weeks before Mrs. Elbaum became ill. Jean Elbaum's daughter and son also testified to similar conversations.*

The trial court ruled against the Elbaums on the grounds of insufficient evidence. The case went to the New York appellate division, which overruled the trial court and found there was "clear and convincing evidence" Mrs. Elbaum would not want tube feeding in this condition. It rejected Grace Plaza's conten-

*tion that the nursing home's interest in maintaining its "ethical integrity" out-
weighed Mrs. Elbaum's wishes, noting that prevailing ethical standards do not
require medical intervention at all costs. The court found it significant that Grace
Plaza failed to make its policy known to the Elbaum family until after the family
requested removal of the feeding tube. Finally the court ruled Grace Plaza had
ten days in which to either transfer Mrs. Elbaum to another facility that would
remove her feeding tube, or allow another physician to enter the nursing home
and remove it.*

The *Elbaum* case is legally significant because it established that thoughtful,
repeated oral statements about not wishing to have life-sustaining treatment
can constitute clear and convincing evidence of a competent decision, as
required by New York law. In an important later development, the trial court
also ruled the Elbaums did not have to pay for Mrs. Elbaum's care because
her treatment was unwanted. This decision could also have a strong impact
on how nursing homes honor their patient's wishes. Any health-care institution would have to proceed very cautiously before administering costly treatment a patient does not want and for which the facility might not be
reimbursed.

There was nothing extraordinary about Grace Plaza's behavior. Many
nursing homes have, and do, act in a similar fashion, protecting their reputa-
tions as *providers* of health care. If you are planning an admission to a nursing
home, it is important to specify your treatment wishes and goals at the outset.
You need to fill out a living will and appoint a health-care proxy *before* you
are admitted. If you fill out an advance directive while in a nursing home, it
must sometimes be witnessed by an ombudsman or other state official, causing
delay when you can ill afford it.

Some nursing homes do not encourage patients to fill out advance directives because the nursing home does not wish to be hindered in any way from
making its own decisions about what is best for patients. Because nursing
home patients are usually frail and elderly and often lack full decision-making
capacity, their end-of-life preferences, like their autonomy, are not always
honored to the extent they should be. This makes it all the more imperative
to have advance directives. Ideally, nursing homes should require a regular
review of patient preferences regarding end-of-life treatment and these preferences should be documented. Your advance directives should also consider
the possibility of transfer from a nursing home to a hospital, which often
happens if life-sustaining technology must be administered. You might say
that you would not wish to be transferred to a hospital unless there was no
other way of keeping you reasonably comfortable. You can also request a not
hospitalize order (DNH).

With the Patient Self-Determination Act, all nursing homes that receive Medicare or Medicaid will have to inform patients on admission if it is their policy not to honor living wills. The nursing home's attitude toward advance directives can thus become an important factor in helping you to choose the best facility for your needs.

HOSPITALS

Of the 2 million plus Americans who died last year, more than 60 percent did so in a hospital. Hospitals tend to be large, complex institutions—there are 6,300 in the United States—especially compared to hospices and nursing homes. As a result, they are generally cautious and bureaucratic entities.

If you're concerned enough about your medical care to complete a living will and a DPAHC, you'll also want to know how you can prevent, solve, or overcome problems that may undermine their effectiveness in a hospital environment. First, let's consider how hospital doctors typically make decisions about life-sustaining medical treatment for their patients. Then we'll look at specific problems you, as a hospital patient, may encounter relating to your living will and durable power of attorney.

THE DECISION-MAKING PROCESS IN HOSPITALS

In making hospital-based decisions about whether to supply, withhold, or withdraw life support technology, there are three basic scenarios:

1. The patient is competent to make a choice.
2. The patient is not competent to make a choice and does not have a living will or durable power of attorney for health care.
3. The patient is not competent to make a choice but does have a living will and a durable power of attorney.

Let's explore each scenario separately.

1. *The patient is competent to make a choice.* The doctor involves the patient directly in the decision-making process, and the patient's decision is final and binding. This activity is technically called seeking the patient's "informed consent." The doctor describes the patient's condition and options for treatment, gives a recommendation, and guides the patient to make a specific treatment choice.

Ideally, this activity takes place as early as possible and is conducted in such a manner that both parties have every opportunity to explain their individual points of view and understand each other. Often, discussions between doctors and their patients about possible life-sustaining treatments occur during office visits prior to the hospitalization itself, so the patient is spared the ordeal of facing a quick, first-time decision in the middle of a hospital crisis.

Regrettably, recent surveys have shown that about half of all physicians feel uncomfortable bringing up the subject of advance directives with their patients. Sometimes there is no discussion of life support until the last minute, when the patient may not have the time to appreciate the true nature of his or her medical situation or of the treatment options available. Yet it is precisely here—at the meeting point between physician and fully conscious, autonomous patient, care giver, and care receiver—that the whole issue must be broached as a matter of routine medical care. Advance directives can stimulate more open conversation about end-of-life treatment between doctors and patients.

There are cases where even a competent patient may run into opposition regarding his or her personal treatment wishes.

Larry McAfee, a young, vigorous man suffered a severe injury to his spinal cord in a 1985 motorcycle accident. The injury left him quadriplegic and totally dependent on a ventilator to breathe, with no chance his condition would improve.

Four years after his accident, Mr. McAfee filed a petition in a Georgia trial court to turn off his respirator. He had devised a timer that would allow him to turn it off by himself. He also asked the court to allow him to take a sedative to alleviate any pain or discomfort that could occur when his respirator was disconnected. Mr. McAfee had made several previous attempts to disconnect his respirator but failed because of the severe discomfort he suffered as a conscious patient deprived of oxygen. No one in the hospital was willing to take the risk of providing sedation.

The trial court approved Mr. McAfee's action, finding that his constitutional rights of privacy and liberty, as found in both the federal and Georgia constitutions, as well as his right to refuse treatment, protected his right as a competent person to make this decision. *The trial court also decided that, although it could not order a medical professional to administer a sedative, no civil or criminal liability would attach to any medical professional who did so.*

The case went to the Georgia Supreme Court—to establish a legal precedent and save others from Mr. McAfee's ordeal—which affirmed the trial court decision. The state supreme court reiterated that competent adults have the right to refuse medical treatment in the absence of conflicting state interests. In this case, the court wrote, the only implicated interest of the state would be the general interest in preserving life, which the state itself conceded did not out-weigh Mr. McAfee's right to make his own decision.

The court also held that Mr. McAfee's right to be free from pain at the time the ventilator is disconnected is inseparable from his right to refuse medical treatment. His right to have a sedative, which the court defined as "a medication that in no way causes or accelerates death," was described as part of his right to control his own medical treatment.

It is interesting to note that, as this book was printed, Mr. McAfee had not yet turned off his ventilator. Perhaps, once Mr. McAfee had won the right to control his own medical destiny he did not feel the same urgency to disconnect his respirator. If one accepts this explanation, then it tells us that the issue of *control,* and a personal sense of *dignity,* is at least as important to some patients as the actual treatment choices made.

2. *The patient is not competent to make a choice and does not have a living will or durable power of attorney for health care.* Much depends on whether the patient's wishes about life support technology are known or not known to the doctor. If the doctor knows the patient's wishes, he or she should—and, most likely, will—follow them, although there's no guarantee this will happen. Most doctors place a very high value on what patients want, but they may feel the need to balance respect for patient autonomy with other competing ethical principles in order to make what they consider the wisest decisions. For instance, if a family member strongly disagrees with the patient's, or the doctor's, wishes, he or she can create a serious obstacle.

If the doctor doesn't know the patient's wishes and the patient has no health-care agent, he or she usually tries to establish whether there is a family member who can convey the patient's wishes. Some doctors (like some states) may require this family member to produce clear and convincing evidence: a written statement on the subject made by the patient, or corroborating testimony from several individuals (friends, coworkers, attorney, clergy). Other doctors in many states will accept a family's "substituted judgment" of what the patient would have wanted based on general knowledge of the patient's values and beliefs. If the doctor is not satisfied the next of kin really knows what the patient would want, or if the patient never had capacity (for example, in the case of a mentally retarded person), the doctor might act according to his or her own sense of what treatment is in the patient's best interests. (*Best interest* refers to a legal standard for making health-care decisions based on what others feel is "best" for the patient when there is no family or friends and no evidence whatsoever of the patient's wishes).

You may find yourself called in to speak for a loved one suddenly struck with a life-threatening injury or illness even if he or she has not appointed you, or anyone else, as a health-care agent. In that case (as well as if you were appointed as the agent), you would first need to ascertain the patient's exact medical condition: (1) Why is the patient unconscious and will he or she ever regain consciousness? (2) If yes, how long will it take to regain consciousness? (3) Should the patient stay on a respirator, be resuscitated if his or her heart stops, receive antibiotics if an infection develops, or be fed by tube if he or she can't swallow? (4) Is the patient in pain now or will the patient be in pain if he or she recovers? (5) If the patient recovers, will the patient be able to recognize people and places or to communicate in any way? (6) Will the patient need round-the-clock care or a guardian to make decisions for him or her?

Once you understand the patient's condition and prognosis, you would have to try to decide what the patient would have wanted. Recall specific conversations—the *Karen Ann Quinlan* and *Nancy Cruzan* cases often stimulate discussion ("if that were ever to happen to me, I would . . .") or else consider the patient's general moral, philosophical, or religious outlook. If the patient ever had personal contact with a friend or relative in a similar terminal condition, his or her feelings, comments, and reactions at that time might supply important clues. If you aren't sure what the patient's feelings or philosophy are, consider the patient's best interests.

3. *The patient is not competent to make a choice but does have a living will and a durable power of attorney for health care.* The doctor, either alone, or in consultation with another doctor, determines whether the medical condition of the patient renders a living will applicable, that is, whether the patient's illness is terminal and/or irreversible. If both doctors agree that it is, certification to that effect is incorporated into the patient's medical record.

The doctor then makes a "reasonable effort" to notify the patient's designated health-care agent. If the health-care agent can't be reached, then the doctor will contact a family member (also standard procedure in the case of patients who have *not* completed a living will and/or durable power of attorney).

In any event, once the patient's living will is located, the doctor is very likely to abide by its directions, even if the state itself does not have a living will statute. Assuming the health-care agent steps in to monitor the patient's medical care, the doctor is also very likely to seek the agent's informed consent in medical treatment decisions just as if the health-care agent were the patient.

PROBLEM SITUATIONS IN A HOSPITAL ENVIRONMENT

Although hospital patients with a living will and a DPAHC usually receive the type of treatment they've requested, problems can and do occur. For all the sophisticated services it provides, a hospital is still a bureaucracy; it wages a never-ending battle with rigid conventions, regulations, red tape, organizational politics, and operational inefficiences. And for all their professionalism, doctors are still human beings, who, like all human beings, sometimes make mistakes, generate conflicts, and succumb to pressures.

Here are the principal reasons why your living will or durable power of attorney for health care directions might not be honored while you are under hospital care.

Your doctor doesn't know about your living will or durable power of attorney for health care or can't locate the documents. With the Patient Self-Determination Act soon in effect, hospitals are legally required to ascertain at the time of your admission whether you have, in fact, completed a living will and a DPAHC. However, even with the Patient Self-Determination Act, if you are suddenly injured in an accident or suffer a stroke and are rushed to the hospital for the first time, there will be no record of your advance directive and no way for you to answer questions concerning its whereabouts.

Reminding the people who are close to you and who may become involved in your medical care about the existence and whereabouts of these documents—especially as your medical condition or treatment changes—is a good idea. Better yet, supply key people—your health-care agent, physician, close friends and relatives, lawyer, religious adviser—with actual, up-to-date copies. Finally, remember that you can register your documents with the Society for the Right to Die (see page 67) so that they will always be available.

The hospital declares your living will or durable power of attorney for health care is not valid. If your hospital has any grounds for rejecting the validity of your living will or DPAHC, there's always the chance it might do so. The most likely motivation would be to protect what the hospital considers to be your best interests; that could happen if all the doctors attending or observing you recommend treatment they think most people would want, even if it conflicts with your living will or health-care agent's instructions.

Another possible motivation may be the hospital's and/or the attending doctor's fear of a lawsuit. From a legal point of view, however, this fear is unjustified. Not one single hospital or doctor has ever been declared civilly (or criminally) liable for honoring a patient's living will directions.

On the contrary, a hospital or physician may be civilly liable for disregarding a patient's wishes and giving life-sustaining treatment without consent. In the 1984 case of *Leach v. Shapiro,* the Ohio Court of Appeals recognized that a civil action for damages due to battery (unconsented touching) could be brought by the estate of a patient who was maintained in a coma on a respirator if there was any evidence that known treatment wishes were ignored, either when the patient was placed on the respirator or while supported on it.

Among the possible grounds a hospital might offer for rejecting a patient's living will or durable power of attorney:

1. *The state has no living will statute.* Even though a state doesn't have a living will statute, hospitals in that state can—and generally do—honor generic living wills. However, if you live in a state without a living will statute and your hospital or attending doctor happens to be philosophically opposed to living wills, or simply ignorant of the law about advance directives, then you, or your health-care agent, may be confronted with this objection.

This is what happened in the case of Dr. Fred Finsterbach.

Ten years before his illness, Dr. Finsterbach wrote a generic living will requesting that he "be allowed to die and not be kept alive by medications, artificial means, or heroic measures." He also wore a bracelet inscribed, "No resuscitation, No IV, No INJ, No Intubation." When hospitalized in 1990, he was started on nasogastric and intravenous tube feeding despite his stated wishes and his daughter's objections. His daughter was told by the court-appointed conservator that New York State had no living will law, and, therefore, the medical treatment team had no alternative but to follow the standard procedure of giving the patient every available form of life support.

Later, when the hospital petitioned the court for permission to replace Dr. Finsterbach's nasogastric tube with a stomach feeding tube, his daughter countered by asking the court to order the removal of all life support systems. By this time, she was better informed about the efficacy of living wills even in states with no living will legislation, and was justifiably convinced the absence of a state living will law did not, in fact, leave a health-care institution with "no alternative" to standard operating procedure.

The court vindicated her position. While acknowledging New York State's stringent standard requiring "clear and convincing" evidence of a patient's wishes, the court held that "[a] hearing is not required when there is a living will or similar written document." Describing a living will as an "ideal situation" for conveying an incompetent person's preferences, the court ordered that Dr. Finsterbach's life support mechanisms be withdrawn. As he had also requested in his living will, medication was to be "mercifully administered" to alleviate his suffering, even if it would shorten his life.

If Dr. Finsterbach had not completed a living will, his wishes, which were well-known to his daughter, might still have prevailed in the long run, although the chances would have been much slimmer. The Finsterbach case clearly af-

firmed that in New York patients who have made out a living will do not have to go to court to have their wishes honored. It is significant that living wills were accorded such high credibility in New York, one of the remaining eight states that does not even have living will legislation! (New Yorkers have since received legislative authority to appoint a health-care proxy.)

Patients in *every* state retain a common law and constitutional right to refuse any kind of treatment; a living will and DPA can legitimately reflect a patient's treatment wishes even in states that do not have legislation, regardless of what you might be told at the hospital. If your health-care agent or a close member of your family speaks in your behalf, this problem can most likely be surmounted. A physician or health-care facility that has a conscientious objection to advance directives is now legally and morally bound to transfer the patient to a health-care provider that will honor them.

2. *Your living will or durable power of attorney is in conflict with current statute regulations.* Some living wills or durable power of attorney documents may be declared invalid because they were written on old, outdated forms. In other cases a patient may want to express treatment wishes not covered by the statute and go further than the legislature granted.

In a recent New York case handled by the Society for the Right to Die, a hospital refused to honor a patient's appointment of a health-care agent because it had been written on an outdated form. The patient had filled out a power of attorney form specifically appointing an agent to make health-care decisions—which was the best form available at the time—but this was superseded when New York passed the Health Care Proxy Bill in 1990. Although the patient had clearly and legally appointed a health-care agent—in this case, her husband—to represent her, she had not reexecuted the new form that had become law just a few months earlier. The hospital, behaving in an extremely narrow and technical fashion, refused to honor the appointment, claiming it needed a court order to do so. The patient died, however, before the issue of the agent's authority was ever resolved. This case underscores the importance of using the latest and most up-to-date forms available in order to avoid the possibility of a technical objection. Being right is small comfort if you have to go to court to prove it.

Other living wills and DPA directives have been declared invalid because they referred to treatments not covered in state law. For example, several state laws exclude artificially supplied nutrition and hydration (tube feeding) from the list of treatments that can be withheld or withdrawn. As we saw, this is what happened in Florida's *Browning* case when the patient refused artificial feeding, a form of life-sustaining treatment not recognized by the Florida living will statute at the time. In most states, courts have supported the patient's request, arguing a constitutional or common law right to refuse treatments that "coexist" with, but are not specified in, the statute. When you write a living will that differs from the statute, you run the risk of having a hospital balk at your request but it is ultimately more important that the document reflect your real wishes.

3. *Your living will or durable power of attorney makes no mention of the particular life support technology at issue or is not specific enough about other issues.* We saw an example of this in the *Wirth* case, where a patient suffering from AIDS related complex (ARC) had not made any specific reference to toxoplasmosis in his living will. Be as precise and concrete as possible; consult your doctor and lawyer for information on which to base your instructions.

4. *Your living will or durable power of attorney for health care is old.* Some hospitals and doctors are automatically suspicious of living wills or durable powers of attorney for health care documents completed a relatively long time before hospital admission—say, more than five years previously—even if the forms are still accurate. After all, it is logical to assume you might have changed your mind about life support treatment since then, particularly if your medical condition altered radically or if new or improved forms of life support technology evolved.

For this reason, it's wise to review and update your living will and durable power of attorney documents at least every few years, or whenever you're advised of new developments in your medical condition or the life support technology potentially available to you. Unless specifically revoked, your living will should be considered valid but it is better not to leave open the possibility that someone might think your preferences had changed.

5. *An emergency situation arises.* In an emergency crisis originating outside of a hospital, like the highway accidents of Nancy Cruzan and Larry McAfee, it is usually impossible to determine immediately the injured person's chances for survival—much less whether he or she has any treatment wishes or documents stating them. Therefore, all possible effort is undertaken to keep the injured person alive, and his or her consent is presumed.

Obviously the more people who know about the existence of an accident victim's living will or DPAHC, the more likely it is the patient's medical-care wishes will be honored in a timely, cooperative, and satisfactory manner. In some emergency cases, the existence of a living will and DPA is known from the start, thanks to a card in the patient's wallet, or even a bracelet on the patient's arm, such as MedicAlert. Some states, like Minnesota, have recently permitted notation of a living will on driver's licenses. Such early warning systems are crucial because the incident rate of life-threatening accidents has steadily risen for all sectors of the population over the last two decades. For those less than forty-five years of age, accidents are the leading cause of death in the United States.

During an emergency situation *inside* a hospital, just like during an emergency situation *outside* a hospital, it is usually impossible to estimate a patient's chances for survival. The patient's consent to any type of life-sustaining machinery is presumed, and the doctor is legally excused from seeking the patient's informed consent.

However, it is generally recognized that even in an emergency, consent will *not* be presumed if the patient has previously refused consent to the precise life-sustaining treatment in question, such as a do not resuscitate order. This is what should have happened in the *Winter* case (Chapter 3). Mr. Winter made out a DNR order after suffering a stroke but was resuscitated nonetheless when he began to experience cardiac arrest. He proceeded to sue the hospital for violating his right to refuse unwanted treatment. Hopelessly ill patients who plan to die at home often make out a prehospital do not resuscitate order but their wishes are too often not followed. Once you dial 911 and emergency medical services arrives on the scene, it is difficult (although not impossible) to control the flow of events. If undesired life-sustaining treatment should be administered to a patient during the course of an emergency because medical personnel are not yet aware of the patient's medical history and treatment preference, then that treatment must be discontinued as soon as information about the patient is available.

Some people worry about *ever* allowing life-sustaining treatment to begin, assuming once it does begin, it is more likely to remain in place. This is not, or should not be, a valid distinction. Legally speaking, there is no difference between "withholding" or "withdrawing" life-sustaining treatment. Through his or her living will directions and health-care agent, a terminally ill patient has just as much right to ask for the cessation of life-sustaining treatment *after* it has been initiated as to reject life-sustaining treatment *before* it is administered.

It has been argued that making it too difficult for patients to *withdraw* life-sustaining treatment once it has been started—using the sanctity of life argument—might paradoxically cause patients to refuse to *initiate* this very treatment when it might still do some good. The Cruzan family agreed to tube feeding while they still thought Nancy had a chance—and found themselves living a nightmare when they could not stop the treatment. They were ignored when they sought to withdraw life support, as if their consent were a one-way street.

It may take several months to arrive at a clear prognosis, and patients should have the opportunity to receive every form of life support while there is still a chance of recuperation. However, once it becomes clear that the patient cannot recover and would not wish to prolong his or her dying, individuals have the right to withdraw unwanted care.

6. *There is conflict within your personal support group—which includes close members of your family and your health-care agent—about whether or not you should receive life-sustaining treatment.* If a patient's spouse, parent, adult children, or health-care agent feels strongly enough that one or more of the patient's living will directions should not be honored, given the situation at hand, that individual may formally challenge the validity of the patient's living will. Following through on such a challenge is an extremely stressful, time-consuming, and costly process. It is rarely pursued. The advent of a loved one's death, however, can always trigger unpredictable reactions, including this one.

It is always best to try to resolve such conflicts without resorting to judicial proceedings. In a New Jersey situation in which the Society for the Right to Die became involved, a woman in a persistent vegetative state had appointed one of her three daughters as her health-care agent. Although both the agent and another daughter agreed with their mother's wishes to withdraw treatment, the third daughter, who was more religious than the other two, objected. The hospital and the agent could have acted within the law and followed the mother's instructions, but they felt uncomfortable without the family's unanimous consent. Several discussions were held with the physician, the hospital administrator, and a lawyer, as well as with the family, until the third daughter accepted that this was what her mother would have wanted.

This case highlights the practical, as opposed to the strictly legal, need to reach a consensus among close family and friends involved with the care of a patient at the end of life. Discuss your advance directive with all relevant parties before it is ever needed so you can preempt such potential objections. Although the New Jersey woman had correctly selected a daughter who agreed with her to carry out her wishes, she should also have discussed her choice with the daughter who objected so there could have been little doubt about her intentions.

Sometimes it is impossible to resolve conflicts within the patient-family-doctor relationship or within the institution, and a more formal objection is launched. Depending on the state, this is what happens when challenging the enforcement of a living will.

Let's suppose controversy arises over whether to honor a patient's living will by turning off a mechanical respirator. The patient wrote that a respirator should be discontinued but the challenger petitions a local court to issue a temporary restraining order preventing the patient's physician from turning off the respirator until the court rules on the will's validity. During this interim period, the court may appoint a "guardian ad litem"—someone with no connection to the patient who is specifically chosen to protect him or her. At a hearing attended by all relevant parties, the court makes its determination.

If the court finds the living will request for no mechanical respiration is, in fact, not valid in the situation at hand, the respirator may not be turned off. If it finds the living will direction valid, the patient's mechanical respirator must be turned off as soon as practical.

What Can Be Done to Resolve Problems

THE APPEAL SYSTEM

If any of the above-listed problems arises concerning your living will or durable power of attorney for health care, it is up to your health-care agent and any close member of your family to try to ensure that your directives are ultimately honored. Let's assume *you* are the one who must step in to defend the rights of a mentally incapacitated loved one. What can you do? To whom can you turn for help?

You must convince anyone who challenges the living will or DPA instructions—other members of the family or the health-care agent, the doctor, or hospital administrators—that the instructions do, in fact, reflect the patient's wishes relevant to the situation at hand. Naturally, any dialogue with someone who has an opposing point of view should be conducted in a calm, rational, even-handed manner. Otherwise, you may do more harm than good. It is important to emphasize this because you will be under tremendous stress and might feel angry with the opposition you encounter.

Prepare yourself beforehand to respond intelligently to the challenger's possible statements and questions; make sure you know his or her exact position and rationale. Assemble all the information you need, including any corroboratory evidence, such as testimony from other friends or relatives who spoke with the patient or any written statement he or she made about treatment wishes. It helps to have as much supporting evidence as you can before you make your way through the health-care setting:

1. The attending physician should always be your first point of contact. Most conflicts begin, and end, at the bedside, in the key exchange between the patient and/or the patient's health-care agent and the physician. Your best bet is to try to persuade the attending physician that his or her objections are not valid or relevant to the individual case at hand (assuming the medical information bears this out). You should always try to speak directly with the physician before taking the next step.

Like most human beings, doctors don't like to have someone go over their heads. You do not want to make the attending physician an antagonist; try to establish a dialogue and win him or her over to your position. It's important to bear in mind that doctors, in general, are not inclined to be opponents but, rather, supporters of advance directive: Recall the 1989 survey conducted by the *Journal of the American Medical Association* that showed almost 80 percent of the physician who responded had positive attitudes toward the use of advance directives. The physician is still your most important ally. Consult with him or her and explain your position as clearly and calmly as possible.

2. When seeking information about the patient, do not neglect to talk to the nursing staff. No one is as intimately and continuously involved with a patient's care as the nurse. Nurses often know more about a patient's true condition—what is on the medical chart and what is not—than anyone else. Unlike doctors they are by the bedside around the clock and have long hours for observation and patient contact. Nurses are also very familiar with hospital politics and policies, and may be a valuable source of information about some of the behind-the-scenes goings-on.

At the same time, nurses and others may become very attached to their patients and occasionally project their own emotions onto them. This is especially true concerning the withdrawal of life-sustaining treatment that might lead to death. Some of Nancy Cruzan's nurses opposed the removal of her feeding tube, convinced she was not in PVS. They claimed to have seen her sit up and smile and swore she understood when they spoke to her. As Dr. Ronald Cranford, the well-known neurologist who examined Nancy Cruzan and confirmed she was incapable of any cognitive function, explained, "Every time you mention removing a feeding tube, some nurses report the patient is talking and eating in bed. And they're not lying. They really believe this, because they can't accept that the person they're caring for is completely vegetative." Keep in mind that personal beliefs and professional roles always influence judgment.

3. Most hospitals have patient representatives and/or social workers to whom you can present your problem. Patient representatives and social workers are specially trained to help family members or health-care agents in a wide variety of conflict-related situations. Frequently they are well versed in the law and can advocate your position to doctors and hospital administrators articulately and convincingly. Seeking out a patient representative should be your first course of appeal if you run into opposition.

But don't automatically assume the patient representative or social worker will go to bat for you. Listen carefully to determine how knowledgeable he or she seems; this area of the law is currently going through a period of rapid transition—some patient representatives and social workers will be better informed than others.

4. If you have not resolved your problem after consulting your patient representative or social worker, try to contact the hospital ethics committee. Many hospitals (about 60 percent) have ethics committees that deliberate and make recommendations on approaches to decision-making matters such as these. The initiator of an ethics committee review in most hospitals can be a doctor, a hospital administrator, a patient, a patient's representative, a social worker, or anyone close to the patient acting in his or her behalf. You will usually be entitled to ask for a meeting at which you can explain and defend the patient's wishes. If no ethics committee exists, you can request that an *ad hoc* group be formed. At some hospitals, there are ethics consultants, individuals who specialize in negotiating the moral and philosophical aspects of a particular medical dilemma.

Consisting of physicians, nurses, social workers, lawyers, theologians, and others, the ethics committee can correct misconceptions or inadequate knowledge for both patients' families and doctors, informing each side about the hospital's policy and practice, current state laws, and the wider ethical consensus relating to the individual medical circumstances. It serves as a forum for reconciling the interests of health professionals with the interests of their patients—without undue stress or antagonism.

Most ethics committees are advisory rather than decision-making bodies, although they can make formal recommendations. They are particularly useful for clarifying options and presenting a larger perspective, explaining when it might be, or might not be, ethically appropriate to withdraw treatment.

In a case handled by the Society for the Right to Die, an elderly man who had suffered a debilitating stroke was maintained on life support for many months despite having a living will. The attending neurologist refused or was unable to give the patient's family a clear reading of the man's condition. He said it would take months to determine whether the stroke was irreversible (which is common with strokes). As time went by, the man's family became anxious about continuing unwanted treatment. They approached the hospital's patient representative, who convened an ethics committee. The proceedings revealed that the neurologist had personal objections to removing life support. Other physicians at the hospital were found who were able to make a definitive diagnosis of irreversible stroke and withdraw life-sustaining treatment.

This case is a good example of how the appeals process can work. It also shows that sometimes professional opinions from members of the health-care team may mask more personal, underlying objections. While remaining respectful, you should not allow yourself to be intimidated by "experts" in seeking to carry out a loved one's wishes.

5. If the hospital does not have an ethics committee, or if the involvement of the ethics committee doesn't further your loved one's cause, go to the hospital administration. Although it varies with the size of the institution, you will usually have access to the director of a hospital department. Risk management is the department frequently involved in this area. Risk managers are responsible for assessing the risk that any course of action poses for the hospital, to insulate it from any liability. But if the issue is a straightforward legal one, you may be able to resolve it at this level. You might wish to do some research into state and hospital policies before meeting with the risk managers. For example, gather data refuting the notion that living wills cannot be honored for the sole reason that the state has no living will statute.

Raise the money issue and the hospital's cost of noncompliance with a patient's wishes. You might refer to the *Elbaum* case (discussed earlier) in which a nursing home was left with an unpaid $100,000 bill for unwanted treatment. In California, a court ruled in the *Bartling* case that a hospital and doctors had to pay a patient's attorney fees of $160,000 for forcing him to go through the court system to affirm his right to refuse life-sustaining treatment. You might suggest that the hospital stands to lose a significant amount of money if it does not honor your loved one's wishes.

6. If you are still unable to resolve the issue after meeting with the hospital administration, there are a number of outside resources you can contact for help. One of these is the Society for the Right to Die, and others are listed in the *Resources* section of this book.

7. Finally, you can ask a lawyer who is very familiar with the relevant state laws to petition a state court for a hearing. This should be your last resort. A legal battle can be quite lengthy, and is certain to be emotionally and financially draining. You should get a clear idea of the patient's overall prognosis before beginning legal proceedings. If there are only a few weeks, the legal process might last longer than the dying process. Time and money spent on lawyers might not be worth it.

Keep in mind, however, that the mere mention of the word *lawyer* will often get you immediate attention in a health-care facility. A physician or a risk manager who has been arguing that it is against hospital policy to honor living wills may suddenly become more responsive when it is clear you are acting on legal advice. You might also ask your lawyer (or anyone else you know) to contact the hospital's president, executive director, or chairman of the medical board to appeal to the hospital at the top.

THE TRANSFER SOLUTION

In some cases, transfering the patient to another institution that will honor his or her advance directives is the best solution. When a hospital denies the validity of a patient's living will or DPAHC, it's as if the patient had never completed these documents. However, it's not always easy to transfer a patient for the purpose of discontinuing life support.

In May of 1986, Danny Delio, a thirty-three-year-old exercise physiologist living in New York, suffered cardiac arrest attack during routine surgery and, as a result, was admitted to Westchester County Medical Center in a vegetative state. A month later, tube feeding was begun. In August, Delio's wife, Julie, with the support of his mother, requested that a state court appoint her "conservator" for her husband and grant her the authority to order tube feeding stopped. Danny Delio had no living will. The hospital claimed withdrawing treatment would violate its mission to preserve life.

The court appointed Julie Delio conservator and also, as customary, appointed a guardian ad litem. In December 1986, after three days of hearings, the judge determined there was "clear and convincing evidence" that Danny Delio, while competent, had vehemently opposed the idea of having his life prolonged solely by means of medical technology. Nevertheless, the judge denied Julie Delio's application to have her husband's tube feeding terminated, citing the absence of "clear legislative or judicial guidance" and implying that Danny Delio's right of self-determination was outweighed by his youth and "nonterminal" medical condition.

In a letter to the New York State Task Force on Life and the Law, Julie Delio wrote in moving terms about the anguish she endured during her eight-month struggle on her husband's behalf:

> *When my husband's diagnosis was clear to me, I requested termination of all medical treatment. The attending physician refused. . . . Not a single reason had anything to do with Danny's wishes or the medical facts. . . .*
>
> *The judicial process was devastating to me and my mother-in-law. The loss of my husband was tragic enough, yet I was then forced to publicly plead to strangers for his death. . . .*
>
> *The guardian ad litem was another source of distress to me and my*

mother-in-law. We feared and resented a stranger who had power over my husband's fate. The fact that an outsider had to be appointed to watch over my husband's interests, rather than my mother-in-law and myself, was terrifying. . . .

When our story and the judge's decision made headlines in Westchester and was carried on New York City radio stations, Danny's mother was devastated. She felt violated that her most private words could be quoted from court transcripts and printed to expose her to the world like that. . . .

My personal tragedy has been compounded and exacerbated by the medical and legal communities.

Julie Delio went on to appeal the trial court's decision. On June 1, 1987, the appellate court authorized the termination of tube feeding. However, the court did not order the hospital to comply with this decision. Perhaps recognizing that such an order would trigger a time consuming appeal on the hospital's part, the court gave the hospital a choice: honor the appeal or permit Danny Delio's transfer to another facility.

The hospital declined to comply with Delio's wishes but did not appeal. At the family's request, the Society for the Right to Die was able to arrange Delio's transfer on June 6. He was cared for in the Palliative Care Program at a New York hospital, which provided for the withholding and withdrawing of all artificial life support. He died peacefully on June 15.

The issue of transferring a patient can be especially thorny when it involves crossing state lines. That is the question raised by the *Christine Busalacchi* case, presently on appeal at the Missouri Supreme Court.

Christine Busalacchi was badly injured in a car accident in 1987, as a high-school junior. A week after the accident, doctors told Pete Busalacchi, Christine's father, that the girl would die unless she underwent a craniotomy and the removal of a section of her right frontal lobe. Pete Busalacchi consented to the operation. A week later he consented to the insertion of a feeding tube. Christine has been said to be in PVS ever since, cared for in the Missouri Rehabilitation Center, the same facility that treated Nancy Cruzan. One crucial difference between Ms. Cruzan and Ms. Busalacchi is that, like most minors, Ms. Busalacchi had never discussed dying and her feelings about life support.

In December 1990, after a three-year ordeal that convinced him his daughter was "gone forever," Pete Busalacchi sought to transfer her to a Minnesota facility, where her neurological condition could be evaluated and removal of her feeding tube would be an option. He was stopped by the Missouri Department of Health, which took him to court to prohibit his daughter's transfer out of state. In the hearing the state questioned whether Ms. Busalacchi was really in PVS—although this is not a requirement for removing tube feeding—and claimed there had been some signs of improvement (a similar claim made by the facility about Nancy Cruzan). Pete Busalacchi contended that as her father, he could seek medical care where he wished. The trial court ruled in Pete Busalacchi's favor, saying the decision to move Christine was properly her guardian's and not the state's.

The state immediately appealed to an intermediate court. William Colby, the attorney who represented Nancy Cruzan before the U.S. Supreme Court, argued on behalf of the Busalacchi family. Colby said parents have a constitutional right and duty to make medical treatment decisions for their minor children and anyone who challenges this right must prove conclusively that the decision constitutes neglect. Colby also asserted that the "right to travel" is a fundamental constitutional right entitling citizens and their families to travel to a sister state to take advantage of that state's laws. In April 1991, however, the Missouri Court of Appeals ruled by a two to one margin that Christine Busalacchi could not be transferred until more information was gathered concerning her exact medical condition. William Colby, on behalf of the Busalacchi family, has appealed to the Missouri Supreme Court.

Regardless of the outcome in the *Busalacchi* case, most patients today have the right to request transfer to another facility within their state if their health care provider refuses to honor their living will or DPAHC requests. According to the Patient Self-Determination Act, every health-care facility that receives federal funding is obligated to follow state law about transfer, which usually mandates that the institution must facilitate transfer of the patient if it cannot comply with his or her advance directives. By stipulating that all such institutions inform patients *in writing* and *on admission* of their own policies concerning advance directives, the Patient Self-Determination Act ensures that patients will have adequate warning about any potential conflict.

Ideally you should learn about your hospital or nursing home's policy toward advance directives *before* entering the facility, so you may choose a sympathetic health-care setting. In the event you do not have advance notice, and find yourself in an institution whose policy does not look favorably on advance directives, you may demand transfer to another facility that will honor your treatment wishes. Do not be shy in asserting your rights. You are protected by law from receiving unwanted treatment.

Guidelines for Avoiding or Overcoming Problems

Living will and DPAHC documents are becoming increasingly familiar and accepted instruments for self-protection. If you've completed these documents carefully and thoughtfully, chances are good that they will not be disregarded or challenged. Certainly you should not assume hospitals will be hostile toward them, nor should you hesitate to take advantage of life-sustaining technology because you're afraid it won't be removed later on.

However, in order to rest assured that your advance directives will be honored, remember simple guidelines:

1. *Keep important people, family, friends, clergy or religious advisers, your doctor and health-care team fully informed about you medical condition, care, and wishes.* Consider registering your living will and DPAHC.

2. *Learn the hospital's policies, procedures, and patient-related resources regarding advance directives.* Thanks to the Patient Self-Determination Act, you should be advised of your hospital's policies at the time of your admission. Demand this information right away if it is not forthcoming. Because patients are not always conscious at the time of admission, learn about your local health-care facility before you ever need it. Ask questions about hospital procedures and patient-related resources, such as:

- What can I do to help make sure my wishes will be honored, even in the event of an emergency, when I can't communicate them personally?
- How and under what circumstances will my family and health-care agent be notified about changes in my health status or treatment?
- In case of an unresolved difference of opinion between my health-care agent and my doctor regarding my treatment wishes, what is the appeal process?
- Do you have patient representatives and/or social workers? Where are they located? How can my health-care agent enlist their help? Are they fully informed about living wills and durable powers of attorney for health care?
- Do you have an ethics committee? How can my health-care agent enlist its help?
- How and under what circumstances can transfers to another health-care institution be arranged?

Persist in your questioning until you have complete answers. This may require some amount of searching for the right source. If you don't receive satisfactory answers, definitely consider another hospital.

Hospital choice may be limited by the community where you reside, or your physician may not have admitting privileges at another hospital and may be unable to follow you. (Some physicians are unwilling to follow patients to nursing homes because they are poorly paid.) Take all these factors into account. Inform yourself *in advance* about your hospital's attitude toward living wills and DPAHC documents.

3. *Don't be put off by statements that it's "against the law" to withhold or withdraw life support technology.* It is *not* against the law for a patient to refuse most types of medical treatment. And even in states without living wills, a living will document is widely recognized as clear and convincing evidence.

Not all health-care professionals realize these facts. After reading this book, you may well know more about the subject than many of them. Also, as in any large and busy institution, there is always a chance someone will give you a perfunctory response like "it's against the law" simply to cut short the conversation or to pass the buck.

4. *Never lose sight of your options.*

Don't give up. Do as much as possible in advance to make sure your treatment wishes will be followed, and to prepare your health-care proxy for a strong advocacy role. You have the right to die as you wish.

CHAPTER FIVE
Beyond the Living Will

> "The knowledge that we must die gives us our perspective for living, our sense of finitude, our conviction of the value of every moment, our determination to live in such a fashion that we transcend our tragic limitation."
>
> —JOHN MCMANNERS

This book describes the most effective and most clear-cut action you can take right now to provide yourself with basic protection in most end-of-life medical situations. This is especially important because new advances in medical technologies over the next three decades will enable doctors to keep more people alive for longer periods of time in compromised health situations—not just terminally ill people but also people experiencing any type of serious injury, infection, illness, or disability.

Beyond living will and durable power statutes, there are other, more involved, ideas and propositions about how to formulate and communicate your medical care wishes, and how to carry them out, whether or not you are in a terminal health situation. These propositions involve not only variations and elaborations on standard documents like living wills, but other fundamental efforts to address our values as moral and social beings.

Cost and Community Values: The Oregon Experiment in Rationing Health Care

The cost of providing health care in the United States has soared in recent years. It now consumes more than 12 percent of the Gross National Product (GNP), or the total value of the nation's output of goods and services. By contrast, we spend 6 percent of the GNP on defense, including all those expensive "star wars" programs.

The United States spends more money than any other industrialized nation in the world on delivering basic health services to its citizens, yet 33 million uninsured Americans are effectively denied access to them. Millions of others who have access are paying increasingly high, even exorbitant, premiums while questioning the quality of the care they do receive. Of the total health-care budget now covered by the government through Medicare and Medicaid, more than half is paid out to patients in the last year of life and close to one-third is consumed in the last thirty days. These facts raise some difficult and vexing questions we as a society must try to answer.

Everyone agrees that U.S. health care is in crisis, but no one knows what to do about it. In a move that could set an example for the nation—or torpedo any similar efforts in the future—the Oregon Health Services Commission has decided to try to make adequate health care available to all Oregonians by rationing and redistributing its Medicaid-supported health services more equitably.

Through a statewide program of meetings run by Oregon Health Decisions, a consensus of community values has emerged that shape health care. Those values are now being used to set priorities for health-care allocations. The commission, after holding public hearings with input from business, community, and professional groups, is ranking health services from the most important to the least important, in a list of twenty-six categories reflecting the comparative benefits of each.

The people of Oregon gave *prevention* its highest possible rating. Prevention was defined as a health-care service that "prevents illness (e.g., immunizations, prenatal care), detects symptoms at an early stage (e.g., mammograms, cholesterol, and blood pressure screenings), or prevents a problem from degenerating to a more severe state (e.g., drug and alcohol treatment, insulin for diabetics)." Participants believed prevention increases the quality of life, is highly cost effective, and often works through education, which is empowering to the individual and benefits large numbers of people. As a result, Oregon will give any health-care service that includes a strong degree of preventive benefits a high priority rating and make it widely accessible.

The condition *appendicitis* and its treatment or service *appendectomy* is high on the list in the "acute imminently life-threatening with full recovery" category. This means an appendectomy meets the value of prevention, as well as other values deemed important by the community, and would be available to any Medicaid-covered citizen who needed it. This prioritized list will effectively determine who gets what care.

The idea of rationing health care is very controversial and provocative.

For many, it is anathema to the very concept of an egalitarian society and smacks of "triage," the idea that when resources are scarce, limits must be set on who is eligible to receive what care. Under Oregon's proposed list, for example, a Medicaid dependent person who has just been diagnosed with AIDS will qualify to receive the expensive drug AZT but an AIDS patient in the late stages of the disease, with a low chance of survival, probably won't.

Many people find this kind of value judgment indefensible. For others, it is, in effect, how the system operates today, although no one is willing to discuss it openly. By publicly admitting that not everyone can have access to everything, and rationing what resources it has—with limits on the most expensive high technology—Oregon hopes to make basic health care available to many more people.

Some have argued that while the Oregon plan represents a more rational use of state money, it increases the disparity between rich and poor—some people with private means and private insurance can still get any treatment they want but those who are forced to rely on Medicaid now have their options limited. Questions were also raised about the makeup of those who attended the community meetings and whether they represented a genuine cross section of the population.

By contrast, in Canada there is a national health policy with full rationing of the entire system; rich and poor receive the same health care and there is no private insurance.

The Oregon experiment has drawn nationwide attention and is closely watched by many other states and health care groups. Regardless of its final outcome, it can teach us a great deal about the search for shared communal values. Oregonians were forced to examine their own values and beliefs and to make difficult choices, both for themselves and for the community, a process you too must go through as you consider some of the larger issues raised by advance directives.

Arriving at Value Judgments: Physician-Assisted Suicide

As medical science develops more and more ways to anticipate and forestall death, Americans are becoming increasingly divided by their ethical attitudes toward dying. Many people believe the most honorable death involves "letting nature take its course." Others claim this attitude is morally irresponsible, given the fact that medical science does have the power to keep life going beyond what used to be its natural course. Still others argue that neither nature nor science should be allowed to have its way if the result is likely to be a long period of agony and/or dehumanized life for the dying individual.

This final, most extreme position challenges a basic taboo in Western civilization: the moral prohibition against committing or assisting suicide. In doing so, it illustrates just how complicated and potentially controversial the decision-making environment surrounding death has become.

Consider the 1990 case of Janet Adkins, who ended her life rather than suffer the gradual deterioration and ravages of Alzheimer's disease. Adkins, fifty-four years old, flew 2,000 miles to kill herself with the aid of a special device invented by a maverick Michigan physician, Dr. Jack Kevorkian. It is easy for many people, including professional bioethicists, to object to this case because of its makeshift and impersonal nature: Dr. Kevorkian didn't know Mrs. Adkins well, and the death itself took place in a van in an abandoned parking lot. But the larger issue—whether it is *ever* ethical for a doctor to help a chronically or terminally ill patient to die—is not so easily resolved.

In the February 28, 1991, issue of the *New England Journal of Medicine,* Dr. Timothy E. Quill of Rochester, New York, described how he helped a long-term patient die in the comfort and privacy of her home. The patient, a forty-five-year-old woman identified in the article as "Diane," had already refused the grueling regimen of chemotherapy and other painful treatments that would have given her, at best, a 25 percent chance of surviving her leukemia. Diane, who had also battled with vaginal cancer, depression, and alcoholism for eight years, conversed calmly and rationally with Dr. Quill and her family about her desire to commit suicide, convincing them of her sincerity and her determination. Dr. Quill described his powerful ambivalence to her plan:

> When the time came, she wanted to take her life in the least painful way possible. Knowing of her desire for independence and her decision to stay in control, I thought this request made perfect sense. I acknowledged and explored this wish but also thought it was out of the realm of currently accepted medical practice and more than I could offer or promise. In our discussion it became clear that preoccupation with fear of a lingering death would interfere with Diane's getting the most out of the time she had left until she found a safe way to ensure her death. I feared the effects of a violent death on her family, the consequences of an ineffective suicide that would leave her lingering in precisely the state she dreaded so much, and the possibility that a family member would be forced to assist her, with all the legal and the personal repercussions that would follow.

After agonizing over what response he should make to Diane's pleas for help, Dr. Quill finally advised her to get information from the Hemlock Society, a group that supports an individual's right to commit suicide under such circumstances. "A week later she phoned me with a request for barbiturates for sleep," Quill recounted. "I knew this was an essential ingredient in a Hemlock Society suicide. I made sure she knew how to use the barbiturates for sleep, and also the amount needed to commit suicide." Two days later, her husband called Quill and told him that Diane had died peacefully after saying good-bye to her family.

In a subsequent interview with Dr. Lawrence K. Altman for *The New York Times,* Dr. Quill suggested that many doctors have helped their patients commit suicide but have not talked about it. He also stated that many other doctors might be willing to assist a suicide in certain situations, but fear to discuss the issue with their patients. Furthermore, he maintained it was right for doctors to assist patients they knew well to die in this manner, if the patients so desired.

The highly complex and controversial issue of doctor-assisted suicide lies beyond the scope of this book. We raise the issue solely because it forces so many people these days to reexamine their values regarding life, death, and acceptable medical care. Is it ever ethical for a physician to assist in the rational suicide of a terminally ill person? What is a rational suicide and who should define it? By assessing your own feelings and thoughts regarding such dramatic cases, you may begin the process of defining with greater precision your own most deeply held values and convictions.

The Values History

In keeping with this growing trend toward self-examination, some groups advocate we should do more than fill out a living will and durable power of attorney for health care; we should also document our personal beliefs and opinions relating to life, death, and health care in general as a matter of medical record in a variety of institutional and living environments.

One such group is the Center of Health Law and Ethics of the Institute of Public Law at the University of New Mexico School of Law. From 1988 through 1990, it conducted the National Values History Project to develop and test a practical mechanism for documenting people's health-related values. The aim was to make a fuller record of individual values and wishes available for the admissions process, both for general purposes and insofar as those values related specifically to making health-care decisions for patients no longer competent. The result is the New Mexico version of the "Values History" form.

The Values History begins by asking individuals whether they have expressed their wishes concerning medical treatment through either a living will or DPAHC, and whether they have any preferences regarding specific medical procedures. It then moves on to discuss values and wishes in other areas, such as personal relationships, overall attitude toward life and thoughts about illness.

You are asked about your attitude toward your current general health before examining your perception of your doctor's role and that of other health-care givers: "Do you like your doctors? Do you trust your doctors? Do you think your doctors should make the final decision concerning any treatment you might need?"

In a series of apparently simple, straightforward questions, you must assess your own feelings, both negative and positive, about doctors and the health care profession. Your answers are helpful to any person involved with your future care, but may also stimulate you to reconsider your present relationship with physicians and what, if any, changes you need to make in that regard.

The questionnaire also probes your thoughts about independence and control and asks important questions about your personal relationships: "Do you expect your friends, family, and/or others will support your decisions regarding medical treatment you may need now or in the future? What, if any, unfinished business from the past are you concerned about (e.g., personal and family relationships, business and legal matters)?"

In assessing your attitude toward death, the Values History inquires about your attitude toward life: "What activities do you enjoy (e.g., hobbies, watching TV)? Are you happy to be alive? How satisfied are you with what you have achieved in your life? What makes you laugh? Cry?"

Your response to these questions will help build a personal profile that could prove invaluable to those entrusted to make the "right" decisions for you. More direct questions about your attitude toward illness, dying, and death ("Where would you prefer to die?"), as well as questions you answered in your living will concerning the use of life-sustaining treatment for terminal illness, permanent coma, and irreversible chronic illness appear.

After covering your religious background and belief ("Does your attitude toward death find support in your religion?") and your "living environment," the Values History asks about your attitude concerning finances: "How much do you worry about having enough money to provide for your care? Would you prefer to spend less money on your care so that more money can be saved for the benefit of your relatives and/or friends? Do you wish to make any general comments concerning your finances and the cost of your health care?"

Once again, the thrust of such questions is twofold: In examining your own attitude toward the cost of your health care, you will not only provide important information to your care givers but you may also gain self-knowledge that could lead to changes in your life now—like acquiring new health insurance or making out a living will.

The Values History has a final series of questions about your wishes concerning your funeral and then poses two optional and provocative questions: "How would you like your obituary (announcement of you death) to read?" and "Write a brief eulogy for yourself."

Answering the questions posed in the Values History form can help you to acknowledge and appreciate your own deepest feelings about life, death, and medical care. This process can be very beneficial for you even if you don't share your answers with anyone else. The creators of the form, however, advise you to give completed copies to close family members, your doctor, your attorney, and anyone else who may become involved in your health care. They also recommend attaching copies to your living will and DPAHC documents. Individual answers may not tell your health-care givers exactly what they should do for you in a specific medical-care situation—the Values History is too long and so subjective that it is open to widely varying interpretations—but the document as a whole can tell them a great deal about your overall preferences, values, and beliefs. See the *Resource* section for more information.

A Multiple-Choice Living Will

Some health-care practitioners believe the living will accepted by most states is too narrow and limited in describing possible medical scenarios. Various modifications and elaborations have been suggested, with a growing consensus on more emphasis for medical outcomes—what condition a patient is in—rather than what treatments are preferred.

This view held by Dr. Charles Culver and Bernard Gert (of Dartmouth Medical School and Dartmouth College, respectively) and Dr. Joanne Lynn (of George Washington University Medical Center), among others, holds that "terminal illness" is too narrow a definition, excluding many other conditions when patients might wish to refuse life-sustaining care. Culver and Gert provide other possibilities patients can list (covered in earlier discussions of medical options and your living will in Chapters 2 and 3.) Lynn points out that laypersons are far more likely to consider concrete examples from their own experience such as "If I become senile like my grandfather and I can't recognize any family or friends, I would not want treatment that only prolonged my dying." Patients should be as emotional as they want and give voice to their strongest, most personal feelings.

These modifications are sensible and may be used by patients who feel they provide a clearer expression of their wishes. One of the Culver/Gert suggestions—that patients can refuse treatment when "permanently unconscious" even if they are not "terminally ill"—is now widely accepted. The most frequent amendments to living will statutes considered in state legislatures now around the country involve precisely this expansion of a terminal condition's definition to include permanent unconsciousness. To a large extent, this change was impelled by the public's concerns arising out of the *Nancy Cruzan* case. Many people were distressed to learn that their own state's living will would not protect them from being sustained in such a vegetative condition, usually because of narrow definitions involving "imminent death."

Dr. Linda Emanuel and Dr. Ezekiel Emanuel (of Massachusetts General Hospital and Harvard University, respectively) have devised a highly detailed living will based on four clinical scenarios, each with thirteen specified interventions. The Emanuels' living will, or medical directive, has received wide publicity for its comprehensiveness and drawn criticism as confusing and impractical. Some have called it a "living will for doctors" because of the degree of medical sophistication involved in filling it out.

The Emanuels describe four basic medical situations: PVS, coma with a chance of recovery, dementia, and dementia with terminal illness. Each scenario has its own page in the living will. On that page, the medical situation is defined more specifically, various treatment alternatives are listed, and the person completing the form is directed to choose the one statement among three or four that best reflects his or her wishes: "I want," "I do not want," "I am undecided," or "I want a trial: if no clear improvement, stop treatment."

In the 1989 article in the *Journal of the American Medical Association* that first presented this medical directive, Dr. Linda Emanuel, an ethicist and fellow in general internal medicine at the Massachusetts General Hospital, emphasized it should be completed only in the context of ongoing discussions between the patient and his or her care givers. In addition, the medical directive is so detailed it must be reviewed and revised frequently as the patient's medical condition changes. Emanuel recommends regular conferences between a patient and his or her physician as soon as the possibility of a crisis arises.

Improved education and communication between physician and patient is an important and worthy goal. However, it may not be feasible for millions of Americans who lack access to basic health care, let alone have a personal physician to whom they can turn. While this kind of informed discussion between doctor and patient should remain an ideal, it cannot be the precondition for filling out an advance directive, because it would exclude too many people who may lack sophisticated medical knowledge but have a pretty good idea of how they wish to be treated at the end of their lives.

Several studies show that while physicians generally seem to be favorably disposed to advance directives, they seem reluctant to initiate discussion about them. In a 1991 *New England Journal of Medicine* study led by Dr. Linda Emanuel, it was found that "of the perceived barriers to issuing advance directives, the lack of physician initiative was among the most frequently mentioned." While we hope, as I'm sure you do, that many of these barriers will come down over time, neither of us would probably wish to pin our hopes for an effective living will on ongoing and detailed discussions with a physician, discussions that may or may not materialize.

No one can accurately predict every possible outcome for a given patient. Even with the exhaustive checklist provided by the Emanuels, there will be new, unforeseen medical situations that are not included in their medical directive. Nevertheless, there are some people who will want the level of medical detail and specificity afforded by this living will. Consult the *Resource* section for more information.

Seeking Uniformity: The Living Will vs. the Durable Power of Attorney

Since the U.S. Supreme Court's decision in the *Cruzan* case, there has been an explosion of interest in advance directives. Not only are more individuals acting to protect themselves, but also more legislators, doctors, and professional organizations are acting to help others protect themselves. Given all the momentum, the next few years are certain to bring forth an unprecedented number of new state living will and DPAHC bills, as well as proposals to strengthen and extend existing laws.

Some noted experts, among them Professor George Annas of Boston University Schools of Medicine and Public Health, have begun to discern a movement away from living wills toward durable powers of attorney for health care. Years ago, the Presidential Commission also felt durable powers might be better for many people because of their great flexibility. Writing in the *New England Journal of Medicine* in April 1991 Professor Annas noted,

> The *Cruzan* case itself which involved facts essentially identical to those in *Quinlan,* gave impetus to the concept of a health-care proxy, just as the *Quinlan* case had previously increased interest in the living will. Physicians are legally and ethically bound to respect the directions of a patient

set forth in a living will, but living wills are limited because no one can accurately foretell the future and interpretation may be difficult.

As we've previously discussed, the durable power of attorney for health care does provide several advantages over a living will; it allows the health-care agent to make treatment decisions for the incapacitated patient in a variety of situations, not just terminal ones, and it appoints a person, rather than a piece of paper, who can advocate more forcefully on behalf of the patient and who can adapt to new circumstances unforeseen in the living will. For those who have someone to appoint—someone who knows their treatment preferences well, and whom they can trust to present those preferences in an effective manner—the DPAHC is indeed a superb document.

However, the DPAHC, while more open-ended than the living will in one respect, is also more limited in another—it is dependent on the appointment of another person. Many individuals, especially but not exclusively the elderly, simply don't have anyone they can designate as their health-care proxy. For numerous reasons—a spouse and other close relatives have died or are unavailable, the patient does not want to burden others or does not trust them or does not wish to relinquish his or her last vestige of autonomy—these individuals cannot make use of the durable power of attorney. For them, it is essentially useless. Everyone can fill out a living will and state their wishes directly, but a health-care proxy is a document that can not be useful to every segment of the population. When it works it is wonderful but it it does not work for everyone.

The answer, of course, is not to choose one document over the other but to fill them both out. The current trend toward the durable power of attorney for health care can be seen as part of that inveterate human desire for simplicity and uniformity. Isn't it confusing to have so many forms! Wouldn't it be nice if we just had one? People are seeking the single all-encompassing form that renders all others obsolete.

The Uniform Rights of the Terminally Ill Act

An evolving legislative approach to the problem of uniformity is a model piece of legislation known as the "Uniform Rights of the Terminally Ill Act" (URTIA). Developed by the National Conference of Commissioners on Uniform State Laws, and approved by the American Bar Association, this act tries to combine all the significant legal protections of the living will, the durable power of attorney for health care, and surrogate decision-making provisions:

(1) It enables a patient to direct a physician to withhold or withdraw life-sustaining treatments.

(2) It enables a patient to designate another individual to make decisions about withholding or withdrawing the patient's life-sustaining treatments.

(3) It gives decision-making authority to certain family members so that patients who do *not* express their wishes in writing can have medical decisions made on their behalf by the people in the best position to know their personal values and treatment preferences.

The Uniform Rights of the Terminally Ill Act was designed to ensure protection for the individual preferences of every citizen regarding life-sustaining treatment. It aims to guarantee that right in a manner that is understandable and, for all practical purposes, acceptable to health-care personnel and institutions. Finally, it attempts to eliminate the current state-by-state inconsistencies that pose serious problems for many hospital patients who are terminally ill and mentally incompetent in a state other than the state in which their living will is legally approved. From the doctor's point of view too, the URTIA is helpful because it tries to bring the patchwork of state laws into alignment with national medical standards.

While a handful of states have adopted the Uniform Rights Act, they have not all adopted it in its entirety. Missouri, for example, followed much of the form and language of the original Act, but took out the right to refuse tube feeding! There are other built-in problems with the Act. Like any "model" piece of legislation, it works better in theory than in practice. Most states are reluctant to cede their law-making powers to an outside group and prefer to shape their own legislative agenda. They want to pass their own living will statutes and define their own terms. In recognition of this intractable diversity, the Uniform State Commissioners—a distinguished group of experts who specialize in establishing uniform laws for the nation—have suggested amending the URTIA to allow for recognition of out-of-state documents. They have given up on the idea that a single uniform law will be accepted by every state.

The Uniform Rights Act is also limited because it only applies to situations of terminal or irreversible illness. Under the URTIA, the health-care proxy cannot make all health-care decisions but only those that relate to life-sustaining treatment. The same restrictions apply to the surrogate decision-maker. The Uniform Commissioners are planning a complete revision that would amalgamate the URTIA with the Uniform Consent Act. The Consent Act covers all medical decisions and would provide clear legal authority for non-terminal health-care decisions. It would make the URTIA even stronger and represent yet another stage in the evolution of this legislative effort to arrive at a national consensus on health-care decision making.

Right now, the best thing you can do to guarantee your personal right to make your own treatment decisions is to fill out a generic living will, a state living will (if applicable), and a durable power of attorney for health care (assuming you know someone who is capable of functioning in that capacity). All you need to take these steps is made available to you in this book. Part Two provides you with the relevant documents for your state.

A nationwide Gallup poll published January 6, 1991, revealed that although 20 percent of Americans have made out living wills, 75 percent of those who have not already written advance directives want to do so "at some point in the future." Why wait for the future? "The readiness," as Prince Hamlet, the great procrastinator, realizes toward the end of Shakespeare's play, "is all." You have only to think about people like Karen Ann Quinlan and Nancy Cruzan to realize the time for action is now.

PART TWO
Making It Legal

Our experience at the Society for the Right to Die suggests there is a big discrepancy between the number of people who request living wills and durable power of attorney for health care forms and the number of people who actually sign them. One explanation: People in general are fundamentally hesitant to sign up for anything. In its most severe form, this hesitancy is known as *signophobia,* the fear of "leaving one's mark." Very few of us become outright signophobes, but we all worry about committing ourselves legally to the statements set forth in a document. We're afraid we may be making a "wrong" decision that will irrevocably bind us or that we may be victimized in the future by "small print" conditions we've somehow overlooked or failed to understand.

When it comes to signing a living will and a DPAHC form, these fears aren't justified. Both are instruments that should be tailored to your precise specifications, personal documents that protect you and extend the time during which you are empowered to make your health-care decisions.

The only person you are bound to is yourself. It is your precise instructions, written in your own hand, that will be used to guide your health-care providers. The living will does not, and cannot, dictate the full program of medical treatment you'll be offered or administered in a given situation. Nor does it attempt to predict the unknowable: how and when you will die or face death in a terminal or irreversible illness. Instead, the scope of a living will is much more limited and knowable. It concerns itself solely with the types of medical treatment you are *sure* you do or do not want in the event you find yourself in an *extreme* medical situation: one where the life remaining to you is severely compromised and can be sustained only by technological means.

The durable power of attorney for health care may, if you so choose, give even broader powers to your health-care agent but these powers can also be explicitly limited by you. In either case, the health-care agent is your spokesperson. You are the one speaking and directing your own health care through the best representative you have, someone hand-picked and carefully coached by you.

Signing a living will and a DPAHC does not by any means represent an *irrevocable* commitment. These advance directives can be revoked or altered by you at any time. As long as you remain competent, you can change any instruction in your living will or DPAHC. While you are under medical care, you can do this orally in the presence of your physician or health-care provider. Your new decisions will be noted on your medical record and respected as your definitive wishes. And you can always make changes in writing, either by amending the documents themselves, or by creating a new document with your own signature and the signature of two witnesses.

One simple fact bears repeating: you must sign these forms and have them properly witnessed before they become legal documents. Don't be a signophobe, afraid to leave your mark—and your personal treatment wishes—for others to follow.

Updating Your Living Will and Durable Power of Attorney for Health Care Forms

Once you complete your living will and durable power of attorney for health care documents, they are valid indefinitely in nearly every state (see state-by-state section). Nevertheless, it's a good idea to review and re-sign your advance directives, and have your two witnesses re-sign them, at least every five years. The more recently the documents are signed, the more likely it is that a doctor, a health-care facility, or a court will accept their terms. You should also update these documents whenever the following situations occur:

1. *Your health status changes.* After completing your living will and medical durable power documents, you may develop an illness or sustain an injury that makes certain situations of physical and medical incompetency and/or certain forms of life-sustaining medical care more likely in your future. If so, you should make sure your living will and DPAHC documents are amended, if necessary, to address these possible scenarios. Your doctor can help you anticipate and describe specific medical conditions and technologies that may be relevant. You should also inform your health-care agent and family members of the change in your health status and any corresponding changes in your living will and medical durable power documents.

2. *The law changes in your state.* If your state doesn't have a living will statute at the time you fill out your generic living will, it may enact one later. When this happens, you should fill out the state-approved form and review your generic living will to make sure it clearly addresses any wishes you have that are *not* covered in the state-approved form.

Assuming your state already has a living will statute and you've completed a state-approved living will form, any number of changes in the state living will law can still occur in the future. The law may be liberalized to include a wide range of medical conditions and medical technologies. Or new requirements may be imposed, such as the need to have a living will notarized.

Whatever the case, there will probably be a new, revised state-approved living will form you will have to fill out in order to comply with the law. Similarly, any change in your state's durable power of attorney for health care law will necessitate completing a new durable power of attorney for health care document. If new forms are not required, it remains in your best interest to review and, if necessary, update your existing documents any time changes are made in your state's laws (see the State-by-State Guide for more information).

3. *There are new developments in life-sustaining medical technology.* Given the incredibly rapid rate of advancement over the last two decades in life-sustaining technologies, the near future is almost certain to bring about a host of new treatments and procedures, many of which we can't even envision. As these treatments and procedures emerge, you may want to address them in your living will and durable power of attorney. Your doctor can keep you apprised of developments and how they may relate to your own future medical care.

4. *Something happens to your health-care agent or proxy, your back-up agent or proxy, or your witnesses.* Once you have appointed a health-care proxy, you need to remain ever aware of that person's fitness to carry out his or her responsibilities. If that individual should move to a distant location, or if you should become socially, emotionally, or ideologically estranged from that person, he or she may no longer be the most appropriate spokesperson for you. If you get divorced, and you named your spouse as health-care agent, then he or she is generally disqualified. In such situations, you should designate a new, more accessible and/or compatible person as your health-care agent.

Of course, you also need to appoint a new health-care agent if your already designated agent should die or become so physically or mentally ill that he or she would be incapable of defending your medical care rights vigorously and effectively. Because there's always a chance your health-care proxy may suddenly die or succumb to a serious illness just when you need his or her services, the safest policy is to designate two or three agents or proxies in order of priority. That way, if something does incapacitate your first designee, another prearranged designee can take over immediately.

There is generally less need to worry in the event that one or both of your witnesses should die. We know of no case in which the witnesses were called to testify to a signature on a living will or durable power of attorney for health care form. However, if you are concerned about this and one of your witnesses dies, you may reexecute your living will.

As in any situation when you alter your living will or durable power of attorney for health care arrangements, you should make sure all parties involved—including your doctor—know the specific changes you have made. In addition to explaining the nature of the changes, you should also explain your reasons for making them, so there will be no misunderstandings regarding your motives or intentions.

5. *You change your mind.* It's always possible you will have second thoughts about having rejected—or requested—a certain form of life-sustaining treatment. If so, it's a simple matter to alter your living will and durable power of attorney documents to reflect your new way of thinking. Your living will should only contain directives to which you are firmly committed. If you're undecided about a particular issue, don't take any stand at all until you are ready.

6. *You move to a new state.* You may need to fill out new, state-approved forms for both a living will and a durable power of attorney for health care. (You would probably also want to name a new health-care agent geographically closer to you.) At the same time, you may want to alter your generic living will so it specifically covers situations or technologies not covered in the state-approved form.

When you travel to a different state, it's a good idea to take a copy of your living will with you in case you need it. Unpleasant as it may be to imagine having a serious accident or succumbing to serious illness while you're far from home, it's important to realize that *any* disturbance in your normal, at-home routine and any excursion into unfamiliar territory opens new possibilities for injury or sickness. This is especially true if your travel plans include athletic activities, such as swimming, hiking, skiing, or scuba-diving.

Think about keeping copies of your living will and durable power of attorney forms permanently available in your automobile glove compartment or in a continually used piece of luggage. It's also wise to take copies of these documents with you when you travel out of the country. Although they may not be binding, they can be very useful as advisory documents.

If you reside in two states, or if you regularly spend time in another specific state each year, it's in your best interest to fill out state-approved forms for both states. Even if you don't fall into this category, it pays to be aware of some of the basic differences among states regarding living will and durable power of attorney for health care legislation. The fewer surprises you encounter in a life-or-death situation, the better off you will be. Also, familiarity with the general range of possibilities regarding living will and durable power of attorney legislation may help you articulate what you do and do not want to happen to you, and what changes you'd like to see in your own state's legislation.

Consult the State-by-State Guide for the appropriate advance directive forms and guidelines for your state. They are up to date as of June 1991 but keep in mind that this is an area of law in constant flux. New statutes and amendments of existing statutes appear virtually every month. As this book goes to print, four states—New Jersey, Ohio, Pennsylvania, and Rhode Island—are close to passing new living will legislation. *Remember:* You must not only complete your living will and durable power of attorney for health care but also maintain each document, changing it whenever necessary to ensure that you get all the protection to which you're entitled.

Keeping abreast of changes in state living will law and durable power of attorney legislation requires time and energy you may not have. If you are a member of the Society for the Right to Die, we automatically inform you of any change, or proposed change, in your state's law and how it applies to you. You can also consult an informed, local attorney or any relevant agency in your state. In light of the Patient Self-Determination Act, all hospitals, nursing homes and other health-care institutions will also have to provide information about advance directives.

What follows are the actual forms for each state and specific instructions pertaining to your state's law:

- Read all forms carefully.
- You may photocopy these forms and use them as valid legal documents when properly signed and witnessed.

- Review Chapter 3 to resolve any questions about the forms.

- You do not need to consult a lawyer, but most local attorneys should be able to answer questions about state forms.

- If you are unsure about specific treatments, you may wish to consult a physician.

- You should give photocopies of the completed forms to your doctor(s) and to family members or close friends who might be involved in decision making for you. Keep the signed originals in a safe, easily accessible place that they know about. Consider registering them with the Society for the Right to Die.

- Initial and date the original forms periodically to show that they continue to represent your wishes.

- Membership in the Society for the Right to Die (renewable annually) entitles you to:
    Appropriate documents for your state and up-to-date information about any changes in your state's law;
    A wallet-sized membership card that also provides a record of your living will and/or health care proxy, complete with name, address, phone number and the exact location of your document;
    The Society's Newsletter three times a year;
    Discounts on all publications, videos and programs such as the Living Will Registration Service.

A list of resources in the appendix will direct you to the appropriate place for further help or guidance.

A State-by-State Guide to Living Will and DPA Statutes as enacted June 1991.

The Living Will and the Alabama Declaration

Alabama recognizes the legal right of any competent adult (nineteen years or older) to sign a written directive instructing his or her physician to withhold or withdraw life-sustaining procedures in the event of a terminal condition. It is important that you understand the specific provisions of this statute:

1. A declaration may be signed by any adult specifying that, in the event of a terminal condition, medical treatment shall not be used solely to prolong life. The declaration should be substantially in the form included in the statute. You may, if you wish, add personal instructions in the space we have provided—for example, regarding particular types of treatment that you may wish to have withheld or withdrawn, such as cardiopulmonary resuscitation or artificial feeding.
2. The declaration shall be in writing, signed and dated by you (or, if you are physically unable to sign, by another person in your presence and at your express direction) in the presence of two or more witnesses at least nineteen years of age.
3. The witnesses *may not* be

   a. Related to you by blood or marriage.
   b. Entitled to any part of your estate by will, codicil, or under law.
   c. Directly financially responsible for your medical care.
   d. The person, if any, whom you directed to sign the declaration on your behalf.

4. You are responsible for informing your physician of the existence of your declaration. The attending physician shall make a photocopy of the declaration part of your medical records.
5. The making of this declaration shall have no effect on the issuance of insurance policies or on the terms of existing policies.
6. The declaration is invalid during pregnancy.

To protect yourself as fully as possible against unwanted treatment we advise that you execute both the Alabama declaration and the generic living will (Chapter 3).

DECLARATION

Declaration made this _____ day of _____ (month, year).

I, _____, being of sound mind, willfully and voluntarily make known my desires that my dying shall not be artificially prolonged under the circumstances set forth below, and do hereby declare:

If at any time I should have an incurable injury, disease, or illness certified to be a terminal condition by two physicians who have personally examined me, one of whom shall be my attending physician, and the physicians have determined that my death will occur whether or not life-sustaining procedures are utilized and where the application of life-sustaining procedures would serve only to artificially prolong the dying process, I direct that such procedures be withheld or withdrawn, and that I be permitted to die naturally with only the administration of medication or the performance of any medical procedure deemed necessary to provide me with comfort care.

Other directions:

In the absence of my ability to give directions regarding the use of such life-sustaining procedures, it is my intention that this declaration shall be honored by my family and physician(s) as the final expression of my legal right to refuse medical or surgical treatment and accept the consequences from such refusal.

I understand the full import of this declaration and I am emotionally and mentally competent to make this declaration.

Signed _____

City, County and State of Residence _____

_____

The declarant has been personally known to me and I believe him or her to be of sound mind. I did not sign the declarant's signature above for or at the direction of the declarant. I am not related to the declarant by blood or marriage, entitled to any portion of the estate of the declarant according to the laws of intestate succession or under any will of declarant or codicil thereto, or directly financially responsible for declarant's medical care.

Witness _____

Witness _____

The Living Will and the Alaska Declaration

Alaska recognizes the legal right of any person eighteen years or older to make a written declaration instructing his or her physician to withhold or withdraw life-sustaining procedures in the event of a terminal condition. It is important that you understand and follow the specific provisions of the law, which are summarized below:

1. *Form of the Declaration.* The declaration may, but need not, be in the form shown here. It must be signed by you or another person at your direction, in the presence of two witnesses or before a person qualified to take acknowledgments under AS 09.63.010, such as a notary public.
2. *Certification.* The declaration may be signed at any time, but it becomes binding only when the attending physician has been provided with a copy of the declaration, has determined that you are in a terminal condition and unable to make treatment decisions, and has recorded the determination and the contents of the declaration in your medical record.
3. *Witnesses.* The witnesses must be at least eighteen years old and may not be related to you by blood or marriage.
4. *Definition of Life-Sustaining Procedures.* Please note that you can state in the declaration whether you want nutrition or hydration by tube; unless you indicate that you do not want it, nutrition and hydration by tube will be deemed "comfort care," and will be administered along with medication to alleviate pain. We have provided room on the form for any other personal instructions you may have. Many people choose to specify that they wish to receive adequate pain control, even if this shortens their life.
5. *Pregnancy Exemption.* The declaration of a patient known to be pregnant is given no effect as long as it is probable that the fetus could develop to the point of live birth with continued application of life-sustaining procedures.
6. *General Provisions.* The making of this declaration does not affect in any way the provisions of life insurance policies. Death resulting from the withholding or withdrawal of life-sustaining procedures in accordance with this law will not, for any purpose, constitute a suicide or a homicide. The declaration can be revoked at any time.

The Alaska declaration is binding on physicians only when you are certified as having a "terminal condition," defined in the statute as a progressive incurable or irreversible condition that, without the administration of life-sustaining procedures, will result in death within a relatively short time. To protect yourself as fully as possible against unwanted treatment, the Society for the Right to Die advises that you execute both the Alaska declaration and the generic living will (Chapter 3).

ALASKA

DECLARATION

If I should have an incurable or irreversible condition that will cause my death within a relatively short time, it is my desire that my life not be prolonged by administration of life-sustaining procedures.

If my condition is terminal and I am unable to participate in decisions regarding my medical treatment, I direct my attending physician to withhold or withdraw procedures that merely prolong the dying process and are not necessary to my comfort or to alleviate pain.

    I [ ] do [ ] do not desire that nutrition or hydration (food and water) be provided by gastric tube or intravenously if necessary.

Other directions:

Signed this _____ day of _____, _____.

Signature _____

Place _____

The declarant is known to me and voluntarily signed or voluntarily directed another to sign this document in my presence.

Witness _____

Address _____

Witness _____

Address _____

State of _____, _____ Judicial District

The foregoing instrument was acknowledged before me this _____ day of _____, _____ by

_____
Name of Person Who Acknowledged

_____
Signature of Person Taking Acknowledgment

_____
Title or Rank

_____
Serial Number, if any

THIS DECLARATION MUST BE EITHER WITNESSED BY TWO PERSONS OR ACKNOWLEDGED
BY A PERSON QUALIFIED TO TAKE ACKNOWLEDGMENTS UNDER AS 09.63.010.

The Arizona Medical Treatment Decisions Act

Arizona recognizes the legal right of any adult (eighteen years or older) to sign a declaration instructing his or her physician to withhold or withdraw life-sustaining procedures in the event of a terminal condition. The Arizona Medical Treatment Decisions Act permits you to add personal instructions, and the form provides a space for these. You may, if you wish, use this additional space to specify treatments that you wish to have withheld or withdrawn, such as cardiopulmonary resuscitation or artificial feeding. Life-sustaining procedures, as defined in the statute, do not include the administration of medication, food or fluids, or other procedures deemed necessary to provide comfort care. *If you want to refuse artificial nutrition and hydration, you should specify this in your document.*

It is important that you understand the specific provisions of the law, which are summarized below:

1. You are responsible for notifying your physician of the existence of your declaration; he or she will then include a photocopy of your declaration in your medical records.
2. The declaration must be signed in the presence of two witnesses (eighteen years or older), neither of whom may be

   a. Related to you by blood or marriage.
   b. Directly responsible for the costs of your medical care.
   c. Entitled to any part of your estate, under your will, a codicil to your will, or by law.
   d. A claimant against any part of your estate.

3. Before your declaration will be legally binding, your terminal condition must be diagnosed and certified in writing by two physicians, one of whom is your attending physician.
4. A declaration may be revoked in writing or verbally by you or by a person designated to act on your behalf; it may also be revoked by the destruction of the document. As long as you are able to make decisions, your own wishes supersede your declaration.
5. The declaration is invalid during pregnancy if it is believed that the fetus could develop to the point of a live birth with the continuation of life-sustaining procedures.
6. The withholding or withdrawal of life-sustaining procedures from a terminal patient in accordance with the instructions of a declaration does not, for any purpose, constitute suicide.
7. The making of a declaration can have no effect on the issuance or continuation of life insurance.

To protect yourself as fully as possible against unwanted treatment, the Society for the Right to Die advises that you execute both the Arizona declaration and the generic living will (Chapter 3).

DECLARATION

Declaration made this _____ day of _____ (month, year).

I, _____, being of sound mind, willfully and voluntarily make known my desire that my dying not be artificially prolonged under the circumstances set forth below and declare that:

> If at any time I should have an incurable injury, disease or illness certified to be a terminal condition by two physicians who have personally examined me, one of whom is my attending physician, and the physicians have determined that my death will occur unless life-sustaining procedures are used and if the application of life-sustaining procedures would serve only to artificially prolong the dying process, I direct that life-sustaining procedures be withheld or withdrawn and that I be permitted to die naturally with only the administration of medication, food or fluids or the performance of medical procedures deemed necessary to provide me with comfort care.

Other instructions:

In the absence of my ability to give directions regarding the use of life-sustaining procedures, it is my intention that this declaration be honored by my family and attending physician as the final expression of my legal right to refuse medical or surgical treatment and accept the consequences of such refusal.

I understand the full import of this declaration and I am emotionally and mentally competent to make this declaration.

Signed _____

City, County and State of Residence _____

_____

The declarant is personally known to me and I believe him/her to be of sound mind.

Witness _____

Witness _____

The Living Will and the Arkansas Rights of the Terminally Ill or Permanently Unconscious Act

The Arkansas Rights of the Terminally Ill or Permanently Unconscious Act recognizes the legal right of any adult (eighteen years or older) to sign a written declaration instructing his or her physician to withhold or withdraw any life-sustaining treatment that serves only to prolong the dying process or maintain a patient in a state of permanent unconsciousness. The Act contains two forms: one covers terminal conditions and the other covers permanent unconsciousness; both forms are shown here.

The following aspects of the act should be noted:

1. The declarations may be signed by any competent adult who wants to specify that life-sustaining treatment not be administered in the event of a terminal illness or permanent unconsciousness.
2. The declarations must be signed in the presence of two adult witnesses.
3. The law permits you to appoint a health-care proxy, that is, an individual who is eighteen years or older and who is designated by you to make decisions regarding the withdrawal or withholding of life-sustaining treatment in the event you are unable to make them yourself. If you decide not to appoint a proxy, you should cross out the proxy clause in ink.
4. The act does not prohibit the withdrawal of artificial feeding; however, the physician's responsibility in this regard is unclear. If you do *not* wish to be sustained by artificial feeding, you should include a specific statement of those wishes in the document.
5. A pregnant woman's declaration must not be honored if it is possible that the fetus could develop to the point of live birth with the application of life-sustaining treatment.
6. A physician who is unwilling to honor the declaration must take steps to transfer the patient to another physician.

We have provided space on each of the declarations that you can use to add your personal instructions—for example, about specific types of treatment, such as artificial feeding or cardiopulmonary resuscitation, that you may wish to have withheld or withdrawn.

The act also allows a guardian, spouse, parent, adult child, and specified others to execute a written request on behalf of a minor or an adult who is unable to make his or her own decisions and has not executed a declaration.

To protect yourself as fully as possible against unwanted treatment, the Society for the Right to Die advises that you execute both the generic living will (Chapter 3) and the Arkansas declarations. Although the Arkansas statute's definition of a terminal condition makes it clear that life support can be ended if your condition would soon lead to death in the absence of treatment, the Terminal Condition Declaration itself is not clear about the point at which life support can be withdrawn. The generic living will applies to conditions—such as advanced Alzheimer's or minimal consciousness after a stroke—in which many people would want life support to be stopped, but which may not fit the declaration's definition of a "terminal condition." This additional document could provide valuable clarification of your wishes.

"TERMINAL CONDITION" DECLARATION

If I should have an incurable or irreversible condition that will cause my death within a relatively short time, and I am no longer able to make decisions regarding my medical treatment, I direct my attending physician, pursuant to the Arkansas Rights of the Terminally Ill or Permanently Unconscious Act, to withhold or withdraw treatment that only prolongs the process of dying and is not necessary to my comfort or to alleviate pain.

Other directions:

I direct my attending physician to follow the instructions of

_____, residing at

_____, as my Health

Care Proxy, to make medical treatment decisions on my behalf consistent with my wishes.*

Signed this _____ day of _____, 19_____.

Signature _____

Address _____

The declarant voluntarily signed this writing in my presence.

Witness _____

Address _____

Witness _____

Address _____

If you do not name a Proxy, it is advisable to draw a line through this portion.

(See other side for Declaration pertaining to Permanent Unconsciousness)

"PERMANENTLY UNCONSCIOUS" DECLARATION

If I should become permanently unconscious, I direct my attending physician, pursuant to the Arkansas Rights of the Terminally Ill or Permanently Unconscious Act, to withhold or withdraw life-sustaining treatments that are no longer necessary to my comfort or to alleviate pain.

Other directions:

I direct my attending physician to follow the instructions of

_____, residing at

_____, as my Health

Care Proxy, to make medical treatment decisions on my behalf consistent with my wishes.*

Signed this _____ day of _____, 19_____.

Signature _____

Address _____

The declarant voluntarily signed this writing in my presence.

Witness _____

Address _____

Witness _____

Address _____

If you do not name a Proxy, it is advisable to draw a line through this portion.

California's Directive to Physicians and Durable Power of Attorney for Health Care

California recognizes the legal right of any adult to sign a written declaration instructing his or her physician to withhold or withdraw life-sustaining procedures in the event of a terminal condition.

The Directive to Physicians must be in the form set forth in the statute, signed and dated by an adult of sound mind, and witnessed by two adults. The directive shown here follows the statutory form.

It is important that you understand the specific provisions of the law:

1. The witnesses to the directive may *not* be

    a. Related to you by blood or marriage.
    b. Entitled to any portion of your estate, by will, codicil, or the laws of inheritance.
    c. Anyone with a claim on your estate.
    d. Your physician.
    e. Employees of either your physician or of a facility in which you are a patient.

    If you are a patient in a nursing facility, one witness *must be* a patient advocate or ombudsman designated by the State Department of Aging and may not be any of the people list above.

2. Unless the directive has been executed at least fourteen days after you have been diagnosed as having a terminal condition, it is only *advisory* to the physician and the physician is not required to comply. If you have been diagnosed as having a terminal condition at least fourteen days before executing or reexecuting the directive, your physician must either honor your directive or take the steps needed to transfer you to the care of a physician who will.

3. The statute does not list artificial nutrition or hydration among the life-sustaining procedures that can be refused. *If you wish to refuse artificial nutrition or hydration you should express this preference clearly in your directive.* The directive has no effect during the course of pregnancy.

4. The directive remains effective for *five years* from the date of its completion, unless you become incompetent or revoke it during that time. After five years, you must either complete a new directive or reexecute the old one.

Because the directive is only advisory if you were not certified as being in a terminal condition at least two weeks before you made it out, the California legislature passed the Keene Health Care Agent Act. This act enables you to name someone to make health-care decisions for you, including decisions to withhold or withdraw life-sustaining treatment, in the event that you are unable to make or express such decisions yourself. This durable power of attorney for health care, with instructions for making it out, is also shown here.

Please read the durable power of attorney for health care document carefully, especially the section titled "Warning to Person Executing This Document," before gathering your witnesses and filling it out. There are important restrictions regarding who may serve as your attorney-in-fact (the person making decisions on your behalf) and who may witness the document. Your durable power of attorney for health care will be legally valid for up to *seven years,* unless you specify a shorter period of time.

To protect yourself as fully as possible against unwanted treatment, the Society for the Right to Die advises that you execute three documents—the California Directive to Physicians, the California power of attorney for health care (if you have someone to appoint), and the generic living will (Chapter 3). The power of attorney is widely recognized and very useful. The California directive may be adequate, however, the generic living will covers a wider range of medical situations than the statutory directive and can be used to state your personal wishes.

DIRECTIVE TO PHYSICIANS

Directive made this _____ day of _____ (month, year).

I, _____ , being of sound mind, willfully and voluntarily make known my desire that my life shall not be artificially prolonged under the circumstances set forth below, and do hereby declare:

1. If at any time I should have an incurable injury, disease, or illness certified to be a terminal condition by two physicians, and where the application of life-sustaining procedures would serve only to artificially prolong the moment of my death and where my physician determines that my death is imminent whether or not life-sustaining procedures are utilized, I direct that such procedures be withheld or withdrawn, and that I be permitted to die naturally.

2. In the absence of my ability to give directions regarding the use of such life-sustaining procedures, it is my intention that this directive shall be honored by my family and physician(s) as the final expression of my legal right to refuse medical or surgical treatment and accept the consequences from such refusal.

3. If I have been diagnosed as pregnant and that diagnosis is known to my physician, this directive shall have no force or effect during the course of my pregnancy.

4. I have been diagnosed at least 14 days ago as having a terminal condition by

    _____ , M.D., whose address is

    _____ , and whose

    telephone number is _____ . I understand that if I have not filled in the physician's name and address, it shall be presumed that I did not have a terminal condition when I made out this directive.

5. This directive shall have no force or effect five years from the date filled in above.

6. I understand the full import of this directive and I am emotionally and mentally competent to make this directive.

Signed _____

City, County and State of Residence _____

The declarant has been personally known to me and I believe him or her to be of sound mind.

Witness _____   Witness _____

This Directive complies in form with the 'Natural Death Act' California Health and Safety Code, Section 7188.

CALIFORNIA
STATUTORY FORM DURABLE POWER OF ATTORNEY
FOR HEALTH CARE
(California Civil Code Section 2500)

> The language in this document is identical to California's Statutory Form Durable Power of Attorney for Health Care, permitting you to designate an agent empowered to make medical decisions on your behalf in the event of incompetency. If you elect to execute this document, we recommend its use in conjunction with the "Directive to Physicians" authorized by the California Natural Death Act of 1976. Forms are available from the Society for the Right to Die.

Warning to Person Executing This Document

This is an important legal document which is authorized by the Keene Health Care Agent Act. Before executing this document, you should know these important facts:

This document gives the person you designate as your agent (the attorney in fact) the power to make health care decisions for you. Your agent must act consistently with your desires as stated in this document or otherwise made known.

Except as you otherwise specify in this document, this document gives your agent the power to consent to your doctor not giving treatment or stopping treatment necessary to keep you alive.

Notwithstanding this document, you have the right to make medical and other health care decisions for yourself so long as you can give informed consent with respect to the particular decision. In addition, no treatment may be given to you over your objection at the time, and health care necessary to keep you alive may not be stopped or withheld if you object at the time.

This document gives your agent authority to consent, to refuse to consent, or to withdraw consent to any care, treatment, service, or procedure to maintain, diagnose, or treat a physical or mental condition. This power is subject to any statement of your desires and any limitations that you include in this document. You may state in this document any types of treatment that you do not desire. In addition, a court can take away the power of your agent to make health care decisions for you if your agent (1) authorizes anything that is illegal, (2) acts contrary to your known desires, or (3) where your desires are not known, does anything that is clearly contrary to your best interests.

Unless you specify a shorter period in this document, this power will exist for seven years from the date you execute this document and, if you are unable to make health care decisions for yourself at the time when this seven-year period ends, this power will continue to exist until the time when you become able to make health care decisions for yourself.

You have the right to revoke the authority of your agent by notifying your agent or your treating doctor, hospital, or other health care provider orally or in writing of the revocation.

Your agent has the right to examine your medical records and to consent to their disclosure unless you limit this right in this document.

Unless you otherwise specify in this document, this document gives your agent the power after you die to (1) authorize an autopsy, (2) donate your body or parts thereof for transplant or therapeutic or educational or scientific purposes, and (3) direct the disposition of your remains.

This document revokes any prior durable power of attorney for health care.

You should carefully read and follow the witnessing procedure described at the end of this form. This document will not be valid unless you comply with the witnessing procedure.

If there is anything in this document that you do not understand, you should ask a lawyer to explain it to you.

Your agent may need this document immediately in case of an emergency that requires a decision concerning your health care. Either keep this document where it is immediately available to your agent and alternate agents or give each of them an executed copy of this document. You may also want to give your doctor an executed copy of this document.

Do not use this form if you are a conservatee under the Lanterman-Petris-Short Act and you want to appoint your conservator as your agent. You can do that only if the appointment document includes a certificate of your attorney.

1. Designation of Health Care Agent.

I, _____

(insert your name and address)

_____

do hereby designate and appoint _____

(Insert name, address and telephone number of one individual only as your agent to make health care decisions for you. None of the following may be designated as your agent: (1) your treating health care provider, (2) a nonrelative employee of your treating health care provider, (3) an operator of a community care facility, (4) a nonrelative employee of an operator of a community care facility, (5) an operator of a residential care facility for the elderly, or (6) a nonrelative employee of an operator of a residential care facility for the elderly.)

as my attorney in fact (agent) to make health care decisions for me as authorized in this document. For the purposes of this document, "health care decision" means consent, refusal of consent, or withdrawal of consent to any care, treatment, service, or procedure to maintain, diagnose, or treat an individual's physical or mental condition.

2. Creation of Durable Power of Attorney for Health Care.

By this document I intend to create a durable power of attorney for health care under Sections 2430 to 2443, inclusive, of the California Civil Code. This power of attorney is authorized by the Keene Health Care Agent Act and shall be construed in accordance with the provisions of Sections 2500 to 2506, inclusive, of the California Civil Code. This power of attorney shall not be affected by my subsequent incapacity.

3. General Statement of Authority Granted.

Subject to any limitations in this document, I hereby grant to my agent full power and authority to make health care decisions for me to the same extent that I could make such decisions for myself if I had the capacity to do so. In exercising this authority, my agent shall make health care decisions that are consistent with my desires as stated in this document or otherwise made known to my agent, including, but not limited to, my desires concerning obtaining or refusing or withdrawing life-prolonging care, treatment, services, and procedures.

(If you want to limit the authority of your agent to make health care decisions for you, you can state the limitations in paragraph 4 ["Statement of Desires, Special Provisions, and Limitations"] below. You can indicate your desires by including a statement of your desires in the same paragraph.)

4. Statement of Desires, Special Provisions, and Limitations.

(Your agent must make health care decisions that are consistent with your known desires. You can, but are not required to, state your desires in the space provided below. You should consider whether you want to include a statement of your desires concerning life-prolonging care, treatment, services, and procedures. You can also include a statement of your desires concerning other matters relating to your health care. You can also make your desires known to your agent by discussing your desires with your agent or by some other means. If there are any types of treatment that you do not want to be used, you should state them in the space below. If you want to limit in any other way the authority given your agent by this document, you should state the limits in the space below. If you do not state any limits, your agent will have broad powers to make health care decisions for you, except to the extent that there are limits provided by law.)

In exercising the authority under this durable power of attorney for health care, my agent shall act consistently with my desires as stated below and is subject to the special provisions and limitations stated below:

(a) Statement of desires concerning life-prolonging care, treatment, services and procedures:

(b) Additional statement of desires, special provisions, and limitations:

(You may attach additional pages if you need more space to complete your statement. If you attach additional pages, you must date and sign EACH of the additional pages at the same time you date and sign this document.)

5. Inspection and Disclosure of Information Relating to My Physical or Mental Health.

Subject to any limitations in this document, my agent has the power and authority to do all of the following:

(a) Request, review, and receive any information, verbal or written, regarding my physical or mental health, including, but not limited to, medical and hospital records.

(b) Execute on my behalf any releases or other documents that may be required in order to obtain this information.

(c) Consent to the disclosure of this information.

(If you want to limit the authority of your agent to receive and disclose information relating to your health, you must state the limitations in paragraph 4 ["Statement of Desires, Special Provisions, and Limitations"] above.)

6. Signing Documents, Waivers, and Releases.

Where necessary to implement the health care decisions that my agent is authorized by this document to make, my agent has the power and authority to execute on my behalf all of the following:

(a) Documents titled or purporting to be a "Refusal to Permit Treatment" and "Leaving Hospital Against Medical Advice."

(b) Any necessary waiver or release from liability required by a hospital or physician.

7. Autopsy; Anatomical Gifts; Disposition of Remains.

Subject to any limitations in this document, my agent has the power and authority to do all of the following:

(a) Authorize an autopsy under Section 7113 of the Health and Safety Code.

(b) Make a disposition of a part or parts of my body under the Uniform Anatomical Gift Act (Chapter 3.5 [commencing with Section 7150] of Part 1 of Division 7 of the Health and Safety Code).

(c) Direct the disposition of my remains under Section 7100 of the Health and Safety Code.

(If you want to limit the authority of your agent to consent to an autopsy, make an anatomical gift, or direct the disposition of your remains, you must state the limitations in paragraph 4 ["Statement of Desires, Special Provisions, and Limitations"] above.)

8. Duration.

(Unless you specify a shorter period in the space below, this power of attorney will exist for seven years from the date you execute this document and, if you are unable to make health care decisions for yourself at the time when this seven-year period ends, the power will continue to exist until the time when you become able to make health care decisions for yourself.)

This durable power of attorney for health care expires on:

_____

(Fill in this space ONLY if you want the authority of your agent to end EARLIER than the seven-year period described above.)

9. Designation of Alternate Agents.

(You are not required to designate any alternate agents but you may do so. Any alternate agent you designate will be able to make the same health care decisions as the agent you designated in paragraph 1, above, in the event that the agent is unable or ineligible to act as your agent. If the agent you designated is your spouse, he or she becomes ineligible to act as your agent if your marriage is dissolved.)

If the person designated as my agent in paragraph 1 is not available or becomes ineligible to act as my agent to make a health care decision for me or loses the mental capacity to make health care decisions for me, or if I revoke that person's appointment or authority to act as my agent to make health care decisions for me, then I designate and appoint the following persons to serve as my agent to make health care decisions for me as authorized in this document, such persons to serve in the order listed below:

A. First Alternate Agent _____

_____

(Insert name, address, and telephone number of first alternate agent)

B. Second Alternate Agent _____

_____

(Insert name, address, and telephone number of second alternate agent)

10. Nomination of Conservator of Person.

(A conservator of person may be appointed for you if a court decides that one should be appointed. The conservator is responsible for your physical care, which under some circumstances includes making health care decisions for you. You are not required to nominate a conservator but you may do so. The court will appoint the person you nominate unless that would be contrary to your best interests. You may, but are not required to, nominate as your conservator the same person you named in paragraph 1 as your health care agent. You can nominate an individual as your conservator by completing the space below.)

If a conservator of the person is appointed for me, I nominate the following individual to serve as conservator of the person:

_____

(Insert name and address of person nominated as conservator of the person)

11. Prior Designations Revoked.

I revoke any prior durable power of attorney for health care.

Date and Signature of Principal
(YOU MUST DATE AND SIGN THIS POWER OF ATTORNEY)

I sign my name to this Statutory Form Durable Power of Attorney for Health Care on

_____ at _____ , _____
   (Date)   (City)   (State)

_____
(You sign here)

(THIS POWER OF ATTORNEY WILL NOT BE VALID UNLESS IT IS SIGNED BY TWO QUALIFIED WITNESSES WHO ARE PRESENT WHEN YOU SIGN OR ACKNOWLEDGE YOUR SIGNATURE. IF YOU HAVE ATTACHED ANY ADDITIONAL PAGES TO THIS FORM, YOU MUST DATE AND SIGN EACH OF THE ADDITIONAL PAGES AT THE SAME TIME YOU DATE AND SIGN THIS POWER OF ATTORNEY.)

Statement of Witnesses

(This document must be witnessed by two qualified adult witnesses. None of the following may be used as a witness: (1) a person you designate as your agent or alternate agent, (2) a health care provider, (3) an employee of a health care provider, (4) the operator of a community care facility, (5) an employee of an operator of a community care facility, (6) the operator of a residential care facility for the elderly, or (7) an employee of an operator of a residential care facility for the elderly. At least one of the witnesses must make the additional declaration set out following the place where the witnesses sign.)

(READ CAREFULLY BEFORE SIGNING. You can sign as a witness only if you personally know the principal or the identity of the principal is proved to you by convincing evidence.)

(To have convincing evidence of the identity of the principal, you must be presented with and reasonably rely on any one or more of the following:

(1) An identification card or driver's license issued by the California Department of Motor Vehicles that is current or has been issued within five years.

(2) A passport issued by the Department of State of the United States that is current or has been issued within five years.

(3) Any of the following documents if the document is current or has been issued within five years and contains a photograph and description of the person named on it, is signed by the person, and bears a serial or other identifying number:

(a) A passport issued by a foreign government that has been stamped by the United States Immigration and Naturalization Service.

(b) A driver's license issued by a state other than California or by a Canadian or Mexican public agency authorized to issue drivers' licenses.

(c) An identification card issued by a state other than California.

(d) An identification card issued by a branch of the armed forces of the United States.

(4) If the principal is a patient in a skilled nursing facility, a witness who is a patient advocate or ombudsman may rely upon the representations of the administrator or staff of the skilled nursing facility, or of family members, as convincing evidence of the identity of the principal if the patient advocate or ombudsman believes that the representations provide a reasonable basis for determining the identity of the principal.)

(Other kinds of proof of identity are not allowed.)

I declare under penalty of perjury under the laws of California that the person who signed or acknowledged this document is personally known to me (or proved to me on the basis of convincing evidence) to be the principal, that the principal signed or acknowledged this durable power of attorney in my presence, that the principal appears to be of sound mind and under no duress, fraud, or undue influence, that I am not the person appointed as attorney in fact by this document, and that I am not a health care provider, an employee of a health care provider, the operator of a community care facility, an employee of an operator of a community care facility, the operator of a residential care facility for the elderly, nor an employee of an operator of a residential care facility for the elderly.

_____
(Signature—Witness I)

_____
(Print Name)

_____
(Residence Address)

_____

_____
(Date)

_____
(Signature—Witness II)

_____
(Print Name)

_____
(Residence Address)

_____

_____
(Date)

(AT LEAST ONE OF THE ABOVE WITNESSES MUST ALSO SIGN THE FOLLOWING DECLARATION.)

I further declare under penalty of perjury under the laws of California that I am not related to the principal by blood, marriage, or adoption, and to the best of my knowledge, I am not entitled to any part of the estate of the principal upon the death of the principal under a will now existing or by operation of law.

Signature: _____   Signature: _____

Statement of Patient Advocate or Ombudsman

(If you are a patient in a skilled nursing facility, one of the witnesses must be a patient advocate or ombudsman. The following statement is required only if you are a patient in a skilled nursing facility—a health care facility that provides the following basic services: skilled nursing care and supportive care to patients whose primary need is for availability of skilled nursing care on an extended basis. The patient advocate or ombudsman must sign both parts of the "Statement of Witnesses" above AND must also sign the following statement.)

I further declare under penalty of perjury under the laws of California that I am a patient advocate or ombudsman as designated by the State Department of Aging and that I am serving as a witness as required by subdivision (f) of Section 2432 of the Civil Code.

Signature: _____

The Living Will and Colorado's Medical Treatment Decision Act

Colorado recognizes the legal right of any competent adult (eighteen years or older) to sign a declaration instructing his or her physician to withhold or withdraw life-sustaining procedures in the event of a terminal condition.

A copy of the Colorado declaration is shown. We have provided room for you to include additional instructions—for example, concerning specific types of treatment that you may wish to forgo, such as cardiopulmonary resuscitation. Please note and read carefully the section on your wishes about artificial feeding. *If you want to refuse artificial feeding, you should specify this in the document.*

1. The declaration may be in the form set forth in the law, but it does not have to be. It must be signed and dated in the presence of two adult witnesses. If you are unable to sign the document, someone may sign it on your behalf, at your direction, in the presence of two witnesses. *The person who signs on your behalf may not be a witness, and neither the person who signs on your behalf nor your witnesses may be any of the following:*

   a. Your attending physician or any other physician.
   b. An employee of your attending physician or of a health-care facility in which you are a patient.
   c. Anyone with a claim against your estate.
   d. Anyone entitled to any portion of your estate by will, codicil, or operation of law.

   If you sign a declaration while you are a patient or resident in a health-care facility, the witnesses may not be patients in that facility.
2. Your declaration must also be notarized.
3. You are responsible for notifying your physician of the existence of your declaration and seeing that a photocopy of it is made part of your medical records.
4. Before your declaration will be legally binding, your terminal condition must be diagnosed and certified in writing by two physicians, one of whom is your attending physician. The physicians must also certify that you have been unable to communicate for at least seven days (as long as you *can* communicate, your express wishes will always supersede your declaration). Once certified, there is a forty-eight hour waiting period before life-sustaining procedures may be withdrawn.
5. A declaration is invalid during pregnancy if it is believed that the fetus could develop to a live birth with the continued application of life-sustaining procedures.
6. The withholding or withdrawal of life support from a terminal patient in accordance with the instructions of a declaration does not, for any purpose, constitute suicide or homicide.
7. The existence of a declaration can have no effect on the issuance or continuation of life insurance.

To protect yourself as fully as possible against unwanted treatment, the Society for the Right to Die advises that you execute both the Colorado declaration and the generic living will (Chapter 3).

COLORADO

DECLARATION AS TO MEDICAL OR SURGICAL TREATMENT

I, _____, being of sound mind and at least eighteen years of age, direct that my life shall not be artificially prolonged under the circumstances set forth below and hereby declare that:

1. If at any time my attending physician and one other qualified physician certify in writing that:

a. I have an injury, disease, or illness which is not curable or reversible and which, in their judgment, is a terminal condition, and

b. For a period of seven consecutive days or more, I have been unconscious, comatose, or otherwise incompetent so as to be unable to make or communicate responsible decisions concerning my person, then

I direct that, in accordance with Colorado law, life-sustaining procedures shall be withdrawn and withheld pursuant to the terms of this declaration, it being understood that life-sustaining procedures shall not include any medical procedure or intervention for nourishment considered necessary by the attending physician to provide comfort or alleviate pain. However, I may specifically direct, in accordance with Colorado law, that artificial nourishment be withdrawn or withheld pursuant to the terms of this declaration.

2. In the event that the only procedure I am being provided is artificial nourishment, I direct that one of the following actions be taken:

____ (Initials of Declarant) a. Artificial nourishment shall not be continued when it is the only procedure being provided; or

____ (Initials of Declarant) b. Artificial nourishment shall be continued for ____ days when it is the only procedure being provided; or

____ (Initials of Declarant) c. Artificial nourishment shall be continued when it is the only procedure being provided.

3. I execute this declaration, as my free and voluntary act, this ____ day of _____, 19____.

By _____
      Declarant

The foregoing instrument was signed and declared by _____ to be his declaration, in the presence of us, who, in his presence, in the presence of each other, and at his request, have signed our names below as witnesses, and we declare that, at the time of the execution of this instrument, the declarant, according to our best knowledge and belief, was of sound mind and under no constraint or undue influence.

Dated at _____, Colorado, this ____ day of _____, 19____.

_____
Name and Address

_____
Name and Address

STATE OF COLORADO)
) ss.
County of _____)

      SUBSCRIBED and sworn to before me by _____,

the declarant, and _____ and _____,

witnesses, as the voluntary act and deed of the declarant this _____ day of _____, 19____.

My commission expires:

                        _____
                                Notary Public

The Living Will and Connecticut's Removal of Life Support Systems Act

Connecticut recognizes the legal right of any competent adult to execute a directive instructing his or her physician to withhold or withdraw life support systems in the event of a terminal condition. The directive should be substantially in the form of the State of Connecticut Directive to Physicians shown here. You may wish to add personal instructions in the space we have provided, for example, about specific types of treatment, such as cardiopulmonary resuscitation or artificial nutrition and hydration. (The state supreme court has interpreted the Connecticut Removal of Life Support Systems Act to permit withdrawal of tube feeding, in the case *McConnell v. Beverly Enterprises.*)

It is important that you understand the specific provisions of the law:

1. Your directive must be signed and dated by you in the presence of two adult witnesses in order to be legally binding. The statute imposes no restrictions on who may serve as your witnesses.
2. Your terminal condition must be confirmed by your attending physician.
3. The statute states that the directive does not apply to pregnant patients.
4. The Connecticut statute provides immunity from liability to physicians or medical facility personnel who withdraw life support from a patient in accordance with the patient's prior wishes *if the informed consent of the patient's next of kin, if known, or legal guardian, if any, is also obtained. It is, therefore, very important that your family as well as your physician understand and support your wishes about terminal care.*

To protect yourself as fully as possible against unwanted treatment, the Society for the Right to Die advises that you use both the Connecticut directive and the generic living will (Chapter 3).

Declaration

If the time comes when I am incapacitated to the point when I can no longer actively take part in decisions for my own life, and am unable to direct my physician as to my own medical care, I wish this statement to stand as a testament of my wishes.

I, _____

request that I be allowed to die and not be kept alive through life support systems if my condition is deemed terminal. I do not intend any direct taking of my life, but only that my dying not be unreasonably prolonged. This request is made, after careful reflection, while I am of sound mind.

Other instructions:

_____ (Signature)

_____ (Date)

_____ (Witness)

_____ (Witness)

The Living Will and the Delaware Death with Dignity Act

The Delaware Death with Dignity Act recognizes the legal right of any competent adult to execute a declaration authorizing the withholding or withdrawal of "maintenance medical treatment" in the event of a terminal condition. (The law defines "medical treatment" as a procedure or intervention that uses mechanical or other artificial means to sustain, restore, or supplant a vital function and that serves only to prolong the dying process). A declaration that meets the requirements of the act is shown. We have provided space for you to enter additional instructions—for example, about any specific types of life-sustaining treatment, such as artificial feeding or cardiopulmonary resuscitation, that you may wish to forgo. You must sign and date the document (or ask someone else to do so for you, in your presence) before two or more adult witnesses. These witnesses *may not:*

1. Be related to you by blood or marriage.
2. Be entitled to any portion of your estate.
3. Have any claim on any portion of your estate.
4. Have financial responsibility for your medical care.
5. Be employees of the hospital or other health-care facility in which you are a patient.

Each witness must state in writing that he or she meets the witnessing requirements. If you are in a sanitorium, rest home, nursing home, boarding home, or related institution when you sign the declaration, one of the witnesses must be a patient advocate or ombudsman designated by the Division of Aging or the public guardian who meets the other witnessing requirements.

The law also permits you to designate someone to make treatment decisions on your behalf in the event you are unable to do so yourself. This person, if you designate one, should know your wishes so that your rights and preferences will be honored.

The declaration has no effect during pregnancy.

A hospital or attending physician is required to make a photocopy of the declaration part of your medical record when it is presented, and to acknowledge the receipt of the declaration.

A death that results from carrying out the provisions in the declaration is neither suicide nor mercy killing. The execution of such a declaration can have no effect on the sale or continuance of any life insurance policy.

To protect yourself as fully as possible against unwanted treatment, the Society for the Right to Die advises that you execute both the Delaware declaration and the generic living will (Chapter 3). The generic living will can apply to "an incurable or irreversible mental or physical condition with no reasonable expectation of recovery" such as advanced Alzheimer's or minimal consciousness after a stroke—situations that may not be encompassed by the Death with Dignity Act.

DECLARATION

I, _____, being an adult of sound mind, make this statement as a directive to be followed if I become unable to participate in decisions regarding my medical care.

If I should be in a terminal condition* as confirmed in writing by two physicians, I direct my attending physician to withhold or withdraw medical maintenance treatment that will serve only to artificially prolong my dying. I further direct that treatment be limited to measures to keep me comfortable and to relieve pain.

Other directions:

These directions express my legal right to refuse treatment. Therefore, I expect my family, doctors, and everyone concerned with my care to regard themselves as legally and morally bound to act in accord with my wishes, and in so doing to be free of any legal liability for having followed my directions.

Date _____   Signed _____

Witness _____

Witness _____

(Please note that witnesses must also sign attestation on reverse side.)

APPOINTMENT OF AN AGENT

(optional)

As provided in §2502 of the Delaware Death with Dignity Act, I hereby appoint:

_____, who resides at:

_____,
as my agent to act on my behalf if, owing to a condition resulting from illness or injury, I am deemed by my attending physician to be incapable of making a decision in the exercise of the right to accept or refuse medical treatment. This authorization includes the right to refuse medical treatment which would extend my life and the duty to act in good faith and with due regard for my benefits and interests.

Date _____   Signed _____

Witness _____

Witness _____

(Please note that witnesses must also sign attestation on reverse side.)

---

*Defined as "any disease, illness or condition sustained by any human being from which there is no reasonable medical expectation of recovery and which, as a medical probability, will result in the death of such human being regardless of the use or discontinuance of medical treatment implemented for the purpose of sustaining life, or the life processes." Del. Code Ann. tit. 16, §2501.

Witnesses' Attestation

I have read the provision of the law Del. Code Ann. tit. 16, §2503(*b*) as reproduced below, and I am not prohibited from being a witness. I am over 18 years of age.

Date _____ Signed _____

Date _____ Signed _____

DELAWARE DEATH WITH DIGNITY ACT

Witnessing Subsection
16 Del. Code Ann. § 2503(*b*)

2503. Written Declaration.

(b) The declaration shall be signed by the declarant in the presence of two subscribing witnesses, neither of whom:

(1) is related to the declarant by blood or marriage;

(2) is entitled to any portion of the estate of the declarant under any will of the declarant or codicil thereto then existing nor, at the time of the declaration, is so entitled by operation of law then existing;

(3) has, at the time of the execution of the declaration, a present or inchoate claim against any portion of the estate of the declarant;

(4) has a direct financial responsibility for the declarant's medical care; or

(5) is an employee of the hospital or other health care facility in which the declarant is a patient.

The Living Will, the D.C. Declaration, and the Durable Power of Attorney for Health Care

The District of Columbia recognizes the legal right of any competent adult (eighteen years or older) to execute a declaration directing that life-sustaining procedures be withheld or withdrawn in the event of a terminal condition. A copy of the declaration suggested by the District of Columbia act is shown. We have provided space for you to include personal instructions—for example, regarding specific types of treatment, such as artificial feeding or cardiopulmonary resuscitation, that you may wish to forgo.

The declaration itself must be dated and signed by you, or by someone in your presence at your direction, before two or more adult witnesses. The witnesses *may not* be

1. The person who signed for you, if you instructed someone else to sign for you.
2. Related to you by blood or marriage.
3. Entitled to any part of your estate.
4. Directly financially responsible for your medical care.
5. Your attending physician or his or her employee or an employee of the health-care facility in which you are a patient.

If you are a patient in an intermediate-care or skilled-care facility, one of the witnesses *must* be a patient advocate or ombudsman and must meet the other witnessing requirements listed above.

A death that results from the withholding or withdrawal of treatment in accordance with the directions of a declaration is neither mercy killing nor suicide. Signing a declaration can have no effect on the issuance or continuation of a life insurance policy.

D.C. law also permits you to appoint someone to make decisions on your behalf, based on what you would wish or what would be in your best interests, through a durable power of attorney for health care (Chapter 3). The durable power of attorney becomes effective if you are unable to make your own health-care decisions. A copy of the suggested form, with instructions, is shown. Be certain to read it carefully—especially the limitations on who may serve as a witness—*before* you fill out, and follow the directions closely.

To protect yourself as fully as possible against unwanted treatment, the Society for the Right to Die advises that you execute the durable power of attorney for health care, the District of Columbia declaration, and the generic living will (Chapter 3). The generic living will covers a wider range of medical situations and treatments than the declaration authorized by D.C. law, and can apply even if your condition is not "terminal" as defined by the D.C. act (for example, in the case of advanced Alzheimer's, or minimal consciousness after a stroke).

DISTRICT OF COLUMBIA

DECLARATION

Declaration made this _____ day of _____ (month, year).

I, _____, being of sound mind, willfully and voluntarily make known my desires that my dying shall not be artificially prolonged under the circumstances set forth below, and do declare:

If at any time I should have an incurable injury, disease or illness certified to be a terminal condition by two (2) physicians who have personally examined me, one (1) of whom shall be my attending physician, and the physicians have determined that my death will occur whether or not life-sustaining procedures are utilized and where the application of life-sustaining procedures would serve only to artificially prolong the dying process, I direct that such procedures be withheld or withdrawn, and that I be permitted to die naturally with only the administration of medication or the performance of any medical procedure deemed necessary to provide me with comfort care or to alleviate pain.

Other directions:

In the absence of my ability to give directions regarding the use of such life-sustaining procedures, it is my intention that this declaration shall be honored by my family and physician(s) as the final expression of my legal right to refuse medical or surgical treatment and accept the consequences from such refusal.

I understand the full import of this declaration and I am emotionally and mentally competent to make this declaration.

Signed _____

Address _____

_____

I believe the declarant to be of sound mind. I did not sign the declarant's signature above for or at the direction of the declarant. I am at least eighteen (18) years of age and am not related to the declarant by blood or marriage, entitled to any portion of the estate of the declarant according to the laws of intestate succession of the District of Columbia or under any will of declarant or codicil thereto, or directly financially responsible for declarant's medical care. I am not the declarant's attending physician, an employee of the attending physician, or an employee of the health facility in which the declarant is a patient.

Witness _____

Witness _____

POWER OF ATTORNEY FOR HEALTH CARE

INFORMATION ABOUT THIS DOCUMENT

This is an important legal document. Before signing this document, it is vital for you to know and understand these facts:

This document gives the person you name as your attorney in fact the power to make health-care decisions for you if you cannot make the decisions for yourself.

After you have signed this document, you have the right to make health-care decisions for yourself if you are mentally competent to do so. In addition, after you have signed this document, no treatment may be given to you or stopped over your objection if you are mentally competent to make that decision.

You may state in this document any type of treatment that you do not desire and any that you want to make sure you receive.

You have the right to take away the authority of your attorney in fact, unless you have been adjudicated incompetent, by notifying your attorney in fact or health-care provider either orally or in writing. Should you revoke the authority of your attorney in fact, it is advisable to revoke in writing and to place copies of the revocation wherever this document is located.

If there is anything in this document that you do not understand, you should ask a social worker, lawyer or other person to explain it to you.

You should keep a copy of this document after you have signed it. Give a copy to the person you name as your attorney in fact. If you are in a health-care facility, a copy of this document should be included in your medical record.

I, _____ , hereby appoint:

_____   _____
(name)   (home address)

_____   _____
(home telephone number)

_____   _____
(work telephone number)

as my attorney in fact to make health-care decisions for me if I become unable to make my own health-care decisions. This gives my attorney in fact the power to grant, refuse, or withdraw consent on my behalf for any health-care service, treatment or procedure. My attorney in fact also has the authority to talk to health-care personnel, get information and sign forms necessary to carry out these decisions.

If the person named as my attorney in fact is not available or is unable to act as my attorney in fact, I appoint the following person to serve in the order listed below:

1. _____   _____
   (name)   (home address)

_____   _____
(home telephone number)

_____   _____
(work telephone number)

2. _____   _____
   (name)   (home address)

_____   _____
(home telephone number)

_____   _____
(work telephone number)

With this document, I intend to create a power of attorney for health care, which shall take effect if I become incapable of making my own health care decisions and shall continue during that incapacity.

My attorney in fact shall make health-care decisions as I direct below or as I make known to my attorney in fact in some other way.

STATEMENT OF DIRECTIVES CONCERNING
LIFE-PROLONGING CARE, TREATMENT, SERVICES AND PROCEDURES:

_____

_____

_____

_____

_____

SPECIAL PROVISIONS AND LIMITATIONS:

_____

_____

_____

_____

_____

BY MY SIGNATURE I INDICATE THAT I UNDERSTAND THE PURPOSE AND EFFECT OF THIS DOCUMENT.

I sign my name to this form on _____
                                    (date)

at:_____
      (address)

                                    _____
                                              (signature)

WITNESSES

I declare that the person who signed or acknowledged this document is personally known to me, that the person signed or acknowledged this durable power of attorney for health care in my presence, and that the person appears to be of sound mind and under no duress, fraud, or undue influence. I am not the person appointed as the the attorney in fact by this document, nor am I a health-care provider of the principal or an employee of the health-care provider of the principal.

First Witness   Second Witness

Signature: _____   Signature: _____

Home Address : _____   Home Address : _____

Print Name : _____   Print Name : _____

Date : _____   Date : _____

(AT LEAST 1 OF THE WITNESSES LISTED ABOVE SHALL ALSO SIGN THE FOLLOWING DECLARATION.)

I further declare that I am not related to the principal by blood, marriage or adoption, and, to the best of my knowledge, I am not entitled to any part of the estate of the principal under a currently existing will or by operation of law.

Signature : _____   Signature:_____

The Florida Declaration and the Living Will

Florida recognizes the legal right of any adult to make a written declaration instructing his or her physician to withhold or withdraw life-sustaining procedures in the event of a terminal condition. The declaration shown here was drafted with the advice of Florida attorneys and draws on the statutory law and case law from the Florida Supreme Court. It is important that you understand and follow the specific provisions of the law, which are summarized below:

1. Your declaration must be signed before two witnesses, one of whom may not be a blood relative or spouse. If you are unable physically to sign, you may instruct one of the witnesses to sign the declaration for you.
2. A space is provided to designate someone to make medical treatment decisions for you if you become incapacitated or incompetent. The statute also establishes a procedure for decision making for family and physicians in the event you have not executed a written or oral declaration or do not designate anyone to make decisions on your behalf.
3. Your declaration becomes effective once you have been diagnosed by your attending physician and one additional doctor as being in a terminally ill condition. The declaration also states that you do not want tube feeding if you are "terminal" or "irreversibly unconscious." If you *do* want tube feeding you should cross out this sentence.
4. It is your responsibility to inform your doctor of the existence of your declaration; your doctor must then place a copy of it in your medical records.
5. You may revoke the declaration at any time, either orally or in writing. Execution of the declaration can have no effect on insurance or health-care policies.

To protect yourself as fully as possible against unwanted treatment, the Society for the Right to Die advises that you execute both the Florida declaration and the generic living will (Chapter 3).

Statutory Citation: Florida Stat. Ann. §§ 7.65.01–765.15. Case Law Citation: *Corbett v. D'Alessandro,* 487 So. 2d 368 (Fla. Dist. Ct. App. 1986).

FLORIDA

DECLARATION

Declaration made this _____ day of _____, 19_____.

I, _____, willfully and voluntarily make known my desire that my dying shall not be artificially prolonged under the circumstances set forth below, and do hereby declare:

If at any time I should have a terminal condition and my attending physician has determined that there can be no recovery from such condition and my death is imminent, where the application of life-prolonging procedures would serve only to artificially prolong the dying process, I direct that such procedures be withheld or withdrawn, and that I be permitted to die naturally with only the administration of medication or the performance of any medical procedure deemed necessary to provide me with comfort care or to alleviate pain.

In addition, whether or not my death is imminent, I direct that, if I have a terminal condition or am irreversibly unconscious, nutrition and hydration (food and water) not be provided by tubing or intravenously.

In the absence of my ability to give directions regarding the use of such life-prolonging procedures, it is my intention that this declaration shall be honored by my family and physician as the final expression of my legal right to refuse medical or surgical treatment and accept the consequences for such refusal.

> Should I become comatose, incompetent or otherwise mentally or physically incapable of communication, I authorize _____
>
> _____
> (name, address and telephone)
>
> to make treatment decisions on my behalf in accordance with my Living Will Declaration. If my designated representative is not readily available, my directions in this Declaration should be carried out without the concurrence of the representative.

If I have been diagnosed as pregnant and that diagnosis is known to my physician, this declaration shall have no force or effect during the course of my pregnancy.

I understand the full import of this Declaration and I am emotionally and mentally competent to make this Declaration.

_____
Signature

The declarant is known to me and I believe her/him to be of sound mind.

_____
Witness

_____
Witness

Important Notes:
- One of the witnesses must not be a spouse or blood relative of the declarant.
- Cross out the third paragraph if you want to be given artificial feeding.

Statutory Citation: Florida Life-Prolonging Procedure Act, § 765.05(2).
Case Law Citation: *Corbett v. D'Alessandro*, 487 So. 2d 368 (Fla. Dist. Ct. App. 1986).

Drafted with the advice and counsel of Shutts & Bowen, West Palm Beach, Florida.

Georgia's Living Will Act and Durable Power of Attorney for Health Care

Georgia's Living Will Act authorizes any competent adult (eighteen years or older) to execute a living will.

The Georgia living will may be written in the form shown here, but in any case, *it must be a separate self-contained document.* It enables you to tell your physician to withhold or withdraw life-sustaining procedures in the event of a terminal condition. Artificial nutrition and hydration are not included in the statutory definition of life-sustaining procedures. If you want to express your preferences about this or any other type of treatment, you should add your personal instructions in the space we have provided in the document for this purpose.

The Georgia living will *must* be signed in the presence of two competent adults who:

1. Are not related to you by blood or marriage.
2. Are not entitled to any part of your estate, under any will or codicil or the laws of inheritance.
3. Are neither the attending physician, an employee of the attending physician, nor an employee of the hospital or skilled nursing facility in which you are a patient.
4. Are not directly financially responsible for your medical care.
5. Do not have a claim against any portion of your estate.

If the Georgia living will is signed in a hospital, you *must* have, as a third witness, the chief of the hospital medical staff or a staff physician not participating in your care; if you sign it in a skilled-nursing facility, the third witness *must* be the medical director or a staff physician not participating in your care.

Georgia also has a durable power of attorney for health care. If you have someone to appoint as your agent, the Georgia durable power of attorney for health care is a better document than the Georgia living will, because it allows your agent to refuse tube feeding and because it covers a range of possible medical conditions (for example, advanced Alzheimer's disease or minimal consciousness after a stroke), whereas the living will applies only to a "terminal condition."

You will need two adult witnesses for the durable power of attorney; if you are currently a patient in a hospital or skilled-nursing facility, your attending physician must serve as a third witness. Other requirements are listed on the durable power of attorney form itself.

If you have both a Georgia living will and a durable power of attorney for health care, the living will is not operative so long as your agent is available to make decisions.

To protect yourself as fully as possible against unwanted treatment, the Society for the Right to Die advises that you execute three documents—the Georgia living will, the durable power of attorney (if you can), and the generic living will (Chapter 3). The generic living will can apply to conditions such as advanced Alzheimer's disease or minimal consciousness after a stroke, which may not fit the Georgia Living Will Act's definition of a "terminal condition." If you do not use the durable power of attorney, it is especially important to document your preferences about tube feeding in the generic living will.

LIVING WILL

Living will made this _____ day of _____ (month, year).

    I, _____, being of sound mind, willfully and voluntarily make known my desire that my life shall not be prolonged under the circumstances set forth below and do declare:

    1. If at any time I should have a terminal condition as defined in and established in accordance with the procedures set forth in paragraph (10) of Code Section 31-32-2 of the Official Code of Georgia Annotated,* I direct that the application of life-sustaining procedures to my body be withheld or withdrawn and that I be permitted to die;

    2. In the absence of my ability to give directions regarding the use of such life-sustaining procedures, it is my intention that this living will shall be honored by my family and physician(s) as the final expression of my legal right to refuse medical or surgical treatment and accept the consequences of such refusal;

    Other instructions:

    3. I understand that I may revoke this living will at any time;

    4. I understand the full import of this living will, and I am at least 18 years of age and am emotionally and mentally competent to make this living will; and

    5. If I am female and I have been diagnosed as pregnant, this living will shall have no force and effect during the course of my pregnancy.

Signed _____

City, County and State of Residence _____

I hereby witness this living will and attest that:

(1) The declarant is personally known to me and I believe the declarant to be at least 18 years of age and of sound mind;

(2) I am at least 18 years of age;

(3) To the best of my knowledge, at the time of the execution of this living will, I:

(A) Am not related to the declarant by blood or marriage;

(B) Would not be entitled to any portion of the declarant's estate by any will or by operation of law under the rules of descent and distribution of this state;

(C) Am not the attending physician of declarant or any employee of the attending physician or an employee of the hospital or skilled nursing facility in which declarant is a patient;

(D) Am not directly financially responsible for the declarant's medical care; and

(E) Have no present claim against any portion of the estate of the declarant;

(4) Declarant has signed this document in my presence as above-instructed, on the date above first shown.

Witness _____ Address _____

Witness _____ Address _____

Additional witness required when living will is signed in a hospital or skilled nursing facility.

I hereby witness this living will and attest that I believe the declarant to be of sound mind and to have made this living will willingly and voluntarily.

Witness _____

(Medical director of skilled nursing facility, or staff physician not participating in the care of the patient, or chief of the hospital medical staff, or staff physician not participating in the care of the patient.)

Paragraph (10), Code Section 31-32-2 of the Official Code of Georgia Annotated provides:

"Terminal condition" means incurable condition caused by disease, illness or injury which, regardless of the application of life-sustaining procedures, would produce death. The procedure for establishing a "terminal condition" is as follows: Two physicians who, after personally examining the declarant, shall certify in writing, based upon conditions found during the course of their examination:

(A) There is no reasonable expectation for improvement in the condition of the declarant; and

(B) Death of the declarant from these conditions is imminent.

GEORGIA

STATUTORY SHORT FORM
DURABLE POWER OF ATTORNEY FOR HEALTH CARE

NOTICE: THE PURPOSE OF THIS POWER OF ATTORNEY IS TO GIVE THE PERSON YOU DESIGNATE (YOUR AGENT) BROAD POWERS TO MAKE HEALTH CARE DECISIONS FOR YOU, INCLUDING POWER TO REQUIRE, CONSENT TO, OR WITHDRAW ANY TYPE OF PERSONAL CARE OR MEDICAL TREATMENT FOR ANY PHYSICAL OR MENTAL CONDITION AND TO ADMIT YOU TO OR DISCHARGE YOU FROM ANY HOSPITAL, HOME, OR OTHER INSTITUTION; BUT NOT INCLUDING PSYCHOSURGERY, STERILIZATION, OR INVOLUNTARY HOSPITALIZATION OR TREATMENT COVERED BY TITLE 37 OF THE OFFICIAL CODE OF GEORGIA ANNOTATED. THIS FORM DOES NOT IMPOSE A DUTY ON YOUR AGENT TO EXERCISE GRANTED POWERS; BUT, WHEN A POWER IS EXERCISED, YOUR AGENT WILL HAVE TO USE DUE CARE TO ACT FOR YOUR BENEFIT AND IN ACCORDANCE WITH THIS FORM. A COURT CAN TAKE AWAY THE POWERS OF YOUR AGENT IF IT FINDS THE AGENT IS NOT ACTING PROPERLY. YOU MAY NAME COAGENTS AND SUCCESSOR AGENTS UNDER THIS FORM, BUT YOU MAY NOT NAME A HEALTH CARE PROVIDER WHO MAY BE DIRECTLY OR INDIRECTLY INVOLVED IN RENDERING HEALTH CARE TO YOU UNDER THIS POWER. UNLESS YOU EXPRESSLY LIMIT THE DURATION OF THIS POWER IN THE MANNER PROVIDED BELOW, OR UNTIL YOU REVOKE THIS POWER OR A COURT ACTING ON YOUR BEHALF TERMINATES IT, YOUR AGENT MAY EXERCISE THE POWERS GIVEN IN THIS POWER THROUGHOUT YOUR LIFETIME, EVEN AFTER YOU BECOME DISABLED, INCAPACITATED, OR INCOMPETENT. THE POWERS YOU GIVE YOUR AGENT, YOUR RIGHT TO REVOKE THOSE POWERS, AND THE PENALTIES FOR VIOLATING THE LAW ARE EXPLAINED MORE FULLY IN CODE SECTIONS 31-36-6, 31-36-9, AND 31-36-10 OF THE GEORGIA "DURABLE POWER OF ATTORNEY FOR HEALTH CARE ACT" OF WHICH THIS FORM IS A PART. THAT ACT EXPRESSLY PERMITS THE USE OF ANY DIFFERENT FORM OF POWER OF ATTORNEY YOU MAY DESIRE. IF THERE IS ANYTHING ABOUT THIS FORM THAT YOU DO NOT UNDERSTAND, YOU SHOULD ASK A LAWYER TO EXPLAIN IT TO YOU.

DURABLE POWER OF ATTORNEY made this _____ day of _____, 19_____.

1. I, _____, (insert name and address of principal) hereby appoint _____ (insert name and address of agent) as my attorney in fact (my agent) to act for me and in my name in any way I could act in person to make any and all decisions for me concerning my personal care, medical treatment, hospitalization, and health care, and to require, withhold, or withdraw any type of medical treatment or procedure, even though my death may ensue. My agent shall have the same access to my medical records that I have, including the right to disclose the contents to others. My agent shall also have full power to make a disposition of any part or all of my body for medical purposes, authorize an autopsy of my body, and direct the disposition of my remains.

THE ABOVE GRANT OF POWER IS INTENDED TO BE AS BROAD AS POSSIBLE SO THAT YOUR AGENT WILL HAVE AUTHORITY TO MAKE ANY DECISION YOU COULD MAKE TO OBTAIN OR TERMINATE ANY TYPE OF HEALTH CARE, INCLUDING WITHDRAWAL OF NOURISHMENT AND FLUIDS AND OTHER LIFE-SUSTAINING OR DEATH-DELAYING MEASURES, IF YOUR AGENT BELIEVES SUCH ACTION WOULD BE CONSISTENT WITH YOUR INTENT AND DESIRES. IF YOU WISH TO LIMIT THE SCOPE OF YOUR AGENT'S POWERS OR PRESCRIBE SPECIAL RULES TO LIMIT THE POWER TO MAKE AN ANATOMICAL GIFT, AUTHORIZE AUTOPSY, OR DISPOSE OF REMAINS, YOU MAY DO SO IN THE FOLLOWING PARAGRAPHS.

2. The powers granted above shall not include the following powers or shall be subject to the following rules or limitations (here you may include any specific limitations you deem appropriate, such as your own definition of when life-sustaining or death-delaying measures should be withheld; a direction to continue nourishment and fluids or other life-sustaining or death-delaying treatment in all events; or instructions to refuse any specific types of treatment that are inconsistent with your religious beliefs or unacceptable to you for any other reason, such as blood transfusion, electroconvulsive therapy, or amputation):

THE SUBJECT OF LIFE-SUSTAINING OR DEATH-DELAYING TREATMENT IS OF PARTICULAR IMPORTANCE. FOR YOUR CONVENIENCE IN DEALING WITH THAT SUBJECT, SOME GENERAL STATEMENTS CONCERNING THE WITHHOLDING OR REMOVAL OF LIFE-SUSTAINING OR DEATH-DELAYING TREATMENT ARE SET FORTH BELOW. IF YOU AGREE WITH ONE OF THESE STATEMENTS, YOU MAY INITIAL THAT STATEMENT, BUT DO NOT INITIAL MORE THAN ONE:

I do not want my life to be prolonged, nor do I want life-sustaining or death-delaying treatment to be provided or continued, if my agent believes the burdens of the treatment outweigh the expected benefits. I want my agent to consider the relief of suffering, the expense involved, and the quality as well as the possible extension of my life in making decisions concerning life-sustaining or death-delaying treatment.

Initialed _____

I want my life to be prolonged, and I want life-sustaining or death-delaying treatment to be provided or continued, unless I am in a coma, including a persistent vegetative state, which my attending physician believes to be irreversible, in accordance with reasonable medical standards at the time of reference. If and when I have suffered such an irreversible coma, I want life-sustaining or death-delaying treatment to be withheld or discontinued.

Initialed _____

I want my life to be prolonged to the greatest extent possible, without regard to my condition, the chances I have for recovery, or the cost of the procedures.

Initialed _____

THIS POWER OF ATTORNEY MAY BE AMENDED OR REVOKED BY YOU AT ANY TIME AND IN ANY MANNER WHILE YOU ARE ABLE TO DO SO. IN THE ABSENCE OF AN AMENDMENT OR REVOCATION, THE AUTHORITY GRANTED IN THIS POWER OF ATTORNEY WILL BECOME EFFECTIVE AT THE TIME THIS POWER IS SIGNED AND WILL CONTINUE UNTIL YOUR DEATH, AND WILL CONTINUE BEYOND YOUR DEATH IF ANATOMICAL GIFT, AUTOPSY, OR DISPOSITION OF REMAINS IS AUTHORIZED, UNLESS A LIMITATION ON THE BEGINNING DATE OR DURATION IS MADE BY INITIALING AND COMPLETING EITHER OR BOTH OF THE FOLLOWING:

3. (   ) This power of attorney shall become effective on _____
(insert a future date or event during your lifetime, such as court determination of your disability, incapacity, or incompetency, when you want this power to first take effect).

4. (   ) This power of attorney shall terminate on _____
(insert a future date or event, such as court determination of your disability, incapacity, or incompetency, when you want this power to terminate prior to your death).

IF YOU WISH TO NAME SUCCESSOR AGENTS, INSERT THE NAMES AND ADDRESSES OF SUCH SUCCESSORS IN THE FOLLOWING PARAGRAPH:

5. If any agent named by me shall die, become legally disabled, incapacitated, or incompetent, or resign, refuse to act, or be unavailable, I name the following (each to act successively in the order named) as successors to such agent:

_____

_____

(insert the name and address of successor agents)

IF YOU WISH TO NAME A GUARDIAN OF YOUR PERSON IN THE EVENT A COURT DECIDES THAT ONE SHOULD BE APPOINTED, YOU MAY, BUT ARE NOT REQUIRED TO, DO SO BY INSERTING THE NAME OF SUCH GUARDIAN IN THE FOLLOWING PARAGRAPH. THE COURT WILL APPOINT THE PERSON NOMINATED BY YOU IF THE COURT FINDS THAT SUCH APPOINTMENT WILL SERVE YOUR BEST INTERESTS AND WELFARE. YOU MAY, BUT ARE NOT REQUIRED TO, NOMINATE AS YOUR GUARDIAN THE SAME PERSON NAMED IN THIS FORM AS YOUR AGENT.

6. If a guardian of my person is to be appointed, I nominate the following to serve as such guardian:

_____

(insert the name and address of nominated guardian of the person)

7. I am fully informed as to all the contents of this form and understand the full import of this grant of powers to my agent.

Signed _____

(Principal)

The principal has had an opportunity to read the above form and has signed the above form in our presence. We, the undersigned, each being over eighteen (18) years of age, witness the principal's signature at the request and in the presence of the principal, and in the presence of each other, on the day and year above set out.

Witnesses: Addresses:

_____   _____

                                              _____

_____   _____

                                              _____

Additional witness required when health care agency is signed in a hospital or skilled nursing facility:

I hereby witness this health care agency and attest that I believe the principal to be of sound mind and to have made this health care agency willingly and voluntarily.

Witness: _____

Attending Physician

Address: _____

_____

YOU MAY, BUT ARE NOT REQUIRED TO, REQUEST YOUR AGENT AND SUCCESSOR AGENTS TO PROVIDE SPECIMEN SIGNATURES BELOW. IF YOU INCLUDE SPECIMEN SIGNATURES IN THIS POWER OF ATTORNEY, YOU MUST COMPLETE THE CERTIFICATION OPPOSITE THE SIGNATURES OF THE AGENTS.

Specimen signature(s) of agent and successor(s):   I certify that the signature(s) of my agent
                                                        and successor(s) is correct:

_____   _____
(Agent)   (Principal)

_____   _____
(Successor agent)   (Principal)

_____   _____
(Successor agent)   (Principal)

Hawaii Medical Treatment Decisions Act

Hawaii recognizes the legal right of any competent adult (eighteen years or older) to make a written declaration instructing his or her physician to withhold or withdraw life-sustaining procedures in the event of a terminal condition. It is important that you understand and follow the specific provisions of the law, which are summarized below:

1. *Form of the Declaration.* The legislature suggested a model declaration shown that you may, but need not, follow. We have provided room for you to include additional instructions—for example, about specific types of life-sustaining treatment, such as artificial feeding or cardiopulmonary resuscitation, that you may wish to forgo. Your document must be in writing and signed and dated by you, or by someone else at your request, in the presence of two or more witnesses. *All of these signatures must be notarized at the same time.*
2. *Witness Requirements.* Witnesses to your declaration must be at least eighteen years of age, not related to you by blood, marriage, or adoption and may not be your attending physician, his or her employee, or an employee of the medical-care facility in which you are a patient.
3. *Physician's Responsibility and Immunity.* A terminal condition must be certified in writing by two physicians, one or both of whom must be your attending physician(s). Once your attending physician receives a photocopy of your completed declaration he or she must make it part of your medical records and, if your condition becomes terminal, is responsible for obtaining the necessary written certification so that the declaration can take effect. If the physician is not willing to honor the declaration, he or she is responsible for transferring you to another physician who will honor your wishes. Any health care provider who honors your declaration is protected from civil or criminal liability.
4. *Pregnancy Exemption.* The Hawaii act states that the declaration can be given no force or effect during the course of pregnancy.
5. *Other Provisions.* The declaration can be revoked at any time, and your desires at all times supersede the effect of the declaration. No one may be forced to sign the declaration either as a condition of insurance or to receive care or admission to a health-care facility.

The Hawaii declaration is binding on physicians only when you are certified as having a "terminal condition." To protect yourself as fully as possible against unwanted treatment, the Society for the Right to Die advises that you execute both the Hawaii declaration and the generic living will (Chapter 3).

DECLARATION

A. STATEMENT OF DECLARANT

Declaration made this _____ day of _____ (month, year).

I, _____, being of sound mind, willfully and voluntarily make known my desire that my dying shall not be artificially prolonged under the circumstances set forth below, and do hereby declare:

If at any time I should have an incurable or irreversible condition certified to be terminal by two physicians who have personally examined me, one of whom shall be my attending physician, and the physicians have determined that I am unable to make decisions concerning my medical treatment, and that without administration of life-sustaining treatment my death will occur in a relatively short time, and where the application of life-sustaining procedures would serve only to prolong artificially the dying process, I direct that such procedures be withheld or withdrawn, and that I be permitted to die naturally with only the administration of medication, nourishment, or fluids or the performance of any medical procedure deemed necessary to provide me with comfort or to alleviate pain.

Other directions:

In the absence of my ability to give directions regarding the use of such life-sustaining procedures, it is my intention that this declaration shall be honored by my family and physician(s) as the final expressions of my legal right to refuse medical or surgical treatment and accept the consequences from such refusal.

I understand the full import of this declaration and I am emotionally and mentally competent to make this declaration.

Signed _____

Address _____

B. STATEMENT OF WITNESSES

I am at least 18 years of age and
—not related to the declarant by blood, marriage, or adoption; and
—not the attending physician, an employee of the attending physician, or an employee of the medical care facility in which the declarant is a patient.
The declarant is personally known to me and I believe the declarant to be of sound mind.

Witness _____

Address _____

Witness _____

Address _____

C. NOTARIZATION

Subscribed, sworn to and acknowledged before me by _____,

the declarant, and subscribed and sworn to before me by _____ and

_____, witnesses, this _____ day of _____, 19____.

(SEAL)   Signed _____

_____
(Official capacity of officer)

Idaho's Natural Death Act and Durable Power of Attorney for Health Care

Idaho's Natural Death Act recognizes the legal right of any adult (eighteen years or older), or emancipated minor, to sign a written living will instructing his or her physician to withhold or withdraw life-sustaining procedures in the event of a condition that makes it impossible to communicate, where such procedures would serve only to postpone the moment of death and where, in the opinion of the attending physician, death is imminent whether or not the procedures are used, or the patient is in a persistent vegetative state. The Natural Death Act also authorizes patients to designate an adult to make medical decisions on their behalf when they become unable to do so, through the use of a durable power of attorney for health care.

Copies of the documents that may be used are shown. The following aspects of the law should be noted:

1. The Idaho living will should be in the form set forth in the statute and signed, dated, and witnessed in accordance with the statute.
2. You should indicate which statement on the directive coincides with your wishes about artificial nutrition or hydration.
3. If you choose *not* to appoint someone as your "proxy/attorney-in-fact," cross out paragraph 2 of the Idaho living will. If you do want to appoint someone, in addition to filling out paragraph 2, you must also execute the Idaho durable power of attorney for health care.

The durable power of attorney enables you to implement the desires expressed in your Idaho living will by designating an adult, known as your health-care agent, to make medical decisions on your behalf when you become incapacitated (see Chapter 3 for more information). It also permits you to name an alternate agent who may act if the first person is unable or unwilling to serve. Instructions are included in the document itself; please read them carefully, especially the witnessing requirements.

The durable power must be signed in the presence of two adult witnesses *or* before a notary public, neither of whom may be: your health-care agent or an alternate; a health-care provider or his or her employee; an operator or employee of an operator of a community-care facility.

At least one of the witnesses may not be: related to you by blood, marriage, or adoption; entitled to any part of your estate under an existing will or by operation of law.

In addition, your health-care agent or alternate may not be: your health-care provider or an operator of a community-care facility; a nonrelative employee of your health-care provider or of an operator of a community care facility.

To protect yourself as fully as possible against unwanted treatment, the Society for the Right to Die advises that you execute three documents—the Idaho living will, the durable power of attorney, and the generic living will (Chapter 3). Idaho's documents apply only when your condition is terminal and death is imminent *with or without the use of life-sustaining procedures.* The generic living will can be used to state your treatment preferences in case of medical conditions that are irreversible, but in which death may not be imminent if life-sustaining procedures are continued, such as permanent unconsciousness or advanced Alzheimer's.

A LIVING WILL

A Directive to Withhold or to Provide Treatment

To my family, my relatives, my friends, my physicians, my employers, and all others whom it may concern:

Directive made this _____ day of _____ 19___

I, _____ (name), being of sound mind, willfully, and voluntarily make known my desire that my life shall not be prolonged artificially under the circumstances set forth below, do hereby declare:

1. If at any time I should have an incurable injury, disease, illness or condition certified to be terminal by two medical doctors who have examined me, and where the application of life-sustaining procedures of any kind would serve only to prolong artificially the moment of my death, and where a medical doctor determines that my death is imminent, whether or not life-sustaining procedures are utilized, or I have been diagnosed as being in a persistent vegetative state, I direct that the following marked expression of my intent be followed and that I be permitted to die naturally, and that I receive any medical treatment or care that may be required to keep me free of pain or distress.

Check One Box

☐ If at any time I should become unable to communicate my instructions, then I direct that all medical treatment, care, and nutrition and hydration necessary to restore my health, sustain my life, and to abolish or alleviate pain or distress be provided to me. Nutrition and hydration shall not be withheld or withdrawn from me if I would die from malnutrition or dehydration rather than from my injury, disease, illness or condition.

☐ If at any time I should become unable to communicate my instructions and where the application of artificial life-sustaining procedures shall serve only to prolong artificially the moment of my death, I direct such procedures be withheld or withdrawn except for the administration of nutrition and hydration.

☐ If at any time I should become unable to communicate my instructions and where the application of artificial life-sustaining procedures shall serve only to prolong artificially the moment of death, I direct such procedures be withheld or withdrawn including withdrawal of the administration of nutrition and hydration.

2. In the absence of my ability to give directions regarding the use of life-sustaining procedures, I hereby appoint

_____ (name) currently residing at _____, as my attorney-in-fact/proxy for the making of decisions relating to my health care in my place; and it is my intention that this appointment shall be honored by him/her, by my family, relatives, friends, physicians and lawyer as the final expression of my legal right to refuse medical or surgical treatment, and I accept the consequences of such a decision. I have duly executed a Durable Power of Attorney for health care decisions on this date.

3. In the absence of my ability to give further directions regarding my treatment, including life-sustaining procedures, it is my intention that this directive shall be honored by my family and physicians as the final expression of my legal right to refuse or accept medical and surgical treatment, and I accept the consequences of such refusal.

4. If I have been diagnosed as pregnant and that diagnosis is known to any interested person, this directive shall have no force during the course of my pregnancy.

5. I understand the full importance of this directive and am emotionally and mentally competent to make this directive. No participant in the making of this directive or in its being carried into effect, whether it be a medical doctor, my spouse, a relative, friend or any other person shall be held responsible in any way, legally, professionally or socially, for complying with my directions.

Signed _____

City, county and state of residence _____
The declarant has been known to me personally and I believe him/her to be of sound mind.

Witness _____ Witness _____

Address _____ Address _____

This Living Will complies with the Idaho Natural Death Act, Idaho Code §§ 39 - 4501 to - 4508 (1977, amend. 1986, 1988).

A DURABLE POWER OF ATTORNEY FOR HEALTH CARE

1. DESIGNATION OF HEALTH CARE AGENT.

I,_____

(Insert your name and address)

_____

do hereby designate and appoint_____

_____

(Insert name, address, and telephone number of one individual only as your agent to make health care decisions for you. None of the following may be designated as your agent: (1) your treating health care provider, (2) a nonrelative employee of your treating health care provider, (3) an operator of a community care facility, or (4) a nonrelative employee of an operator of a community care facility.)

as my attorney in fact (agent) to make health care decisions for me as authorized in this document. For the purposes of this document, "health care decision" means consent, refusal of consent, or withdrawal of consent to any care, treatment, service, or procedure to maintain, diagnose, or treat an individual's physical condition.

2. CREATION OF DURABLE POWER OF ATTORNEY FOR HEALTH CARE.
By this document I intend to create a durable power of attorney for health care. This power of attorney shall not be affected by my subsequent incapacity.

3. GENERAL STATEMENT OF AUTHORITY GRANTED.
Subject to any limitations in this document, I hereby grant to my agent full power and authority to make health care decisions for me to the same extent that I could make such decisions for myself if I had the capacity to do so. In exercising this authority, my agent shall make health care decisions that are consistent with my desires as stated in this document or otherwise made known to my agent, including, but not limited to, my desires concerning obtaining or refusing or withdrawing life-prolonging care, treatment, services, and procedures.

(If you want to limit the authority of your agent to make health care decisions for you, you can state the limitations in paragraph 4 ["Statement of Desires, Special Provisions, and Limitations"] below. You can indicate your desires by including a statement of your desires in the same paragraph.)

4. STATEMENT OF DESIRES, SPECIAL PROVISIONS, AND LIMITATIONS.

(Your agent must make health care decisions that are consistent with your known desires. You can, but are not required to, state your desires in the space provided below. You should consider whether you want to include a statement of your desires concerning life-prolonging care, treatment, services, and procedures. You can also include a statement of your desires concerning other matters relating to your health care. You can also make your desires known to your agent by discussing your desires with your agent or by some other means. If there are any types of treatment that you do not want to be used, you should state them in the space below. If you want to limit in any other way the authority given your agent by this document, you should state the limits in the space below. If you do not state any limits, your agent will have broad powers to make health care decisions for you, except to the extent that there are limits provided by law.)

In exercising the authority under this durable power of attorney for health care, my agent shall act consistently with my desires as stated below and is subject to the special provisions and limitations stated in the living will. Additional statement of desires, special provisions, and limitations:

_____

_____

_____

_____

_____

_____

(You may attach additional pages if you need more space to complete your statement. If you attach additional pages, you must date and sign each of the additional pages at the same time you date and sign this document.)

5. INSPECTION AND DISCLOSURE OF INFORMATION RELATING TO MY PHYSICAL OR MENTAL HEALTH. Subject to any limitations in this document, my agent has the power and authority to do all of the following:
   (a) Request, review, and receive any information, verbal or written, regarding my physical or mental health, including, but not limited to, medical and hospital records.
   (b) Execute on my behalf any releases or other documents that may be required in order to obtain this information.
   (c) Consent to the disclosure of this information.
   (d) Consent to the donation of any of my organs for medical purposes.

(If you want to limit the authority of your agent to receive and disclose information relating to your health, you must state the limitations in paragraph 4 ["Statement of Desires, Special Provisions, and Limitations"] above.)

6. SIGNING DOCUMENTS, WAIVERS, AND RELEASES. Where necessary to implement the health care decisions that my agent is authorized by this document to make, my agent has the power and authority to execute on my behalf all of the following:
   (a) Documents titled or purporting to be a "Refusal to Permit Treatment" and "Leaving Hospital Against Medical Advice."
   (b) Any necessary waiver or release from liability required by a hospital or physician.

7. DESIGNATION OF ALTERNATE AGENTS.

(You are not required to designate any alternate agents but you may do so. Any alternate agent you designate will be able to make the same health care decisions as the agent you designated in paragraph 1, above, in the event that agent is unable or ineligible to act as your agent. If the agent you designated is your spouse, he or she becomes ineligible to act as your agent if your marriage is dissolved.)

If the person designated as my agent in paragraph 1 is not available or becomes ineligible to act as my agent to make a health care decision for me or loses the mental capacity to make health care decisions for me, or if I revoke that person's appointment or authority to act as my agent to make health care decisions for me, then I designate and appoint the following persons to serve as my agent to make health care decisions for me as authorized in this document, such persons to serve in the order listed below:

A. First Alternate Agent _____
              (Insert name, address, and telephone number
                    of first alternate agent)

_____

B. Second Alternate Agent _____
              (Insert name, address, and telephone number
                   of second alternate agent)

_____

8. PRIOR DESIGNATIONS REVOKED. I revoke any prior durable power of attorney for health care.

DATE AND SIGNATURE OF PRINCIPAL
(You Must Date and Sign this Power of Attorney)

I sign my name to this Statutory Form Durable Power of Attorney for Health Care on _____ at_____, _____
              (Date)   (City)   (State)
_____
                        (You sign here)

(This Power of Attorney will not be valid unless it is signed by two qualified witnesses who are present when you sign or acknowledge your signature. If you have attached any additional pages to this form, you must date and sign each of the additional pages at the same time you date and sign this Power of Attorney.)

STATEMENT OF WITNESSES

(This document must be witnessed by two qualified adult witnesses. None of the following may be used as a witness: (1) a person you designate as your agent or alternate agent, (2) a health care provider, (3) an employee of a health care provider, (4) the operator of a community care facility, (5) an employee of an operator of a community care facility. At least one of the witnesses must make the additional declaration set out following the place where the witnesses sign.)

I declare under penalty of perjury under the laws of Idaho that the person who signed or acknowledged this document is personally known to me (or proved to me on the basis of convincing evidence) to be the principal, that the principal signed or acknowledged this durable power of attorney in my presence, that the principal appears to be of sound mind and under no duress, fraud, or undue influence, that I am not the person appointed as attorney in fact by this document, and that I am not a health care provider, an employee of a health careprovider, the operator of a community care facility, nor an employee of an operator of a community care facility.

Signature: _____

Print name: _____

Date: _____ Residence address: _____

Signature: _____

Print name: _____

Date: _____ Residence address: _____
(At least one of the above witnesses must also sign)

    I further declare under penalty of perjury under the laws of Idaho that I am not related to the principal by blood, marriage, or adoption, and, to the best of my knowledge, I am not entitled to any part of the estate of the principal upon the death of the principal under a will now existing or by operation of law.

Signature: _____

Signature: _____

NOTARY

(Signer of instrument may either have it witnessed as above or have his/her signature notarized as below, to legalize this instrument.)

State of Idaho
County of _____ ss.

On this _____ day of _____ 19 _____

before me personally appeared _____
(Full name of signer of instrument)

to me known (or proved to me on basis of satisfactory evidence) to be the person whose name is subscribed to this instrument, and acknowledged that he/she executed it. I declare under penalty of perjury that the person whose name is subscribed to this instrument appears to be of sound mind and under no duress, fraud or undue influence.

                    _____
                      (Signature of Notary)

[1894L-0688]

The Illinois Power of Attorney for Health Care Form

Illinois has a Living Will Act but because it is much more limited than the Statutory Short Form Power of Attorney for Health Care and contains contradictory and confusing language. We recommend that you use the generic living will outlined in Chapter 3. Illinois attorneys advise us that the power of attorney for health care, along with the generic living will, will ensure the best legal protection of your right to refuse unwanted medical treatment. The power of attorney form shown here complies with the statute. Read the witnessing and execution requirements carefully.

ILLINOIS
STATUTORY SHORT FORM POWER OF ATTORNEY
FOR HEALTH CARE

(NOTICE: THE PURPOSE OF THIS POWER OF ATTORNEY IS TO GIVE THE PERSON YOU DESIGNATE (YOUR "AGENT") BROAD POWERS TO MAKE HEALTH CARE DECISIONS FOR YOU, INCLUDING POWER TO REQUIRE, CONSENT TO OR WITHDRAW ANY TYPE OF PERSONAL CARE OR MEDICAL TREATMENT FOR ANY PHYSICAL OR MENTAL CONDITION AND TO ADMIT YOU TO OR DISCHARGE YOU FROM ANY HOSPITAL, HOME OR OTHER INSTITUTION. THIS FORM DOES NOT IMPOSE A DUTY ON YOUR AGENT TO EXERCISE GRANTED POWERS; BUT WHEN POWERS ARE EXERCISED, YOUR AGENT WILL HAVE TO USE DUE CARE TO ACT FOR YOUR BENEFIT AND IN ACCORDANCE WITH THIS FORM AND KEEP A RECORD OF RECEIPTS, DISBURSEMENTS AND SIGNIFICANT ACTIONS TAKEN AS AGENT. A COURT CAN TAKE AWAY THE POWERS OF YOUR AGENT IF IT FINDS THE AGENT IS NOT ACTING PROPERLY. YOU MAY NAME SUCCESSOR AGENTS UNDER THIS FORM BUT NOT CO-AGENTS, AND NO HEALTH CARE PROVIDER MAY BE NAMED. UNLESS YOU EXPRESSLY LIMIT THE DURATION OF THIS POWER IN THE MANNER PROVIDED BELOW, UNTIL YOU REVOKE THIS POWER OR A COURT ACTING ON YOUR BEHALF TERMINATES IT, YOUR AGENT MAY EXERCISE THE POWERS GIVEN HERE THROUGHOUT YOUR LIFETIME, EVEN AFTER YOU BECOME DISABLED. THE POWERS YOU GIVE YOUR AGENT, YOUR RIGHT TO REVOKE THOSE POWERS AND THE PENALTIES FOR VIOLATING THE LAW ARE EXPLAINED MORE FULLY IN SECTIONS 4-5, 4-6, 4-9 AND 4-10(b) OF THE ILLINOIS "POWERS OF ATTORNEY FOR HEALTH CARE LAW" OF WHICH THIS FORM IS A PART. THAT LAW EXPRESSLY PERMITS THE USE OF ANY DIFFERENT FORM OF POWER OF ATTORNEY YOU MAY DESIRE. IF THERE IS ANYTHING ABOUT THIS FORM THAT YOU DO NOT UNDERSTAND, YOU SHOULD ASK A LAWYER TO EXPLAIN IT TO YOU.)

POWER OF ATTORNEY made this _____ day of _____
                                                                (month)   (year)

1. I, _____ ,
                          (insert name and address of principal)

hereby appoint: _____

_____
                          (insert name and address of agent)

as my attorney-in-fact (my "agent") to act for me and in my name (in any way I could act in person) to make any and all decisions for me concerning my personal care, medical treatment, hospitalization and health care and to require, withhold or withdraw any type of medical treatment or procedure, even though my death may ensue. My agent shall have the same access to my medical records that I have, including the right to disclose the contents to others. My agent shall also have full power to make a disposition of any part or all of my body for medical purposes, authorize an autopsy and direct the disposition of my remains.

(THE ABOVE GRANT OF POWER IS INTENDED TO BE AS BROAD AS POSSIBLE SO THAT YOUR AGENT WILL HAVE AUTHORITY TO MAKE ANY DECISION YOU COULD MAKE TO OBTAIN OR TERMINATE ANY TYPE OF HEALTH CARE, INCLUDING WITHDRAWAL OF FOOD AND WATER AND OTHER LIFE-SUSTAINING MEASURES, IF YOUR AGENT BELIEVES SUCH ACTION WOULD BE CONSISTENT WITH YOUR INTENT AND DESIRES. IF YOU WISH TO LIMIT THE SCOPE OF YOUR AGENT'S POWERS OR PRESCRIBE SPECIAL RULES OR LIMIT THE POWER TO MAKE AN ANATOMICAL GIFT, AUTHORIZE AUTOPSY OR DISPOSE OF REMAINS, YOU MAY DO SO IN THE FOLLOWING PARAGRAPHS.)

2. The powers granted above shall not include the following powers or shall be subject to the following rules or limitations (here you may include any specific limitations you deem appropriate, such as: your own definition of when life-sustaining measures should be withheld; a direction to continue food and fluids or life-sustaining treatment in all events; or instructions to refuse any specific types of treatment that are inconsistent with your religious beliefs or unacceptable to you for any other reason, such as blood transfusion, electro-convulsive therapy, amputation, psychosurgery, voluntary admission to a mental institution, etc.):

_____

_____

_____

_____

(THE SUBJECT OF LIFE-SUSTAINING TREATMENT IS OF PARTICULAR IMPORTANCE. FOR YOUR CONVENIENCE IN DEALING WITH THAT SUBJECT, SOME GENERAL STATEMENTS CONCERNING THE WITHHOLDING OR REMOVAL OF LIFE-SUSTAINING TREATMENT ARE SET FORTH BELOW. IF YOU AGREE WITH ONE OF THESE STATEMENTS, YOU MAY INITIAL THAT STATEMENT; BUT DO NOT INITIAL MORE THAN ONE):

I do not want my life to be prolonged nor do I want life-sustaining treatment to be provided or continued if my agent believes the burdens of the treatment outweigh the expected benefits. I want my agent to consider the relief of suffering, the expense involved and the quality as well as the possible extension of my life in making decisions concerning life-sustaining treatment.

Initialed _____

I want my life to be prolonged and I want life-sustaining treatment to be provided or continued unless I am in a coma which my attending physician believes to be irreversible, in accordance with reasonable medical standards at the time of reference. If and when I have suffered irreversible coma, I want life-sustaining treatment to be withheld or discontinued.

Initialed _____

I want my life to be prolonged to the greatest extent possible without regard to my condition, the chances I have for recovery or the cost of the procedures.

Initialed _____

(THIS POWER OF ATTORNEY MAY BE AMENDED OR REVOKED BY YOU IN THE MANNER PROVIDED IN SECTION 4-6 OF THE ILLINOIS "POWERS OF ATTORNEY FOR HEALTH CARE LAW." ABSENT AMENDMENT OR REVOCATION, THE AUTHORITY GRANTED IN THIS POWER OF ATTORNEY WILL BECOME EFFECTIVE AT THE TIME THIS POWER IS SIGNED AND WILL CONTINUE UNTIL YOUR DEATH, AND BEYOND IF ANATOMICAL GIFT, AUTOPSY OR DISPOSITION OF REMAINS IS AUTHORIZED, UNLESS A LIMITATION ON THE BEGINNING DATE OR DURATION IS MADE BY INITIALING AND COMPLETING EITHER OR BOTH OF THE FOLLOWING:)

3. ( ) This power of attorney shall become effective on _____

_____

(insert a future date or event during your lifetime, such as court determination of your disability, when you want this power to first take effect)

4. ( ) This power of attorney shall terminate on _____

_____

(insert a future date or event, such as court determination of your disability, when you want this power to terminate prior to your death)

(IF YOU WISH TO NAME SUCCESSOR AGENTS, INSERT THE NAMES AND ADDRESSES OF SUCH SUCCESSORS IN THE FOLLOWING PARAGRAPH.)

5. If any agent named by me shall die, become incompetent, resign, refuse to accept the office of agent or be unavailable, I name the following (each to act alone and successively, in the order named) as successors to such agent:

_____

_____

For purposes of this paragraph 5, a person shall be considered to be incompetent if and while the person is a minor or an adjudicated incompetent or disabled person or the person is unable to give prompt and intelligent consideration to health care matters, as certified by a licensed physician. (IF YOU WISH TO NAME YOUR AGENT AS GUARDIAN OF YOUR PERSON, IN THE EVENT A COURT DECIDES THAT ONE SHOULD BE APPOINTED, YOU MAY, BUT ARE NOT REQUIRED TO, DO SO BY RETAINING THE FOLLOWING PARAGRAPH. THE COURT WILL APPOINT YOUR AGENT IF THE COURT FINDS THAT SUCH APPOINTMENT WILL SERVE YOUR BEST INTERESTS AND WELFARE. STRIKE OUT PARAGRAPH 6 IF YOU DO NOT WANT YOUR AGENT TO ACT AS GUARDIAN.)

6. If a guardian of my person is to be appointed, I nominate the agent acting under this power of attorney as such guardian, to serve without bond or security:

_____

_____

(insert name and address of nominated guardian of the person)

7. I am fully informed as to all the contents of this form and understand the full import of this grant of powers to my agent.

Signed _____
(principal)

The principal has had an opportunity to read the above form and has signed the form or acknowledged his or her signature or mark on the form in my presence.

_____   Residing at _____
(witness)

_____

(YOU MAY, BUT ARE NOT REQUIRED TO, REQUEST YOUR AGENT AND SUCCESSOR AGENTS TO PROVIDE SPECIMEN SIGNATURES BELOW. IF YOU INCLUDE SPECIMEN SIGNATURES IN THIS POWER OF ATTORNEY, YOU MUST COMPLETE THE CERTIFICATION OPPOSITE THE SIGNATURES OF THE AGENTS.)

Specimen signatures of agent (and successors).   I certify that the signatures of my agent (and successors) are correct.

_____   _____
(agent)   (principal)

_____   _____
(successor agent)   (principal)

_____   _____
(successor agent)   (principal)

Indiana's Living Wills and Life-Prolonging Procedures Act

Indiana's Living Wills and Life-Prolonging Procedures Act recognizes your right to make two kinds of declaration: 1) The Living Will Declaration stating that you do not want your dying artificially prolonged by the use of life-sustaining procedures. This declaration will become applicable whenever your attending physician and one other doctor confirm that your condition is terminal.

In addition, the statute provides for: 2) a Life-Prolonging Procedures Declaration that can be used to request the use of life-prolonging procedures. Both forms are shown here. Please read them carefully to ensure that you are using the one that reflects your wishes. You may, if you wish, add personalized directions, and we have provided space for these. You might wish to consider listing the particular treatments to be given, withheld, or withdrawn—for example, cardiac resuscitation, a respirator, or tube feeding.

Your declaration must be signed in the presence of two witnesses, neither of whom may be

1. Your parent, spouse, or child.
2. Directly responsible for costs of your medical care.
3. Entitled to any part of your estate.

Properly signed and witnessed, your declaration will remain in effect until or unless you revoke it. As long as you are able to communicate your preferences, your own expressed wishes always supersede your declaration. To protect yourself as fully as possible against unwanted treatment, the Society for the Right to Die advises that you execute both the Indiana declaration of your choice and the generic living will (Chapter 3).

LIVING WILL DECLARATION

Declaration made this _____ day of _____ (month, year).

I, _____, being at least eighteen (18) years old and of sound mind, willfully and voluntarily make known my desires that my dying shall not be artificially prolonged under the circumstances set forth below, and I declare:

If at any time I have an incurable injury, disease, or illness certified in writing to be a terminal condition by my attending physician, and my attending physician has determined that my death will occur within a short period of time, and the use of life-prolonging procedures would serve only to artificially prolong the dying process, I direct that such procedures be withheld or withdrawn, and that I be permitted to die naturally with only the provision of appropriate nutrition and hydration and the administration of medication and the performance of any medical procedure necessary to provide me with comfort care or to alleviate pain.

Other instructions:

In the absence of my ability to give directions regarding the use of life-prolonging procedures, it is my intention that this declaration be honored by my family and physician as the final expression of my legal right to refuse medical or surgical treatment and accept the consequences of the refusal.

I understand the full import of this declaration.

Signed _____

City, County and State of Residence _____

The declarant has been personally known to me, and I believe (him/her) to be of sound mind. I did not sign the declarant's signature above for or at the direction of the declarant. I am not a parent, spouse, or child of the declarant. I am not entitled to any part of the declarant's estate or directly financially responsible for the declarant's medical care. I am competent and at least eighteen (18) years old.

Witness _____ Date _____

Witness _____ Date _____

Iowa's Life-sustaining Procedures Act and Durable Power of Attorney for Health Care

Iowa recognizes the legal right of any adult (eighteen years or older) to make a written declaration instructing his or her physician to withhold or withdraw life-sustaining procedures in the event of a terminal condition. A copy of the suggested form of declaration is shown. It is important that you understand these specific provisions of the law:

1. Your declaration may, but need not, follow the form set forth in the suggested declaration shown. It must, however, be signed and dated by you in the presence of two adult witnesses.
2. Before your declaration will be legally binding, your terminal condition must be confirmed by your attending physician and one other physician and recorded on your medical chart.
3. A declaration is not effective during pregnancy as long as the fetus could develop to the point of a live birth with continued application of life-sustaining procedures.
4. Some of the statute's language suggests that life-sustaining procedures in this act might not include sustenance or pain medication. *If you want artificial nutrition and hydration to be withheld or withdrawn, you should specify this in your document.* We have provided space on the form for you to add instructions—for example, about this and other specific types of treatment, such as cardiopulmonary resuscitation.
5. You may revoke the declaration at any time.
6. In the absence of a declaration, life-sustaining procedures may be withheld or withdrawn by your physician in consultation with your attorney-in-fact, family, and others specified by the statute. There must be a witness present at the time of such a consultation. Nonetheless, we strongly recommend that you execute a written declaration, so that your own wishes will be clear.

Iowa law also provides for a durable power of attorney for health care (DPAHC). The DPAHC includes space for you to add personal instructions, such as your wishes about particular types of treatment. If your wishes are not known, your agent must act in your best interests.

Read the DPAHC carefully—especially the witnessing provisions—*before* you gather your witnesses.

You *may not* designate your health-care provider, or an employee of your health-care provider, as your health-care agent. However, if you have nobody else to appoint as your agent, you may be able to appoint an employee of your health-care provider; if you want to do so you should consult a local attorney.

To protect yourself as fully as possible against unwanted treatment, the Society for the Right to Die advises that you execute three documents—the Iowa declaration, the Iowa durable power of attorney for health care and the generic living will (Chapter 3). We recommend that you complete the generic living will as an added protection, *especially if you wish to refuse artificial feeding.*

Note: The new durable power of attorney for health care was not available as this book went to press. Please contact the Society for the Right to Die to obtain the form.

DECLARATION

If I should have an incurable or irreversible condition that will cause my death within a relatively short time, it is my desire that my life not be prolonged by administration of lifesustaining procedures. If my condition is terminal and I am unable to participate in decisions regarding my medical treatment, I direct my attending physician to withhold or withdraw procedures that merely prolong the dying process and are not necessary to my comfort or freedom from pain.

Other instructions:

Signed this _____ day of _____, _____.

Signature _____

City, County and State of Residence _____

The declarant is known to me and voluntarily signed this document in my presence.

Witness _____

Address _____

Witness _____

Address _____

The Kansas Declaration to Physicians, and the Durable Power of Attorney for Health Care

Kansas recognizes the legal right of any competent adult (eighteen years or older) to sign a written declaration instructing his or her physician to withhold or withdraw life-sustaining procedures in the event of a terminal condition. It is important that you understand the specific provisions of this statute:

1. The declaration must be substantially in the form shown, but we have provided room for you to add personal instructions—for example, regarding particular types of treatment that you may wish to refuse, such as cardiopulmonary resuscitation or tube feeding. The declaration must be in writing, signed and dated by you, or by another person in your presence and at your express direction.
2. "Life-sustaining procedures" can only be withheld or withdrawn after you have been certified in writing as having a terminal condition by two physicians who have personally examined you, one of whom is your attending physician.
3. The declaration must be witnessed by two adults. The witnesses *may not* be: a. The person, if any, whom you directed to sign the declaration on your behalf; b. Anyone related to your by blood or marriage; c. Anyone entitled to any part of your estate, by will, codicil, or the laws of inheritance; d. Anyone directly financially responsible for your medical care.
4. The declaration is not effective during a declarant's pregnancy.

Kansas law also provides for a durable power of attorney for health care (see Chapter 3). You may not name any of the following people as your agent: 1. A treating health-care provider; 2. An employee of a treating health-care provider; 3. An employee, owner, director, or officer of a health-care facility.

Your durable power of attorney must be witnessed, *either* by two witnesses *or* by a notary public. If you choose witnesses, sign and date the document in their presence. The witnesses must be at least eighteen years old, and *may not* be: 1. A person you named as your agent; 2. Related to you by blood, marriage, or adoption; 3. Entitled to any portion of your estate by will, codicil, or the laws of inheritance; 4. Directly financially responsible for your health care.

If you choose a notary, sign and date the document in the notary's presence.

Kansas law permits you to have the durable power of attorney become effective immediately, if you want it to; the law also permits you to personalize the manner in which the power can be revoked. Consult a local attorney if you are interested in these options.

To protect yourself as fully as possible against unwanted treatment, the Society for the Right to Die advises that you execute three documents—the Kansas declaration, the durable power of attorney (if you have someone to appoint), and the generic living will (Chapter 3). The generic living will can apply to conditions that may not fit the Kansas statute's definition of "terminal condition"—for example, advanced Alzheimer's disease.

KANSAS

DECLARATION

Declaration made this _____ day of _____(month, year).

I, _____, being of sound mind, wilfully and voluntarily make known my desires that my dying shall not be artificially prolonged under the circumstances set forth below, and do hereby declare:

If at any time I should have an incurable injury, disease, or illness certified to be a terminal condition by two physicians who have personally examined me, one of whom shall be my attending physician, and the physicians have determined that my death will occur whether or not life-sustaining procedures are utilized and where the application of life-sustaining procedures would serve only to artificially prolong the dying process, I direct that such procedures be withheld or withdrawn, and that I be permitted to die naturally with only the administration of medication or the performance of any medical procedure deemed necessary to provide me with comfort care.

In the absence of my ability to give directions regarding the use of such life-sustaining procedures, it is my intention that this declaration shall be honored by my family and physician(s) as the final expression of my legal right to refuse medical or surgical treatment and accept the consequences from such refusal.

I understand the full import of this declaration and I am emotionally and mentally competent to make this declaration.

Other directions:

Signed _____

City, County, and State of Residence _____

The declarant has been personally known to me and I believe him or her to be of sound mind. I did not sign the declarant's signature above for or at the direction of the declarant. I am not related to the declarant by blood or marriage, entitled to any portion of the estate of the declarant according to the laws of intestate succession or under any will of declarant or codicil thereto, or directly financially responsible for the declarant's medical care.

Witness _____

Witness _____

This Declaration complies with Kansas laws of 1979. However, additional specific directions may be included by declarer.

KANSAS

DURABLE POWER OF ATTORNEY FOR HEALTH CARE DECISIONS
GENERAL STATEMENT OF AUTHORITY GRANTED

I, _____, designate and appoint:

Name: _____ Address: _____

_____ Telephone Number: _____

or, in the event the person I appoint above is unable, unwilling or unavailable to serve,

Name: _____ Address: _____

_____ Telephone Number: _____

to be my agent for health care decisions and pursuant to the language stated below, on my behalf to:

(1) Consent, refuse consent, or withdraw consent to any care, treatment, service or procedure to maintain, diagnose or treat a physical or mental condition, and to make decisions about organ donation, autopsy and disposition of the body;

(2) make all necessary arrangements at any hospital, psychiatric hospital or psychiatric treatment facility, hospice, nursing home or similar institution; to employ or discharge health care personnel, to include physicians, psychiatrists, psychologists, dentists, nurses, therapists or any other person who is licensed, certified or otherwise authorized or permitted by the laws of this state to administer health care, as the agent shall deem necessary for my physical, mental and emotional well being; and

(3) request, receive and review any information, verbal or written, regarding my personal affairs or physical or mental health, including medical and hospital records, and to execute any releases of other documents that may be required in order to obtain such information.

In exercising the grant of authority set forth above my agent for health care decisions shall:

_____

_____

_____

(Here may be inserted any special instructions or statement of the principal's desires to be followed by the agent in exercising the authority granted).

LIMITATIONS OF AUTHORITY

(1) The powers of the agent herein shall be limited to the extent set out in writing in this durable power of attorney for health care decisions, and shall not include the power to revoke or invalidate any previously existing declaration made in accordance with the natural death act.

(2) The agent shall be prohibited from authorizing consent for the following items:

_____

_____

(3) This durable power of attorney for health care decisions shall be subject to the additional following limitations:

_____

_____

EFFECTIVE TIME

This power of attorney for health care decisions shall become effective upon the occurrence of my disability or incapacity.

REVOCATION

Any durable power of attorney for health care decisions I have previously made is hereby revoked.

This durable power of attorney for health care decisions shall be revoked by an instrument in writing executed, witnessed or acknowledged in the same manner as required herein.

EXECUTION

Executed this _____, at _____, Kansas.

              Date   County

_____

                                 Principal

This document must be: (1) Witnessed by two individuals of lawful age who are not the agent, not related to the principal by blood, marriage or adoption, not entitled to any portion of the principal's estate and not financially responsible for the principal's health care; OR (2) acknowledged by a notary public.

_____   _____

Witness   Witness

_____   _____

Address   Address

(OR)

STATE OF KANSAS   )

COUNTY OF   ) ss.

This instrument was acknowledged before me on _____

                                                  Date

by _____

        Name of Principal

_____

                    Signature of Notary Public

(Seal, if any)

My appointment expires: _____

Copies:

Kentucky's Living Will Act

The Kentucky Living Will Act recognizes your right to fill out a living will declaration setting out your treatment wishes in the event of a terminal condition.

However, because the Kentucky declaration only covers a narrow range of medical situations—described below—we strongly suggest that you also fill out a generic living will (Chapter 3), which covers more medical situations and types of treatment than Kentucky's declaration.

You may also want to appoint an agent to make medical decisions for you when you cannot make them yourself. You can do this by using the "proxy designation clause" in the generic living will and by filling out a Kentucky Designation of Health Care Surrogate form. Make sure that you appoint the same health-care agent in both documents, so there will be no confusion about which person has your authorization.

When Your Declaration Becomes Effective. The declaration will only be honored if you are in a terminal condition, which Kentucky law describes as a condition that is "incurable and irreversible, and will result in death within a relatively short time." That means that the document probably will not apply if you have senile dementia, advanced Alzheimer's, or are permanently unconscious. If you would not want to be sustained in these situations, you should fill out a generic living will.

What Treatments Are Covered. Kentucky law states that any "procedure deemed necessary . . . for nutrition and hydration" is not considered to be life-prolonging treatment. If you would *not* want artificial nutrition and hydration, you can refuse it through the generic living will.

Revocation. You may revoke the living will at any time, either orally or in writing.

How to Fill Out the Kentucky Declaration

1. *Other instructions.* Add any personal instructions you wish, such as the name of your health-care agent and whether you also have a generic living will. Indicate any particular treatment you do not want.
2. *Witnessing Requirements.* You must have two adult witnesses, who may *not* be

   a. A blood relative who would be your beneficiary.
   b. Anyone else who would inherit from you under Kentucky law.
   c. An employee of a health-care facility in which you are a patient.
   d. Your attending physician.
   e. Any person directly financially responsible for your health care.

How to Use the Kentucky Designation of Health Care Surrogate Form

Read the instructions and the document carefully. Your health-care surrogate will have the power to consent to or withdraw consent for any medical procedure, treatment, or intervention, with some limitations. Be sure to print your name.

Naming Your Health Care Surrogate

a. Print the name(s), address(es), and telephone number(s) of your agent and any alternate agent(s) you wish to appoint. Alternates are advisable in case your first choice agent is not available when decisions must be made.

b. You may designate more than one person to make decisions for you, but if more than one person is serving at the same time, all decisions must be by unanimous consent. It is preferable to name one person at a time, because sometimes one of your surrogates will be unavailable.

c. You may not name as your agent an employee, owner, director, or officer of a health-care facility where you are a resident, unless that person is a relative.

d. You can have your document witnessed by either two adult witnesses *or* a notary public. If you choose witnesses, make sure both of your witnesses are present when you sign and date the document. If you choose a notary, sign the document in the presence of the notary.

Your surrogate can make almost all health-care decisions for you, in accordance with accepted medical practice. Your decisionmaker must consider the attending physician's recommendation, the decision you would want made, and the decision that would be in your best interests.

Note that a decision to withhold or withdraw nutrition and hydration is only allowed if inevitable death is imminent or if artificial feeding cannot be physically assimilated or the burden of providing artificial nutrition and hydration outweighs its benefits.

DECLARATION

Declaration made this _____ day of _____ (month, year).

I, _____, willfully and voluntarily make known my desire that my dying shall not be artificially prolonged under the circumstances set forth below, and do hereby declare:

If at any time I should have a terminal condition and my attending and one (1) other physician, in their discretion, have determined such condition is incurable and irreversible and will result in death within a relatively short time, and where the application of life-prolonging treatment would serve only to artificially prolong the dying process, I direct that such treatment be withheld or withdrawn, and that I be permitted to die naturally with only the administration of medication or the performance of any medical treatment deemed necessary to alleviate pain or for nutrition or hydration.

Other instructions:

In the absence of my ability to give directions regarding the use of such life-prolonging treatment, it is my intention that this declaration shall be honored by my attending physician and my family as the final expression of my legal right to refuse medical or surgical treatment, and I accept the consequences of such refusal.

If I have been diagnosed as pregnant and that diagnosis is known to my attending physician, this directive shall have no force or effect during the course of my pregnancy.

I understand the full import of this declaration and I am emotionally and mentally competent to make this declaration.

STATE OF KENTUCKY   )
) Sct.

COUNTY OF   )

Before me, the undersigned authority, on this day personally appeared _____

_____, Living Will Declarant, and _____

and _____, known to me to be witnesses whose names are each signed to the foregoing instrument, and all these persons being first duly sworn,

_____, Living Will Declarant, declared to me and to the witnesses in my presence that the instrument is the Living Will Declaration of the Declarant and that the Declarant has willingly signed, and that such Declarant executed it as a free and voluntary act for the purposes therein expressed; and each of the witnesses stated to me, in the presence and hearing of the Living Will Declarant, that the declarant signed the Declaration as witness and to the best of such witness' knowledge, the Living Will Declarant was eighteen (18) years of age or over, of sound mind and under no constraint or undue influence.

Living Will Declarant: _____

Witness: _____

Address: _____

Witness: _____

Address: _____

Subscribed, sworn to and acknowledged before me by _____,

Living Will Declarant, and subscribed and sworn to before me by _____

and _____, witnesses, on this the _____ day of _____.
                                                             (month, year)

Notary Public State at Large _____

Date my commission expires: _____

KENTUCKY

DESIGNATION OF HEALTH CARE SURROGATE

I designate _____ as
my health care surrogate(s) to make any health care decisions for me when I no longer have decisional capacity.
If _____ refuses or is not
able to act for me, I designate _____ as
my health care surrogate(s).

Any prior designation is revoked.

Signed this _____ day of _____, 19_____.

Signature and address of the grantor:

_____

_____

In our joint presence, the grantor, who is of sound mind and eighteen years of age or older, voluntarily dated and signed this writing or directed it to be dated and signed for the grantor.

Signature and address of the witnesses:

_____   _____

_____   _____

— OR —

STATE OF KENTUCKY)
)
COUNTY OF)

Before me, the undersigned authority, came the grantor who is of sound mind and eighteen (18) years of age or older, and acknowledged that he voluntarily dated and signed this writing or directed it to be dated and signed as above.

Done this _____ day of _____, 19_____.

Signature of Notary Public or other person authorized to administer oaths:

_____

Date commission expires:_____

Louisiana Life-Sustaining Procedures Act

Louisiana's Life-Sustaining Procedures Act recognizes your right as an adult to make a declaration instructing your physician to withhold or withdraw life-sustaining procedures in the event you are in a terminal and irreversible condition or a continual profound comatose state with no reasonable chance of recovery, as diagnosed by two physicians.

The form shown here complies with the suggested declaration form given in the statute. You may, if you wish, add personalized directions, and we have provided space for these. You may wish to list the particular treatments to be withheld or withdrawn—for example, cardiopulmonary resuscitation or artificial feeding. The right to name a proxy is specified in the statute. Although a proxy designation clause is not contained in the act's suggested declaration, we have added it to the document in case you want to make use of it. We strongly recommend that you do, if you have someone you trust to act on your behalf.

Your declaration must be signed in the presence of *two adult witnesses, neither of whom may be entitled to any part of your estate on your death.*

Properly signed and witnessed, your declaration will remain in effect until or unless you revoke it. To protect yourself as fully as possible against unwanted treatment, the Society for the Right to Die advises that you execute the Louisiana declaration and the generic living will. The generic living will can apply to situations that may not fit the Louisiana definition of terminal and irreversible condition.

DECLARATION

Declaration made this _____ day of _____(month, year).

I, _____, being of sound mind, willfully and volun-
tarily make known my desire that my dying shall not be artificially prolonged under the circumstances set forth
below and do hereby declare:

If at any time I should have an incurable injury, disease, or illness certified to be a terminal and irreversible
condition, or a continual profound comatose state with no reasonable chance of recovery, by two physicians who
have personally examined me, one of whom shall be my attending physician, and the physicians have determined
that the application of life-sustaining procedures would serve only to prolong artificially the dying process, I direct
that such procedures be withheld or withdrawn, and that I be permitted to die naturally with only the administration
of medication or the performance of any medical procedures deemed necessary to provide me with comfort care.

Other directions:

In the absence of my ability to give directions regarding the use of such life-sustaining procedures, it is my
intention that this declaration shall be honored by my family and physician(s) as the final expression of my legal
right to refuse medical or surgical treatment and accept the consequences from such refusal.

I understand the full import of this declaration and I am emotionally and mentally competent to make this
declaration.

Designation Clause*

I, _____, authorize

_____, residing

at _____,
to make treatment decisions on my behalf should I be (1) diagnosed as suffering from
a terminal condition or (2) comatose, incompetent or otherwise mentally or physically
incapable of communication. I have discussed my desires concerning terminal care
with this person, and I trust his/her judgment on my behalf. I understand that if I have
not filled in any name in this clause, my declaration will nevertheless be given effect
should the appropriate circumstances arise.

Signed _____

City, Parish and State of Residence _____

The declarant has been personally known to me and I believe him or her to be of sound mind.

Witness _____

Witness _____

*Designation of a proxy is an optional provision in Louisiana's Life-Sustaining Procedures Act, Section
1299.58.3, which does not specify its form. Wording of the clause is suggested by the Society for the Right to
Die. If you choose not to use the Designation Clause, it is advisable to draw a line through it.

The Maine Uniform Rights of the Terminally Ill Act and the Living Will

The Maine Uniform Rights of the Terminally Ill Act recognizes your right to fill out a declaration setting out your wishes about medical treatment in the event of a terminal condition. It also allows you to appoint another person (known as your health-care agent) to make decisions on your behalf to withhold or withdraw medical treatment in the event you are in a terminal condition and cannot make or express such decisions yourself. We suggest that you fill out both declarations if you have someone whom you trust as an agent and who is available to make such decisions for you. Your documents must be witnessed by two adults, who must sign their names and write their addresses. Maine law does not have any restrictions on who may serve as your witnesses.

If you have personal wishes that are not covered by the Maine declaration, be sure also to fill out the generic living will (Chapter 3) and specify your personal instructions.

When Your Maine Declaration Becomes Effective. Your declaration will only be honored if you are no longer able to make or express decisions about life support and you are in a terminal condition, which Maine law defines as "an incurable and irreversible condition that, without the administration of life-sustaining treatment, will . . . result in death within a relatively short time." This definition should cover conditions such as senile dementia, advanced Alzheimer's, or permanent unconsciousness. However, if you would not want to be sustained in those situations, you should make your preferences clear by stating your views in the space provided on the Maine declaration, and also by filling out a generic living will.

The Treatments Covered. The Maine declaration applies to life-sustaining treatment that would serve only to prolong the process of dying. The law states that *if you want to reject artificially administered nutrition and hydration you must indicate your wishes in writing.* The form contains an optional provision allowing you to do this.

The Health-Care Provider's Responsibility. It is your responsibility (or that of your spokesperson) to let your physician know that you have completed a declaration (and a living will, if applicable). Your physician must make the copies part of your medical record. Health-care providers who honor declarations are protected from charges of unprofessional conduct, or civil or criminal liability. If a health-care provider is unwilling to honor a declaration, the patient or spokesperson must be promptly told. The physician must then take all reasonable steps as promptly as practicable to transfer the patient to the care of someone who would be willing to honor the declaration.

Revocation. You may revoke the declaration and/or the living will at any time.

Other Information. Maine law also allows certain relatives to make decisions for patients in a terminal condition who have not documented their wishes, but *artificially administered nutrition and hydration cannot be refused or stopped without a written directive from the patient.*

The making of a declaration does not affect your life insurance policy.

MAINE

DECLARATION

If I should have an incurable and irreversible condition that, without the administration of life-sustaining treatment, will, in the opinion of my attending physician, cause my death within a relatively short time, and I am no longer able to make or communicate decisions regarding my medical treatment, I direct my attending physician, pursuant to the Uniform Rights of the Terminally Ill Act of this State, to withhold or withdraw such treatment that only prolongs the process of dying and is not necessary for my comfort or to alleviate pain.

> **OPTIONAL:** I direct my attending physician to withhold or withdraw artificially administered nutrition and hydration which only prolongs the process of dying.
>
> Signature _____
>
> **NOTE:** This optional provision must be signed to be effective.

Special instructions:

Signed this _____ day of _____, 19_____.

Signature _____

Address _____

The declarant voluntarily signed this writing in my presence.

Witness _____

Address _____

Witness _____

Address _____

> **NOTE:** Maine law provides that artificially administered nutrition and hydration does not constitute a life-sustaining treatment that may be withheld or withdrawn pursuant to a living will declaration **unless the declarant elects otherwise in the declaration itself.**

DECLARATION
APPOINTING A DECISIONMAKER

If I should have an incurable and irreversible condition that, without the administration of life-sustaining treatment, will, in the opinion of my attending physician, cause my death within a relatively short time, and I am no longer able to make or communicate decisions regarding my medical treatment, I appoint _____ or, if he or she is not reasonably available or is unwilling to serve, _____, to make decisions on my behalf regarding withholding or withdrawal of such treatment that only prolongs the process of dying and is not necessary for my comfort or to alleviate pain, pursuant to the Uniform Rights of the Terminally Ill Act of this State.

> **OPTIONAL:** If the individual(s) I have so appointed is not reasonably available or is unwilling to serve, I direct my attending physician, pursuant to the Uniform Rights of the Terminally Ill Act of this State, to withhold or withdraw such treatment that only prolongs the process of dying and is not necessary for my comfort or to alleviate pain.
>
> Signature _____
>
> **NOTE:** This optional provision must be signed to be effective.
>
> **OPTIONAL:** I direct my attending physician to withhold or withdraw artificially administered nutrition and hydration which only prolongs the process of dying.
>
> Signature _____
>
> **NOTE:** This optional provision must be signed to be effective.

Signed this _____ day of _____, 19_____.

> Signature _____
>
> Address _____

The declarant voluntarily signed this writing in my presence.

> Witness _____
>
> Address _____
>
> Witness _____
>
> Address _____

Name and address of designee(s).

> Name _____
>
> Address _____
>
> Name _____
>
> Address _____

> **NOTE:** Maine law provides that artificially administered nutrition and hydration does not constitute a life-sustaining treatment that may be withheld or withdrawn pursuant to a living will declaration **unless the declarant elects otherwise in the declaration itself.**

Maryland's Life-Sustaining Procedures Act

Maryland's Life-Sustaining Procedures Act recognizes your right to make a declaration stating that you do not want your dying artificially prolonged by the use of life-sustaining procedures. The declaration will be given effect whenever your attending physician and one other doctor confirm that your condition is terminal. Medical procedures or interventions to provide comfort or alleviate pain cannot be withheld or withdrawn.

The form shown here complies with the suggested declaration form given in the statute. The act also permits personalized additions, and we have provided space for these. You might wish to consider listing the particular treatments to be withheld or withdrawn—for example, cardiac resuscitation or artificial feeding. An opinion by the Maryland attorney general has made it clear that you can refuse artificial feeding, but you must expressly state in your declaration that you do not want this form of treatment.

You might want to name a proxy—someone you trust to make the treatment decisions you would make if you could. You might want to emphasize your desire to be kept comfortable and pain free, even though medication might shorten your life.

Your declaration must be signed in the presence of two witnesses, neither of whom may be

1. Related to you by blood or marriage.
2. A person or employee of a person financially or otherwise responsible for your medical care.
3. A creditor, or any person entitled to any part of your estate by inheritance, or to any financial benefit as a result of your death.

Properly signed and witnessed, your declaration will remain in effect until or unless you revoke it. As long as you are able to express your preferences, your own expressed wishes always supersede your declaration.

The Maryland attorney general has indicated that durable powers of attorney can be used to direct an agent to carry out specific directives concerning specific medical treatments, including the withholding or withdrawing of artificial feeding or the agent can be empowered to make all medical decisions. A Maryland Durable Power of Attorney for Medical Treatment form is shown here. We have left space in the form for your personal wishes if you choose to include them. Please read the form and witnessing requirements carefully before you gather witnesses together and sign it.

MARYLAND

DECLARATION

Declaration made this _____ day of _____ *(month, year)*.

I, _____, being of sound mind, willfully and voluntarily direct that my dying shall not be artificially prolonged under the circumstances set forth in this declaration.

If at any time I should have an incurable injury, disease, or illness certified to be a terminal condition by two (2) physicians who have personally examined me, one (1) of whom shall be my attending physician, and the physicians have determined that my death is imminent and will occur whether or not life-sustaining procedures are utilized and where the application of such procedures would serve only to artificially prolong the dying process, I direct that such procedures be withheld or withdrawn, and that I be permitted to die naturally with only the administration of medication, the administration of food and water, and the performance of any medical procedure that is necessary to provide comfort care or alleviate pain. In the absence of my ability to give directions regarding the use of such life-sustaining procedures, it is my intention that this declaration shall be honored by my family and physician(s) as the final expression of my right to control my medical care and treatment.

Other instructions :

I am legally competent to make this declaration, and I understand its full import.

Signed _____

Address _____

Under penalty of perjury, we state that this declaration was signed by

_____ in the presence of the undersigned who, at his/her request, in his/her presence, and in the presence of each other, have hereunto signed our names and witnessed this _____ day of _____, 19_____. Further each of us, individually, states that: The declarant is known to me, and I believe the declarant to be of sound mind. I did not sign the declarant's signature to this declaration. Based upon information and belief, I am not related to the declarant by blood or marriage, a creditor of the declarant, entitled to any portion of the estate of the declarant under any existing testamentary instrument of the declarant, entitled to any financial benefit by reason of the death of the declarant, financially or otherwise responsible for the declarant's medical care, or an employee of any such person or institution.

_____ Address _____

_____ Address _____

DURABLE POWER OF ATTORNEY FOR MEDICAL TREATMENT

> **INFORMATION ABOUT THIS DOCUMENT**
> This is an important legal document. Before signing this document, it is vital for you to know and understand these facts:
> This document gives the person you name as your agent the power to make health care decisions for you if you can't make decisions for yourself. Even after you have signed this document, you have the right to make health care decisions for yourself so long as you are able to do so. Your agent will be able to make decisions for you only after two physicians have certified that you are incapable of making them yourself. You have the right to revoke (take away) the authority of your agent by notifying your agent or your health care provider orally or in writing of this desire.

I, _____,
　　　　　　　　　　　　　　　　　　　　(your name)

hereby appoint: _____
　　　　　　　　　　　　　　　　　　(agent's name)

_____
　　　　　　　　　　(agent's address and telephone)

as my agent to make health care decisions for me if and when I am unable to make my own health care decisions. This gives my agent the power to consent to giving, withholding or stopping any health care, treatment (including life-sustaining treatment), service, or diagnostic procedure. I specifically authorize my agent to make decisions for me about artificially supplied nutrition and hydration (tube feeding). My agent also has the authority to talk with health care personnel, get information, and sign forms necessary to carry out those decisions.

If the person named as my agent is not available or is unable to act as my agent, then I appoint the following person(s) to serve in the order listed below:

1. _____
　　　　　　　　　　　　　　(agent's name)

_____
　　　　　　　　　　　(address and telephone)

2. _____
　　　　　　　　　　　　　　(agent's name)

_____
　　　　　　　　　　　(address and telephone)

By this document I intend to create a power of attorney for health care which shall take effect upon my incapacity to make my own health care decisions and shall continue during that incapacity.

I have discussed my wishes with my agent, and he or she shall make all health care decisions on my behalf, including decisions to withhold or withdraw all forms of life-sustaining treatment, including artificially administered hydration and nutrition.

My particular wishes are:

_____

_____

_____

_____

_____

_____

_____

BY SIGNING HERE I INDICATE THAT I UNDERSTAND THE PURPOSE OF THIS DOCUMENT

I sign my name to this form on _____
　　　　　　　　　　　　　　　　　　　　(date)

at: _____
　　　　　　　　　　　　　　(address)

_____
　　　　　　　　　　(You sign here)

WITNESSES

I declare that the person who signed or acknowledged this document is personally known to me, that he/she signed or acknowledged this durable power of attorney in my presence, and that he/she appears to be of sound mind and under no duress, fraud, or undue influence. I am not the person appointed as agent by this document, nor am I the patient's health care provider, or an employee of the patient's health care provider.

I further declare that I am not related to the patient by blood, marriage, or adoption, and, to the best of my knowledge, I am not entitled to any part of his/her estate under a will now existing or by operation of law.

FIRST WITNESS　　　　　　　　　　**SECOND WITNESS**

Signature: _____　　Signature: _____

Home Address: _____　　Home Address: _____

Print Name: _____　　Print Name: _____

Date: _____　　Date: _____

The Massachusetts Health Care Proxy by Individuals Act and the Living Will

Massachusetts has enacted a statute that permits any competent adult (eighteen years or older) to execute a Health Care Proxy. This document lets you express your instructions concerning your health care and designate an individual (known as your "health-care agent" or "proxy") to carry out your desires in the event you are unable to make or express health-care decisions. You still retain the right to consent to or refuse treatment, for as long as you are able.

To protect yourself as fully as possible against unwanted treatment, the Society for the Right to Die advises that you execute both the Massachusetts Health Care Proxy, drafted by a Task Force of Massachusetts organizations, and the generic living will (Chapter 3). The living will lets you state your wishes about medical care in the event of an incurable or irreversible mental or physical condition with no reasonable expectation of recovery, and it includes space for you to add personal instructions—for example, about specific treatments that you would want to refuse or to receive, such as tube feeding or cardiopulmonary resuscitation. *If you do not have anyone to appoint as your agent, it is important for you to use the generic living will in order to document your preferences about life support.*

MASSACHUSETTS HEALTH CARE PROXY

1 I, _____ , residing at

(Principal -- PRINT your name)

_____
(Street)   (City or Town)   (State)

appoint as my **Health Care Agent**: _____
(Name of person you choose as Agent)

of _____
(Street)   (City/town)   (State)   (Phone)

(OPTIONAL: If my Agent is unwilling or unable to serve, then I appoint as my **Alternate**:

_____ , of
(Name of person you choose as Alternate)

_____ .)
(Street)   (City/town)   (State)   (Phone)

2 My Agent shall have the authority to make all health care decisions for me, including decisions about life-sustaining treatment, subject to any limitations I state below, if I am unable to make health care decisions myself. My Agent's authority becomes effective if my attending physician determines in writing that I lack the capacity to make or to communicate health care decisions. My Agent is then to have the same authority to make health care decisions as I would if I had the capacity to make them **EXCEPT** (here list the limitations, if any, you wish to place on your Agent's authority):

I direct my Agent to make health care decisions based on my Agent's assessment of my personal wishes. If my personal wishes are unknown, my Agent is to make health care decisions based on my Agent's assessment of my best interests. Photocopies of this Health Care Proxy shall have the same force and effect as the original.

3   Signed:_____

Complete only if Principal is physically unable to sign: I have signed the Principal's name above at his/her direction in the presence of the Principal and two witnesses.

_____   _____
(Name)   (Street)

                                        _____
                                         (City/town)   (State)

4 **WITNESS STATEMENT:** We, the undersigned, each witnessed the signing of this Health Care Proxy by the Principal or at the direction of the Principal and state that the Principal appears to be at least 18 years of age, of sound mind and under no constraint or undue influence. Neither of us is named as the Health Care Agent or Alternate in this document. In our presence this _____ day of _____ , 199___.

Witness #1 _____   Witness #2 _____
(Signature)   (Signature)

Name (print) _____   Name (print) _____

Address: _____   Address: _____

_____   _____

Health Care Agent: I have been named by the Principal as the Principal's **Health Care Agent** by this Health Care Proxy. I have read this document carefully, and have personally discussed with the Principal his/her health care wishes at a time of possible incapacity. I know the Principal and accept this appointment freely. I am not an operator, administrator or employee of a hospital, clinic, nursing home, rest home, Soldiers Home or other health facility where the Principal is presently a patient or resident or has applied for admission. Or if I am a person so described, I am also related to the Principal by blood, marriage, or adoption. If called upon and to the best of my ability, I will try to carry out the Principal's wishes.

(Signature of **Health Care Agent**) _____

Alternate: I have been named by the Principal as the Principal's **Alternate** by this Health Care Proxy. I have read this document carefully, and have personally discussed with the Principal his/her health care wishes at a time of possible incapacity. I know the Principal and accept this appointment freely. I am not an operator, administrator or employee of a hospital, clinic, nursing home, rest home, Soldiers Home or other health facility where the Principal is presently a patient or resident or has applied for admission. Or if I am a person so described, I am also related to the Principal by blood, marriage, or adoption. If called upon and to the best of my ability, I will try to carry out the Principal's wishes.

(Signature of **Alternate**) _____

✶   ✶   ✶   ✶   ✶

Model Health Care Proxy form developed by a Task Force of the following organizations:

Boston University Schools of Medicine and Public Health:
   Law, Medicine, and Ethics Program
Hospice Federation of Massachusetts
Massachusetts Bar Association
Massachusetts Department of Public Health
Massachusetts Executive Office of Elder Affairs
Massachusetts Federation of Nursing Homes
Massachusetts Health Decisions
Massachusetts Hospital Association

Massachusetts Medical Society
Massachusetts Nurses Association
Medical Center of Central Massachusetts
Deaconess Hospital ElderCare Program
Suffolk University Law School:
   Elder Law Clinic
University of Massachusetts at Boston:
   The Gerontology Institute
Visiting Nurse Associations of Massachusetts

For quantity orders, please write:
Massachusetts Health Decisions, Publications, PO Box 417, Sharon, MA 02067-0417

Michigan Designation of Patient Advocate for Health Care

Michigan does not have a specific living will form. We recommend that you use the generic living will outlined in Chapter 3. Michigan *does* have a Patient Advocate for Health Care form, however. Although some specific instructions for filling out this form follow, we suggest that you review Chapter 3 for more general information about durable powers of attorney for health care.

Print the name(s), address(es) and telephone number(s) of your patient advocate and any successor advocate(s) you wish to appoint. Successor advocates are advisable in case your first choice advocate is not available when decisions must be made.

Your document must be witnessed by two individuals. Your witnesses must be at least eighteen years of age. Your witnesses must not be any of the following:

1. Your spouse.
2. Your parent.
3. Your child.
4. Your grandchild.
5. Your sibling.
6. Your physician.
7. A person who might inherit property from you.
8. A beneficiary of your will.
9. Your patient advocate.
10. An employee of your life or health insurer.
11. An employee of a health facility treating you.
12. An employee of a home for the aged treating you.

Before acting as a patient advocate, your proposed patient advocate and successor advocate must sign an acceptance to your designation of patient advocate. Your patient advocate and successor advocate should sign the acceptance as soon as possible after or at the same time that you sign the designation of patient advocate. Keep your designation of patient advocate and the advocate acceptance statement together and make them part of your medical record.

MICHIGAN

DESIGNATION OF PATIENT ADVOCATE FOR HEALTH CARE

I, _____ ,

(name and home address)

am of sound mind, and I voluntarily make this designation.

I designate _____ , residing at _____

_____ ,

(address and phone number)

as my patient advocate to make care, custody, or medical treatment decisions for me only when I become unable to participate in medical treatment decisions. The determination of when I am unable to participate in medical treatment decisions shall be made by my attending physician and another physician or licensed psychologist.

If the first individual is unable, unwilling, or unavailable to serve as my patient advocate, then I designate _____ , residing at _____

_____ ,

(address and phone number of successor)

to serve as my patient advocate.

I authorize my patient advocate to decide to withhold or withdraw medical treatment which could or would allow me to die. I am fully aware that such a decision could or would lead to my death.

In making decisions for me, my patient advocate shall be guided by my wishes, whether expressed orally, in a living will, or in this designation. If my wishes as to a particular situation have not been expressed, my patient advocate shall be guided by his or her best judgment of my probable decision, given the benefits, burdens and consequences of the decision, even if my death, or the chance of my death, is one consequence.

My patient advocate shall have the same authority to make care, custody and medical treatment decisions as I would if I had the capacity to make them EXCEPT *(here list the limitations, if any, you wish to place on your patient advocate's authority)*:

_____

_____

_____

This designation of patient advocate shall not be affected by my disability or incapacity. This designation of patient advocate is governed by Michigan law, although I request that it be honored in any state in which I may be found. I reserve the power to revoke this designation at any time by communicating my intent to revoke it in any manner in which I am able to communicate.

Photostatic copies of this document, after it is signed and witnessed, shall have the same legal force as the original document.

I voluntarily sign this designation of patient advocate after careful consideration. I accept its meaning and I accept its consequences.

_____
(your signature)

_____
(your street address)

_____
(city, Michigan, zip code)

_____
(date)

Notice Regarding Witnesses

You must have two adult witnesses who should be disinterested individuals and should not be your spouse, parent, child, grandchild, sibling, a person who might inherit property from you or a beneficiary of your will at the time of the witnessing, physician, patient advocate, an employee of your life or health insurance provider, an employee of a health facility that is treating you, or an employee of a home for the aged in which you reside.

Statement of Witnesses

We sign below as witnesses. This designation was signed in our presence. The designator appears to be of sound mind, and to be making this designation voluntarily, and under no duress, fraud, or undue influence.

Witness 1   Signature: _____

_____
(print or type full name)

Address: _____

Witness 2   Signature: _____

_____
(print or type full name)

Address: _____

Acceptance by Patient Advocate and Successor Advocate (If Any)

(A) This designation shall not become effective unless the patient is unable to participate in treatment decisions.

(B) A patient advocate shall not exercise powers concerning the patient's care, custody and medical treatment that the patient, if the patient were able to participate in the decision, could not have exercised on his or her own behalf.

(C) This designation cannot be used to make a medical treatment decision to withhold or withdraw treatment from a patient who is pregnant that would result in the pregnant patient's death.

(D) A patient advocate may make a decision to withhold or withdraw treatment which would allow a patient to die only if the patient has expressed in a clear and convincing manner that the patient advocate is authorized to make such a decision, and that the patient acknowledges that such a decision could or would allow the patient's death.

(E) A patient advocate shall not receive compensation for the performance of his or her authority, rights, and responsibilities, but a patient advocate may be reimbursed for actual and necessary expenses incurred in the performance of his or her authority, rights, and responsibilities.

(F) A patient advocate shall act in accordance with the standards of care applicable to fiduciaries when acting for the patient and shall act consistent with the patient's best interests. The known desires of the patient expressed or evidenced while the patient is able to participate in medical treatment decisions are presumed to be in the patient's best interests.

(G) A patient may revoke his or her designation at any time or in any manner sufficient to communicate an intent to revoke.

(H) A patient advocate may revoke his or her acceptance to the designation at any time and in any manner sufficient to communicate an intent to revoke.

(I) A patient admitted to a health facility or agency has the rights enumerated in Section 20201 of the Public Health Code, Act No. 368 of the Public Acts of 1978, being section 333.20201 of the Michigan Compiled Laws.

I understand the above conditions and I accept the designation as patient advocate for _____
_____.

Dated: _____   Signed: _____

I understand the above conditions and I accept the designation as successor patient advocate for _____
_____.

Dated: _____   Signed: _____

Minnesota Adult Health Care Decisions Act

The Minnesota Adult Health Care Decisions Act recognizes your right to make a declaration stating that you do not want your dying to be artificially prolonged by the use of life-sustaining procedures. By stating your preferences regarding health-care decisions in this document, or by appointing a proxy to make these decisions on your behalf, your desires can be respected and followed even when you are no longer able to express them.

Your declaration becomes effective when you are diagnosed as in a terminal condition and become unable to participate in decisions regarding your health care.

The document shown here complies with the statutory form. In the spaces provided, you can state your personal instructions about the treatment you do and do not want and the circumstances in which the declaration is to apply. The law says you must specifically write in your wishes about the artificial administration of nutrition and hydration. If you do not want to receive artificially administered nutrition and hydration, you *must* state this in section (6). As an alternative, you can also state in section (6) that you wish your proxy, if you appoint one, to make decisions regarding the artificial administration of nutrition and hydration.

To be valid, your declaration must be signed in the presence of two witnesses or a notary public. Neither of the witnesses may be someone entitled to any part of your estate, and neither the witnesses nor the notary may be named as your proxy.

Properly signed and witnessed, your declaration will remain in effect until or unless you revoke it. As long as you are able to make treatment decisions, your own expressed wishes supersede your written statements.

MINNESOTA

Health Care Declaration

NOTICE:

This is an important legal document. Before signing this document, you should know these important facts:

(a) This document gives your health care provider or your designated proxy the power and guidance to make health care decisions according to your wishes when you are in a terminal condition and cannot do so. This document may include what kind of treatment you want or do not want and under what circumstances you want these decisions to be made. You may state where you want or do not want to receive any treatment.

(b) If you name a proxy in this document and that person agrees to serve as your proxy, that person has a duty to act consistently with your wishes. If the proxy does not know your wishes, the proxy has the duty to act in your best interests. If you do not name a proxy, your health care providers have a duty to act consistently with your instructions or tell you that they are unwilling to do so.

(c) This document will remain valid and in effect until and unless you amend or revoke it. Review this document periodically to make sure it continues to reflect your preferences. You may amend or revoke the declaration at any time by notifying your health care providers. (d) Your named proxy has the same right as you have to examine your medical records and to consent to their disclosure for purposes related to your health care or insurance unless you limit this right in this document.

(e) If there is anything in this document that you do not understand, you should ask for professional help to have it explained to you.

TO MY FAMILY, DOCTORS, AND ALL THOSE
CONCERNED WITH MY CARE:

I, _____, being an adult of sound mind, willfully and voluntarily make this statement as a directive to be followed if I am in a terminal condition and become unable to participate in decisions regarding my health care. I understand that my health care providers are legally bound to act consistently with my wishes, within the limits of reasonable medical practice and other applicable law. I also understand that I have the right to make medical and health care decisions for myself as long as I am able to do so and to revoke this declaration at any time.

(1) The following are my feelings and wishes regarding my health care (you may state the circumstances under which this declaration applies):

(2) I particularly want to have all appropriate health care that will help in the following ways (you may give instructions for care you do want):

(3) I particularly do not want the following (you may list specific treatment you do not want in certain circumstances):

(4) I particularly want to have the following kinds of life-sustaining treatment if I am diagnosed to have a terminal condition (you may list the specific types of life-sustaining treatment that you do want if you have a terminal condition):

(5) I particularly do not want the following kinds of life-sustaining treatment if I am diagnosed to have a terminal condition (you may list the specific types of life-sustaining treatment that you do not want if you have a terminal condition):

(6) I recognize that if I reject artificially administered sustenance, then I may die of dehydration or malnutrition rather than from my illness or injury. The following are my feelings and wishes regarding artificially administered sustenance should I have a terminal condition (you may indicate whether you wish to receive food and fluids given to you in some other way than by mouth if you have a terminal condition):

(7) Thoughts I feel are relevant to my instructions. (You may, but need not, give your religious beliefs, philosophy, or other personal values that you feel are important. You may also state preferences concerning the location of your care.)

(8) PROXY DESIGNATION. (If you wish, you may name someone to see that your wishes are carried out, but you do not have to do this. You may also name a proxy without including specific instructions regarding your care. If you name a proxy, you should discuss your wishes with that person.)

If I become unable to communicate my instructions, I designate the following person(s) to act on my behalf consistently with my instructions, if any, as stated in this document. Unless I write instructions that limit my proxy's authority, my proxy has full power and authority to make health care decisions for me. If a guardian or conservator of the person is to be appointed for me, I nominate my proxy named in this document to act as guardian or conservator of my person.

Name: _____

Address: _____

Phone Number: _____

Relationship: (If any) _____

If the person I have named above refuses or is unable or unavailable to act on my behalf, or if I revoke that person's authority to act as my proxy, I authorize the following person to do so:

Name: _____

Address: _____

Phone Number: _____

Relationship: (If any) _____

I understand that I have the right to revoke the appointment of the person named above to act on my behalf at any time by communicating that decision to the proxy or my health care provider.

DATE: _____

SIGNED: _____

STATE OF _____

COUNTY OF _____

Subscribed, sworn to, and acknowledged before me by

_____ on this _____ day of _____, 19_____

_____

NOTARY PUBLIC

OR

(Sign and date here in the presence of two adult witnesses, neither of whom is entitled to any part of your estate under a will or by operation of law, and neither of whom is your proxy.)

I certify that the declarant voluntarily signed this declaration in my presence and that the declarant is personally known to me. I am not named as a proxy by the declaration, and to the best of my knowledge, I am not entitled to any part of the estate of the declarant under a will or by operation of law.

Witness_____ Address_____

Witness_____ Address_____

Reminder: Keep the signed original with your personal papers. Give signed copies to your doctors, family, and proxy.

The Mississippi Declaration and the Mississippi Durable Power of Attorney for Health Care

Mississippi recognizes the right of any competent adult to make an advance declaration authorizing withdrawal of life-sustaining treatment if you are in a terminal physical condition causing severe distress or unconsciousness, and your attending physician and two other doctors agree that there is no expectation of your recovering consciousness or a state of health that is meaningful to you and that but for the use of life-sustaining mechanisms your death would be imminent.

The form shown here follows the Mississippi State Department of Health format created by the statute.

In order to be legally valid, your declaration must be filed with the Mississippi State Department of Health, Division of Public Health Statistics. Payment of a $10 filing fee is required.

Also shown is Mississippi's form for a durable power of attorney for health care, which permits you to appoint someone to make medical decisions for you, including decisions about the use of life support if at any time you become unable to make them yourself. If you have someone to appoint, the durable power of attorney for health care is particularly useful because it covers all medical decisions, not just those at the end of life. It does not have to be filed with the Mississippi State Department of Health. If you wish to use the durable power of attorney for health care, you should first review Chapter 3.

You may not name any of the following as your agent(s):

1. A treating health-care provider.
2. An employee of a treating health-care provider.

You can have your durable power of attorney for health care document witnessed by either two witnesses *or* a notary public. *If you choose witnesses,* make sure both of your witnesses are present when you sign and date the document. Neither of your witnesses may be

1. A person you named as your agent.
2. A health-care provider.
3. An employee of a health-care provider or facility.

At least one of your witnesses must be a person who is neither related to you by blood, marriage, or adoption nor entitled to inherit from you under any existing will, codicil, or by operation of law. *If you choose a notary,* sign the document in the presence of the notary.

Although Mississippi has particular requirements for its declaration (and requires filing), the Society for the Right to Die recommends that you also use the generic living will (Chapter 3), which covers a wider range of medical situations and treatments. The generic living also has space for you to add personal instructions, which cannot be added to the Mississippi declaration.

MISSISSIPPI

DECLARATION

DECLARATION made on _____ (date)

by _____ (name)

of _____ (address)

_____ (Social Security No.)

Next of kin _____

Address _____

I, _____, being of sound mind, declare that if at any time I should suffer a terminal physical condition which causes me severe distress or unconsciousness, and my physician, with the concurrence of two (2) other physicians, believes that there is no expectation of my regaining consciousness or a state of health that is meaningful to me and but for the use of life-sustaining mechanisms my death would be imminent, I desire that the mechanisms be withdrawn so that I may die naturally. However, if I have been diagnosed as pregnant and that diagnosis is known to my physician, this declaration shall have no force or effect during the course of my pregnancy. I further declare that this declaration shall be honored by my family and my physician as the final expression of my desires concerning the manner in which I die.

Other directions:

Signed _____

I hereby witness this declaration and attest that:
    (1) I personally know the Declarant and believe the Declarant to be of sound mind.
    (2) To the best of my knowledge, at the time of the execution of this declaration, I:
        (a) Am not related to the Declarant by blood or marriage.
        (b) Do not have any claim on the estate of the Declarant.
        (c) Am not entitled to any portion of the Declarant's estate by any will or by operation of law, and
        (d) Am not a physician attending the Declarant or a person employed by a physician attending the Declarant.

Witness _____

Address _____

_____ Soc. Sec. No. _____

Witness _____

Address _____

_____ Soc. Sec. No. _____

This declaration complies with Miss. Code Ann. §§ 41-41-101 to 41-41-121, signed into law April 17, 1984. The law requires that it be filed with the Mississippi State Department of Health—Public Health Statistics, PO. Box 1700, Jackson, MS 39215-1700.

MISSISSIPPI

DURABLE POWER OF ATTORNEY FOR HEALTH CARE

NOTICE TO PERSONS EXECUTING THIS DOCUMENT:

This is an important legal document. Before executing this document, you should know these important facts:

This document gives the person you designate as the attorney-in-fact (your agent) the power to make health care decisions for you. This power exists only as to those health care decisions to which you are unable to give informed consent. The attorney-in-fact must act consistently with your desires as stated in this document or otherwise made known.

Except as you otherwise specify in this document, this document gives your agent the power to consent to your doctor not giving treatment or stopping treatment necessary to keep you alive.

Notwithstanding this document, you have the right to make medical and other health care decisions for yourself so long as you can give informed consent with respect to the particular decision. In addition, no treatment may be given to you over your objection, and health care necessary to keep you alive may not be stopped or withheld if you object at the time.

The document gives your agent authority to consent, to refuse to consent or to withdraw consent to any care, treatment, service or procedure to maintain, diagnose or treat a physical or mental condition. This power is subject to any statement of your desires and any limitations that you include in this document. You may state in this document any types of treatment that you do not desire. In addition, a court can take away the power of your agent to make health care decisions for you if your agent (a) authorizes anything that is illegal, (b) acts contrary to your known desires, or (c) where your desires are not known, does anything that is clearly contrary to your best interests.

You have the right to revoke the authority of your agent by notifying your agent or your treating doctor, hospital or other health care provider in writing of the revocation.

Your agent has the right to examine your medical records and to consent to this disclosure unless you limit this right in this document.

Unless you otherwise specify in this document, this document gives your agent the power after you die to (a) authorize an autopsy, (b) donate your body or parts thereof for transplant or for educational, therapeutic or scientific purposes, and (c) direct the disposition of your remains.

If there is anything in this document that you do not understand, you should ask your lawyer to explain it to you.

This power of attorney will not be valid for making health care decisions unless it is either (a) signed by two (2) qualified adult witnesses who are personally known to you and who are present when you sign or acknowledge your signature or (b) acknowledged before a notary public in the state.

1)   I, _____,

(Name of principal)

of _____

(Address)

hereby appoint _____

(Name of attorney-in-fact)

of _____

(Address and telephone of attorney-in-fact)

as my attorney-in-fact to express and carry out my specific and general instructions and desires with respect to medical treatment.

2)   In the event the person I appoint above is unable, unwilling or unavailable to act as my health care agent, I hereby appoint _____

(Name of alternate attorney-in-fact)

of _____.

(Address and telephone of alternate attorney-in-fact) .

3)   I have discussed my wishes with my attorney-in-fact and my alternate attorney-in-fact, and authorize him/her to make all and any health care decisions for me, including decisions to with-hold or withdraw any form of life support. I expressly authorize my agent (and alternate agent) to make decisions for me about tube feeding and medication. Other specific instructions:

4)   This power of attorney becomes effective when I can no longer make my own medical deci-sions and shall not be affected by subsequent disability or incompetence. The determination of whether I can make my own medical decisions is to be made by my attorney-in-fact, or if he or she is unable, unwilling or unavailable to act, by my alternate attorney-in-fact.

IN WITNESS WHEREOF, I have set my hand this _____ day of _____, 19____.

_____

(Signature of principal)

"I declare under penalty of perjury under the laws of Mississippi that the principal is personally known to me, that the principal signed or acknowledged this durable power of attorney in my presence, that the principal appears to be of sound mind and under no duress, fraud or undue influence, that I am not the person appointed as attorney in fact by this document, and that I am not a health care provider, nor an employee of a health care provider or facility."

_____
(First witness' signature)

_____
(First witness' name and address)

_____
(Second witness' signature)

_____
(Second witness' name and address)

"I further declare under penalty of perjury under the laws of Mississippi that I am not related to the principal by blood, marriage, or adoption, and to the best of my knowledge, I am not entitled to any part of the estate of the principal upon the death of the principal under a will now existing or by operation of law."

_____
(Signature of first or second witness)

– OR –

State of Mississippi   )
)
County of   )

On this _____ day of _____, in the year 19____, before me,

_____, personally appeared
(insert name of notary public)

_____, personally known to me (or proved
(insert name of principal)

to me on the basis of satisfactory evidence) to be the person whose name is subscribed to this instrument, and acknowledged that he or she executed it. I declare under the penalty of perjury that the person whose name is subscribed to this instrument appears to be of sound mind and under no duress, fraud or undue influence.

(NOTARY SEAL)

_____
(Signature of notary public)

Missouri Life Support Declarations Act

The Missouri Life Support Declarations Act recognizes your right as an adult to make a declaration stating that you do not want your dying artificially prolonged by the use of "death-prolonging procedures." The declaration takes effect if or when your attending physician has certified in writing that your condition is terminal, and that with or without such procedures, your death will occur "within a short time."

The form shown here complies with the suggested declaration form given in the statute. You may, if you wish, add personalized directions, and we have provided space for these. You might wish to consider listing the particular treatments to be withheld or withdrawn—for example, cardiac resuscitation or surgery. If you are also opposed to being artificially fed in a terminal condition, add this to your list of unwanted treatment. Unfortunately, there is language in the Missouri act that would appear to mandate the administration of nutrition and hydration. Your best course nevertheless is to specify your refusal of it if that is your preference. You may also want to name a proxy—someone you trust to make treatment decisions on your behalf.

Your declaration must be signed in the presence of two witnesses who are at least eighteen years old.

Properly signed and witnessed, your declaration will remain in effect until or unless you revoke it. As long as you are competent, your own expressed wishes always supersede your declaration. To protect yourself as fully as possible against unwanted medical treatment, the Society for the Right to Die advises that you execute both the Missouri declaration and the generic living will (Chapter 3).

Note: On May 17, 1991, Missouri passed a durable power of attorney for health care that was not available as this book went to press. Please contact the Society for the Right to Die to obtain the new document.

DECLARATION

I have the primary right to make my own decisions concerning treatment that might unduly prolong the dying process. By this declaration I express to my physician, family and friends my intent. If I should have a terminal condition it is my desire that my dying not be prolonged by administration of death-prolonging procedures. If my condition is terminal and I am unable to participate in decisions regarding my medical treatment, I direct my attending physician to withhold or withdraw medical procedures that merely prolong the dying process and are not necessary to my comfort or to alleviate pain. It is not my intent to authorize affirmative or deliberate acts or omissions to shorten my life rather only to permit the natural process of dying.

Other instructions:

Signed this _____ day of _____, _____.

Signature _____

City, County and State of Residence _____

The declarant is known to me, is eighteen years of age or older, of sound mind and voluntarily signed this document in my presence.

Witness _____

Address _____

Witness _____

Address _____

REVOCATION PROVISION

I hereby revoke the above declaration.

Signed _____
(Signature of Declarant)

Date _____.

The Montana Rights of the Terminally Ill Act

Montana recognizes the legal right of any adult to make a declaration instructing his or her physician to withhold or withdraw life-sustaining procedures in the event of a terminal condition. You may also designate someone to make decisions about life-sustaining treatment for you if you are in a terminal condition and lose the ability to make such decisions yourself.

The document shown has both statutory forms on it. One is to be used if you have someone to designate as your decision maker (that person will be known as your designee, or agent); the other is to be used if you are *not* designating anyone. If you have someone to name as your designee whom you trust and who is willing to serve in that capacity, we recommend that option.

We have provided space on the forms for you to write in any personal instructions you may have—for example, to specify particular treatments that you may wish to refuse or to receive, such as tube feeding, cardiopulmonary resuscitation, or a respirator.

It is important that you understand some of the specific provisions of this statute:

1. Your declaration must be signed and dated by you (or if you are physically unable to sign, by someone else at your direction) in the presence of two adult witnesses. There are no restrictions on who may act as a witness, but we recommend that you *do not* use your agent as a witness.
2. It is your responsibility to notify your physician or health-care provider about your declaration and to provide a photocopy of the completed form for your medical records.
3. A declaration is not effective during pregnancy, as long as it is probable that the fetus will develop to the point of a live birth with the continued application of life-sustaining treatment.
4. You may revoke your declaration at any time and in any manner. Revocation becomes effective when it is communicated to your attending physician or health-care provider, by you or by a witness to the revocation.
5. Death resulting from withholding or withdrawal of life-sustaining procedures pursuant to a declaration is not considered suicide or homicide.
6. Your declaration does not in any way affect the issuance or continuation of your life insurance.

DECLARATION WITH APPOINTMENT OF AGENT

(fill out Declaration on reverse side if you have no one to appoint)

If I should have an incurable or irreversible condition that, without the administration of life-sustaining treatment, will, in the opinion of my attending physician, cause my death within a relatively short time and I am no longer able to make decisions regarding my medical treatment, I appoint _____ or, if he or she is not reasonably available or is unwilling to serve, _____, to make decisions on my behalf regarding withholding or withdrawal of treatment that only prolongs the process of dying and is not necessary for my comfort or to alleviate pain, pursuant to the Montana Rights of the Terminally Ill Act.

If the individual I have appointed is not reasonably available or is unwilling to serve, I direct my attending physician, pursuant to the Montana Rights of the Terminally Ill Act, to withhold or withdraw treatment that only prolongs the process of dying and is not necessary for my comfort or to alleviate pain.

Signed this _____ day of _____, _____.

Signature _____

City, County, and State of Residence _____

The declarant voluntarily signed this document in my presence.

Witness _____

Address _____

Witness _____

Address _____

Name and address of designee (agent).

Name _____

Address _____

DECLARATION

(fill out Declaration on reverse side if you have an agent to appoint)

If I should have an incurable or irreversible condition that, without the administration of life-sustaining treatment, will, in the opinion of my attending physician, cause my death within a relatively short time and I am no longer able to make decisions regarding my medical treatment, I direct my attending physician, pursuant to the Montana Rights of the Terminally Ill Act, to withhold or withdraw treatment that only prolongs the process of dying and is not necessary to my comfort or to alleviate pain.

Signed this _____ day of _____, _____.

Signature _____

City, County, and State of Residence _____

The declarant voluntarily signed this document in my presence.

Witness _____

Address _____

Witness _____

Address _____

Nebraska Living Will and Durable Power of Attorney

Nebraska does not have a specific living will form. We recommend that you use the generic living will outlined in Chapter 3. The Nebraska Durable Power of Attorney Statute makes no mention of medical decisions, and, therefore, is not reprinted. If you want to fill out a durable power of attorney for health care, consult a local attorney.

Directive to Physicians Authorized by the Nevada Withholding or Withdrawal of Life-Sustaining Procedures Act

The Directive to Physicians shown here is a legal form authorized by the state of Nevada allowing any adult to make a written directive instructing his or her physician to withhold or withdraw procedures that serve only to prolong dying. Nevada also has a Durable Power of Attorney for Health Care Decisions form, which can provide you with additional protection.

Although your directive must be "substantially" in the form included in the law, it may include additional directions, and we have provided space for these. You may want to consider listing the particular treatments to be withheld or withdrawn—for example, "I especially do not want surgery, cardiac resuscitation, a respirator, antibiotics, artificially administered nutrition and hydration." You may want to emphasize your desire to be kept comfortable and pain free, even though medication might shorten your life.

Your directive must be witnessed by two people. A witness may *not* be

1. Anyone related to you by blood or marriage.
2. Anyone who has a claim against your estate.
3. Your doctor or any of your doctor's employees.

If you are a patient in a hospital or other health-care facility when you sign the directive, employees of the facility *cannot* act as witnesses.

In the event that you are in a terminal condition and also incompetent or otherwise unable to communicate with your physician, the physician will give weight to your directive, but may also consider other factors in determining whether circumstances warrant following these directions.

Properly signed and witnessed, your declaration will remain valid until or unless you revoke it. Your own expressed wishes always supersede your directive.

Nevada's Durable Power of Attorney for Health Care Decisions permits you to appoint a person the law calls an "attorney-in-fact" specifically authorized to make medical treatment decisions on your behalf in the event you lack the capacity to make and communicate such decisions for yourself. Because the requirements regarding the power of attorney are all spelled out in accordance with the statute, there is no necessity for you to consult a lawyer in order to execute the form.

NEVADA

DIRECTIVE TO PHYSICIANS

Date _____

I, _____, being of sound mind, intentionally and voluntarily declare:

1. If at any time I am in a terminal condition and become comatose or am otherwise rendered incapable of communicating with my attending physician, and my death is imminent because of an incurable disease, illness or injury, I direct that life-sustaining procedures be withheld or withdrawn, and that I be permitted to die naturally.

Other directions:

2. It is my intention that this directive be honored by my family and attending physician as the final expression of my legal right to refuse medical or surgical treatment and to accept the consequences of my refusal.

3. If I have been found to be pregnant, and that fact is known to my physician, this directive is void during the course of my pregnancy.

I understand the full import of this directive, and I am emotionally and mentally competent to execute it.

Signed _____

City, County and State of Residence _____

The declarant has been personally known to me and I believe _____
to be of sound mind.

Witness _____

Witness _____

WARNING TO PERSON EXECUTING THIS DOCUMENT

THIS IS AN IMPORTANT LEGAL DOCUMENT. IT CREATES A DURABLE POWER OF ATTORNEY FOR HEALTH CARE. BEFORE EXECUTING THIS DOCUMENT, YOU SHOULD KNOW THESE IMPORTANT FACTS:

1. This document gives the person you designate as your attorney-in-fact the power to make health care decisions for you. This power is subject to any limitations or statement of your desires that you include in this document. The power to make health care decisions for you may include consent, refusal of consent, or withdrawal of consent to any care, treatment, service, or procedure to maintain, diagnose, or treat a physical or mental condition. You may state in this document any types of treatment or placements that you do not desire.

2. The person you designate in this document has a duty to act consistent with your desires as stated in this document or otherwise made known or, if your desires are unknown, to act in your best interests.

3. Except as you otherwise specify in this document, the power of the person you designate to make health care decisions for you may include the power to consent to your doctor not giving treatment or stopping treatment which would keep you alive.

4. Unless you specify a shorter period in this document, this power will exist indefinitely from the date you execute this document and, if you are unable to make health care decisions for yourself, this power will continue to exist until the time when you become able to make health care decisions for yourself.

5. Notwithstanding this document, you have the right to make medical and other health care decisions for yourself so long as you can give informed consent with respect to the particular decision. In addition, no treatment may be given to you over your objection, and health care necessary to keep you alive may not be stopped if you object.

6. You have the right to revoke the appointment of the person designated in this document to make health care decisions for you by notifying that person of the revocation orally or in writing.

7. You have the right to revoke the authority granted to the person designated in this document to make health care decisions for you by notifying the treating physician, hospital, or other provider of health care orally or in writing.

8. The person designated in this document to make health care decisions for you has the right to examine your medical records and to consent to their disclosure unless you limit this right in this document.

9. This document revokes any prior durable power of attorney for health care.

10. If there is anything in this document that you do not understand, you should ask a lawyer to explain it to you.

1. DESIGNATION OF HEALTH CARE AGENT.

I, _____ (insert your name)

do hereby designate and appoint: Name: _____

Address: _____ Phone: _____
as my attorney-in-fact to make health care decisions for me as authorized in this document.

(Insert the name and address of the person you wish to designate as your attorney-in-fact to make health care decisions for you. None of the following may be designated as your attorney-in-fact: (1) your treating provider of health care, (2) an employee of your treating provider of health care, (3) an operator of a health care facility, or (4) an employee of an operator of a health care facility.)

2. CREATION OF DURABLE POWER OF ATTORNEY FOR HEALTH CARE.

By this document I intend to create a durable power of attorney by appointing the person designated above to make health care decisions for me. This power of attorney shall not be affected by my subsequent incapacity.

3. GENERAL STATEMENT OF AUTHORITY GRANTED.

In the event that I am incapable of giving informed consent with respect to health care decisions, I hereby grant to the attorney-in-fact named above full power and authority to make health care decisions for me before or after my death, including: consent, refusal of consent, or withdrawal of consent to any care, treatment, service, or procedure to maintain, diagnose, or treat a physical or mental condition, subject only to the limitations and special provisions, if any, set forth in paragraph 4 or 6.

4. SPECIAL PROVISIONS AND LIMITATIONS.
(Your attorney-in-fact is not permitted to consent to any of the following: commitment to or placement in a mental health treatment facility, convulsive treatment, psychosurgery, sterilization, or abortion. If there are any other types of treatment or placement that you do not want your attorney-in-fact's authority to give consent for or other restrictions you wish to place on his or her attorney-in-fact's authority, you should list them in the space below. If you do not write any limitations, your attorney-in-fact will have the broad powers to make health care decisions on your behalf which are set forth in paragraph 3, except to the extent that there are limits provided by law.)
In exercising the authority under this durable power of attorney for health care, the authority of my attorney-in-fact is subject to the following special provisions and limitations:

_____

_____

_____

_____

5. DURATION.
I understand that this power of attorney will exist indefinitely from the date I execute this document unless I establish a shorter time. If I am unable to make health care decisions for myself when this power of attorney expires, the authority I have granted my attorney-in-fact will continue to exist until the time when I become able to make health care decisions for myself.
(IF APPLICABLE)
I wish to have this power of attorney end on the following date: _____

6. STATEMENT OF DESIRES.
(With respect to decisions to withhold or withdraw life-sustaining treatment, your attorney-in-fact must make health care decisions that are consistent with your known desires. You can, but are not required to, indicate your desires below. If your desires are unknown, your attorney-in-fact has the duty to act in your best interests; and, under some circumstances, a judicial proceeding may be necessary so that a court can determine the health care decision that is in your best interests. If you wish to indicate your desires, you may INITIAL the statement or statements that reflect your desires and/or write your own statements in the space below.)

(If the statement reflects your desires, initial the box next to the statement.)

1. I desire that my life be prolonged to the greatest extent possible, without regard to my condition, the chances I have for recovery or long term survival, or the cost of the procedures.   [_____]

2. If I am in a coma which my doctors have reasonably concluded is irreversible, I desire that life-sustaining or prolonging treatments not be used. (Also should utilize provisions of NRS . 449.610 et seq.--Nevada Withholding or Withdrawal of Life Sustaining Procedures Act "Directive to Physicians"-- if this subparagraph is initialed.)   [_____]

3. If I have an incurable or terminal condition or illness and no reasonable hope of long term recovery or survival, I desire that life sustaining or prolonging treatments not be used. (Also should utilize provisions of NRS 449.610 et seq. if this subparagraph is initialed.)   [_____]

4. I do not desire treatment to be provided and/or continued if the burdens of the treatment outweigh the expected benefits. My attorney-in-fact is to consider the relief of suffering, the preservation or restoration of functioning, and the quality as well as the extent of the possible extension of my life.   [_____]

(If you wish to change your answer, you may do so by drawing an "X" through the answer you do not want, and circling the answer you prefer.)

Other or Additional Statements of Desires:

_____

_____

_____

_____

7. DESIGNATION OF ALTERNATE ATTORNEY-IN-FACT.
(You are not required to designate any alternative attorney-in-fact but you may do so. Any alternative attorney-in-fact you designate will be able to make the same health care decisions as the attorney-in-fact designated in paragraph 1, page 2, in the event that he or she is unable or unwilling to act as your attorney-in-fact. Also, if the attorney-in-fact designated in paragraph 1 is your spouse, his or her designation as your attorney-in-fact is automatically revoked by law if your marriage is dissolved.)

If the person designated in paragraph 1 as my attorney-in-fact is unable to make health care decisions for me, then I designate the following persons to serve as my attorney-in-fact to make health care decisions for me as authorized in this document, such persons to serve in the order listed below:

A. First Alternative Attorney-in-fact

Name: _____

Address: _____

_____ Phone _____

B. Second Alternative Attorney-in-fact

Name: _____

Address: _____

_____ Phone _____

8. PRIOR DESIGNATIONS REVOKED. I revoke any prior durable power of attorney for health care.

(YOU MUST DATE AND SIGN THIS POWER OF ATTORNEY)

I sign my name to this Durable Power of Attorney for Health care on

_____ at _____
        (date)   (city and state)

_____
                (Signature)

(THIS POWER OF ATTORNEY WILL NOT BE VALID FOR MAKING HEALTH CARE DECISIONS UNLESS IT IS EITHER (1) SIGNED BY AT LEAST TWO QUALIFIED WITNESSES WHO ARE PERSONALLY KNOWN TO YOU AND WHO ARE PRESENT WHEN YOU SIGN OR ACKNOWLEDGE YOUR SIGNATURE OR (2) ACKNOWLEDGED BEFORE A NOTARY PUBLIC.)

CERTIFICATE OF ACKNOWLEDGEMENT OF NOTARY PUBLIC

(You may use acknowledgment before a notary public instead of the statement of witnesses.)

State of Nevada _____)
)ss.
County of _____)

On this _____ day of _____, in the year _____, before me,

_____, personally
                    (name of notary public)

appeared _____,
                    (name of principal)
personally known to me (or proved to me on the basis of satisfactory evidence) to
be the person whose name is subscribed to this instrument, and acknowledged that
he or she executed it. I declare under penalty of perjury that the person whose
name is ascribed to this instrument appears to be of sound mind and under no
duress, fraud, or undue influence.

NOTARY SEAL
                          _____
                              (Signature of Notary Public)

STATEMENT OF WITNESSES

(You should carefully read and follow this witnessing procedure. This document
will not be valid unless you comply with the witnessing procedure. If you elect
to use witnesses instead of having this document notarized you must use two
qualified adult witnesses. None of the following may be used as a witness: (1) a
person you designate as the attorney-in-fact, (2) a provider of health care, (3)
an employee of a provider of health care, (4) the operator of health care
facility, (5) an employee of an operator of a health care facility. At least one
of the witnesses must make the additional declaration set out following the place
where the witnesses sign.)

I declare under penalty of perjury that the principal is personally known to
me, that the principal signed or acknowledged this durable power of attorney in my
presence, that the principal appears to be of sound mind and under no duress,
fraud, or undue influence, that I am not the person appointed as attorney-in-fact
by this document, and that I am not a provider of health care, an employee of a
provider of health care, the operator of a community care facility, nor an
employee of an operator of a health care facility.

Signature: _____   Date: _____

Print Name: _____

Address: _____

Signature: _____   Date: _____

Print Name: _____

Address: _____

(AT LEAST ONE OF THE ABOVE WITNESSES
MUST ALSO SIGN THE FOLLOWING DECLARATION.)

I declare under penalty of perjury that I am not related to the principal by
blood, marriage, or adoption, and to the best of my knowledge I am not entitled to
any part of the estate of the principal upon the death of the principal under a
will now existing or by operation of law.

Signature: _____

Print Name: _____   Date: _____

Address: _____

COPIES: You should retain an executed copy of this document and give one to your
attorney-in-fact. The power of attorney should be available so a copy may be
given to your providers of health care.

New Hampshire's Terminal Care Document Act

New Hampshire's Terminal Care Document Act recognizes your right to make a declaration stating that you do not want your dying artificially prolonged by the use of life-sustaining procedures. The declaration will be given effect whenever your attending physician and one other doctor confirm that your condition is terminal. Medical procedures or interventions to provide comfort or alleviate pain cannot be withheld or withdrawn.

The form shown here complies with the suggested declaration form given in the statute, which "may be, but need not be" followed. You may, if you wish, add personalized directions, and we have provided space for these. You might wish to consider listing the particular treatments to be withheld or withdrawn—for example, cardiac resuscitation or a respirator. You might want to name a proxy—someone you trust to make the treatment decisions you would make if you could. You might want to emphasize your desire to be kept comfortable and pain free, even though medication might shorten your life.

Your declaration must be signed in the presence of a notary public, justice of the peace, or other official authorized to administer oaths in the place of execution, and two witnesses, neither of whom may be

1. Your spouse.
2. Your heir.
3. Your attending physician or a person acting under the direction of your attending physician.
4. Anyone who has at the time of witnessing any claims against your estate.

Properly signed and witnessed, your declaration will remain in effect until or unless you revoke it. As long as you are capable of decision making, your own expressed wishes always supersede your declaration. To protect yourself fully against unwanted treatment, the Society for the Right to Die advises that you execute both the New Hampshire Terminal Care Document and the generic living will (Chapter 3). The generic living will can apply to an incurable or irreversible mental or physical condition with no reasonable expectation of recovery such as advanced Alzheimer's or minimal consciousness after a stroke—situations that may not be covered by the New Hampshire act.

Note: On May 20, 1991, New Hampshire passed a durable power of attorney for health care that was not available as this book went to press. Please contact the Society for the Right to Die to obtain this new document.

DECLARATION

Declaration made this _____ day of _____ (month, year).

I, _____, being of sound mind, willfully and voluntarily make known my desire that my dying shall not be artificially prolonged under the circumstances set forth below, do hereby declare:

If at any time I should have an incurable injury, disease, or illness certified to be a terminal condition by 2 physicians who have personally examined me, one of whom shall be my attending physician, and the physicians have determined that my death will occur whether or not life-sustaining procedures are utilized and where the application of life-sustaining procedures would serve only to artificially prolong the dying process, I direct that such procedures be withheld or withdrawn, and that I be permitted to die naturally with only the administration of medication, sustenance, or the performance of any medical procedure deemed necessary to provide me with comfort care.

Other directions:

In the absence of my ability to give directions regarding the use of such life-sustaining procedures, it is my intention that this declaration shall be honored by my family and physicians as the final expression of my right to refuse medical or surgical treatment and accept the consequences of such refusal.

I understand the full import of this declaration, and I am emotionally and mentally competent to make this declaration.

Signed _____

State of _____, _____ County

We, the declarant and witnesses, being duly sworn each declare to the notary public or justice of the peace or other official signing below as follows:

1. The declarant signed the instrument as a free and voluntary act for the purposes expressed, or expressly directed another to sign for him.

2. Each witness signed at the request of the declarant, in his presence, and in the presence of the other witness.

3. To the best of my knowledge, at the time of the signing the declarant was at least 18 years of age, and was of sane mind and under no constraint or undue influence.

_____ Declarant

_____ Witness

_____ Witness

The affidavit shall be made before a notary public or justice of the peace or other official authorized to administer oaths in the place of execution, who shall not also serve as a witness, and who shall complete and sign a certificate in content and form substantially as follows:

Sworn to and signed before me by _____, *declarant,*

_____ *and* _____, *witnesses,*

on _____.

_____
Signature

_____
Official Capacity

New Jersey's Medical Power of Attorney

Although New Jersey has not yet enacted living will legislation,* its courts have recognized the legal right of adult residents of the state to have life-sustaining treatment withheld or withdrawn in the event of a terminal condition. The New Jersey Supreme Court has indicated that a living will may be the "best evidence" of a patient's preferences regarding life-sustaining treatment. The same court has also recognized your right to use a durable power of attorney to authorize someone to make any and all medical decisions on your behalf, if you lose the ability to make or express such decisions yourself.

We suggest you use the generic living will outlined in Chapter 3 and follow the guidelines listed there.

The appointment of an agent to make health-care decisions was approved by the New Jersey Supreme Court in *In re Peter,* decided in June 1987. The form shown here, which was drafted by our legal staff in conjunction with a New Jersey law firm, permits you to appoint an agent to make medical decisions on your behalf, including decisions to withdraw or withhold life-support if you yourself are no longer able to be involved in decision making.

Your agent should sign the form in acknowledgment of acceptance. Both signatures—your agent's as well as your own—must be witnessed by a notary public. See Chapter 3 for more information about this form and how to choose an agent.

*As this book went to press, New Jersey passed living will legislation awaiting Governor Florio's signature. Please contact the Society for the information.

MEDICAL POWER OF ATTORNEY

I, _____ , residing at

_____ , as

principal, hereby designate and appoint _____ ,

residing at _____ ,

as my agent for all matters relating to my health care including, but not limited to full power
to give, refuse or revoke consent to all medical, surgical and hospital care. Specifically, I
authorize my agent to order the refusal, discontinuation or withdrawal of all forms of
life-sustaining treatment if my agent determines that based upon his/her knowledge of my
personal instructions, beliefs, and value system I would not want to have such treatment
instituted or continued. This power of attorney shall not be affected by any disability of the
principal.

Signed, sealed and
delivered in the presence
of:

_____   _____
          Agent's signature   Principal's signature

STATE OF NEW JERSEY   )
) ss.:
COUNTY OF   )

BE IT REMEMBERED THAT ON THIS _____ day of _____ 19 ___ ,

before me the subscriber, a Notary Public of New Jersey, personally appeared_____

_____ ,

who I am satisfied is the person named in and who executed the within Power of Attorney and
he acknowledged that he signed, sealed and delivered said Power of Attorney as his/her
voluntary act and deed, for the uses and purposes therein expressed.

_____
                              Notary Public

New Mexico Right to Die Act

New Mexico's Right to Die Act recognizes your right to execute a directive stating that you do not want maintenance medical treatment used for the prolongation of your life if you are terminally ill or in irreversible coma. Although the statute contains no suggested directive form, the declaration shown here may be used to give such directions to your physician. Two witnesses are required.

You will notice that we have provided space for you to include your own specific additions regarding treatment in the event of a terminal condition or irreversible coma. You might wish to consider listing the particular measures to be withheld or withdrawn—for example, "I do not want surgery, cardiac resuscitation, a respirator, artificial feeding." You might want to name a proxy—someone you trust to make the treatment decisions you would make if you could.

Your declaration will not take effect until after a diagnosis of a terminal condition or irreversible coma has been certified in writing by two physicians, one of whom is the attending physician.

As long as you are competent, your own expressed wishes always supersede your declaration.

To protect yourself fully against unwanted treatment, the Society for the Right to Die advises that you execute both the New Mexico Directive and the generic living will (Chapter 3). The generic living will can apply to an incurable or irreversible mental or physical condition with no reasonable expectation of recovery, such as advanced Alzheimer's or minimal consciousness after a stroke—situations that may not be covered by the New Mexico act.

DECLARATION

Declaration made this _____ day of _____, 19_____.

I, _____, being of sound mind, willfully and voluntarily make known my desire that my life shall not be prolonged under the circumstances set forth below, and do hereby declare:

1. If at any time I should be certified in writing by two physicians, one of whom is my attending physician, to be suffering from a terminal illness, or be in an irreversible coma, I direct that maintenance medical treatment shall not be utilized for the prolongation of my life.

2. By maintenance medical treatment I mean any medical treatment that is designed solely to sustain the life processes without effecting a real improvement in my condition. I mean to include within maintenance medical treatment the administration of antibiotics and the artificial provision of nutrients and hydration, but I do not mean to include medication or other measures administered for the purpose of easing pain and discomfort.

3. In the absence of my ability to give directions regarding the use of such medical maintenance treatment, it is my intention that this directive shall be honored by my family and physicians as the final expression of my legal right to refuse medical and surgical treatment and accept the consequences from such refusal.

4. I understand the full import of this directive and I am emotionally and mentally competent to make this directive.

5. I understand that I may revoke this directive at any time.

Other directions:

Proxy Designation Clause*

Should I become unable to communicate my instructions as stated above, I designate the following person to act in my behalf:

Name _____

Address _____

If the person I have named above is unable to act in my behalf, I authorize the following person to do so:

Name _____

Address _____

---

*If you do not name a proxy, it is advisable to draw a line through this portion.

WITNESSES MUST SIGN

Declarant _____

Address _____

We, the undersigned witnesses, hereby attest that the declarant signed and executed the foregoing instrument as the declarant's free and voluntary act for the purposes therein expressed; that each of the undersigned witnesses saw the declarant sign the foregoing instrument; that in the presence of the declarant and in the presence of each other, each of the undersigned has signed this instrument as witness; and that to the best of the knowledge of each of the undersigned the declarant has reached the age of majority, is of sound mind and is under no constraint or undue influence.

Witness _____

Address _____

Witness _____

Address _____

This Declaration complies with the New Mexico Right to Die Act, N.M. Stat. Ann. §§ 24-7-1 to -11 (1986).

New York Health Care Proxy Appointment and the Living Will

New York now has a health-care proxy law, which permits you to appoint someone to make medical decisions for you when you become unable to make them yourself. If you have someone to appoint, we urge you to make use of the proxy law. It is particularly useful because it covers all medical decisions, not only those at the end of life. Instructions for its completion are on the form shown here. Please read them carefully before preparing to sign the form.

The Society for the Right to Die has also prepared a living will designed specifically for New York residents, shown here. A living will has particular significance for New Yorkers because of a series of New York court decisions. The New York living will has been prepared to conform with the law announced by the state's highest court, the court of appeals. The court stated that a living will can be an "ideal" expression of your wishes. The living will is especially important for those people who have no one to appoint or do not wish to appoint a proxy. Even if you do have a proxy, a living will can provide useful information to him or her.

We recommend that, if possible, you appoint a proxy *and* complete a living will. It is important that you discuss your wishes regarding medical treatment with your proxy. The living will can serve to guide your proxy if he or she is required to make medical treatment decisions for you. You should keep the originals of these documents yourself, but be sure that your proxy has copies of both. Also give your physician a copy of the proxy form and have a copy put in your medical records.

If you are *not* appointing a health-care proxy, it is especially important that you prepare a living will so that your wishes regarding medical treatment at the end of life are known. It is important that the living will express your own wishes in as much detail as possible: write in any personal instructions you may have. Sign and date it in the presence of two adult witnesses, who must also sign. Be sure to give a copy to your physician and *discuss* it with him or her, as well as to anyone else who might at some point be involved with your health care.

New York Living Will

*This Living Will has been prepared to conform to the law in the State of N
York, as set forth in the case of <u>In re Westchester County Medical Center,</u>
N.Y.2d 517 (1988). In that case the Court approved the use of a Living W
stating that the "ideal situation is one in which the patient's wishes w
expressed in some form of writing, perhaps a 'living will.' "*

I, _____, being of sound mi
make this statement as a directive to be followed if I become permanen
unable to participate in decisions regarding my medical care. These instr
tions reflect my firm and settled commitment to decline medical treatm
under the circumstances indicated below:

I direct my attending physician to withhold or withdraw treatment t
serves only to prolong the process of my dying, if I should be in an incura
or irreversible mental or physical condition with no reasonable expectat
of recovery.

These instructions apply if I am a) in a terminal condition; b) permane
unconscious; or c) if I am conscious but have irreversible brain damage
will never regain the ability to make decisions and express my wishes.

I direct that treatment be limited to measures to keep me comfortable
to relieve pain, including any pain that might occur by withholding
withdrawing treatment.

While I understand that I am not legally required to be specific about fut
treatments, if I am in the condition(s) described above I feel especi
strongly about the following forms of treatment:

I do not want cardiac resuscitation.
I do not want mechanical respiration.
I do not want tube feeding.
I do not want antibiotics.

I do want maximum pain relief.

Other directions (insert personal instructions):_____
_____
_____
_____

These directions express my legal right to refuse treatment, under the law
New York. I intend my instructions to be carried out, unless I have rescin
them in a new writing or by clearly indicating that I have changed my mi

Signed: _____ Date: _____

Witness: _____

  Address: _____

  _____

Witness: _____

  Address: _____

_____

*Keep the signed original with your personal papers at home. Give copies of the sig
original to your doctor, family, lawyer and others who might be involved in your c*

Health Care Proxy

(1) I, _____

hereby appoint _____

(name, home address and telephone number)

_____

as my health care agent to make any and all health care decisions for me, except to the extent that I state otherwise. This proxy shall take effect when and if I become unable to make my own health care decisions.

(2) Optional instructions: I direct my proxy to make health care decisions in accord with my wishes and limitations as stated below, or as he or she otherwise knows. (Attach additional pages if necessary).

_____

_____

(Unless your agent knows your wishes about artificial nutrition and hydration [feeding tubes], your agent will not be allowed to make decisions about artificial nutrition and hydration. See the preceding instructions for samples of language you could use.)

(3) Name of substitute or fill-in proxy if the person I appoint above is unable, unwilling or unavailable to act as my health care agent.

_____

(name, home address and telephone number)

_____

(4) Unless I revoke it, this proxy shall remain in effect indefinitely, or until the date or condition stated below. This proxy shall expire (specific date or conditions, if desired):

_____

(5) Signature _____

Address _____

Date _____

Statement by Witnesses (must be 18 or older)

I declare that the person who signed this document is personally known to me and appears to be of sound mind and acting of his or her own free will. He or she signed (or asked another to sign for him or her) this document in my presence.

Witness 1_____

Address _____

Witness 2_____

Address _____

New York State Department of Health

North Carolina Right to a Natural Death Act

North Carolina's Right to a Natural Death Act recognizes your right to execute a declaration stating that you do not want your dying artificially prolonged by the use of life-sustaining procedures. The declaration will be given effect whenever your attending physician and one other doctor have verified in writing that your condition is terminal.

The form shown here complies with the suggested declaration form given in the statute. The act also permits personalized additions, and we have provided space for these. You might wish to consider listing the particular treatment to be withheld or withdrawn—for example, "I do not want surgery, cardiac resuscitation, a respirator, artificial feeding." You might want to name a proxy—someone you trust to make the treatment decisions you would make if you could. You might want to emphasize your desire to be kept comfortable and pain free, even though medication might shorten your life.

Your declaration must be signed in the presence of two witnesses, neither of whom may be

1. Related to you by blood or marriage.
2. Entitled to any part of your estate, by inheritance or other claim.
3. Your attending physician or his or her employee.
4. An employee of the health facility, nursing home, or other group-care facility in which you are a patient or a resident.

The declaration must also be "proved"—that is, sworn to by the two witnesses before a notary public or before a clerk of the superior court of North Carolina. Space for this is included in the form shown here.

Properly signed and witnessed, your declaration will remain in effect until or unless you revoke it. As long as you are competent, your own expressed wishes always supersede your declaration.

To protect yourself fully against unwanted treatment, the Society for the Right to Die advises that you execute both the North Carolina declaration and the generic living will (Chapter 3). The generic living will can apply to an incurable or irreversible mental or physical condition with no reasonable expectation of recovery such as advanced Alzheimer's or minimal consciousness after a stroke—situations that may not be covered by the North Carolina act.

DECLARATION OF A DESIRE FOR A NATURAL DEATH

I _____, being of sound mind, desire that my life not be prolonged by extraordinary means if my condition is determined to be terminal and incurable. I am aware and understand that this writing authorizes a physician to withhold or discontinue extraordinary means.

Other directions:

This the _____ day of _____, _____.

Signature _____

I hereby state that the declarant, _____, being of sound mind signed the above declaration in my presence and that I am not related to the declarant by blood or marriage and that I do not know or have a reasonable expectation that I would be entitled to any portion of the estate of the declarant under any existing will or codicil of the declarant or as an heir under the Intestate Succession Act if the declarant died on this date without a will. I also state that I am not the declarant's attending physician or an employee of the declarant's attending physician, or an employee of a health facility in which the declarant is a patient or an employee of a nursing home or any group-care home where the declarant resides. I further state that I do not now have any claim against the declarant.

Witness _____

Witness _____

This Declaration complies with the 'Right to Natural Death,' North Carolina laws of 1977, amended in 1979, 1981, and 1983.

The clerk or the assistant clerk, or a notary public, may, upon proper proof, certify the declaration as follows:

CERTIFICATE

I, _____, Clerk (Assistant Clerk) of Superior Court or Notary Public (circle one as appropriate) for _____ County hereby certify that _____, the declarant appeared before me and swore to me and to the witnesses in my presence that this instrument is his Declaration of A Desire for A Natural Death, and that he had willingly and voluntarily made and executed it as his free act and deed for the purpose expressed in it.

I further certify that _____ and _____, witnesses, appeared before me and swore that they witnessed _____, declarant, sign the attached declaration, believing him to be of sound mind; and also swore that at the time they witnessed the declaration (i) they were not related within the third degree to the declarant or to the declarant's spouse, and (ii) they did not know or have a reasonable expectation that they would be entitled to any portion of the estate of the declarant upon the declarant's death under any will of the declarant or codicil thereto then existing or under the Intestate Succession Act as it provides at that time, and (iii) they were not a physician attending the declarant or an employee of an attending physician or an employee of a health facility in which the declarant was a patient or an employee of a nursing home or any group-care home in which the declarant resided, and (iv) they did not have a claim against the declarant. I further certify that I am satisfied as to the genuineness and due execution of the declaration.

This the _____ day of _____

Clerk (Assistant Clerk) of Superior Court or Notary Public (circle one as appropriate) for the County of _____

North Dakota's Declaration and Durable Power of Attorney for Health Care

North Dakota's Natural Death Act recognizes the legal right of any competent adult (eighteen years or older) to make a declaration governing the use, withholding, or withdrawal of life-sustaining procedures in the event of a terminal condition. The law provides for two separate declarations, one for the withholding or withdrawal of life-prolonging treatment (Declaration A), the other for the use of such treatment (Declaration B). Both forms are shown here. *You should cross out the one you do not use.*

The North Dakota definition of a terminal condition *does not cover* senility, Alzheimer's disease, or chronic mental or physical impairment, including permanent unconsciousness that will not lead to imminent death. The statute excludes artificial nutrition and hydration (tube feeding) from the list of procedures patients may refuse, except when the nutrition or hydration cannot be absorbed, or causes the patient harm or unreasonable pain. A terminally ill pregnant woman may not refuse life-sustaining treatment unless a doctor certifies that it is not possible to maintain the woman to permit a live birth.

It is important that you understand the specific provisions of the law, which are summarized below:

1. You must sign and date your declaration in the presence of two adult witnesses, who *may not* be

   a. Related to you by blood or marriage.
   b. Entitled to any portion of your estate under any will or codicil or by operation of law.
   c. Claimants against any portion of your estate.
   d. Directly financially responsible for your medical care.
   e. Your attending physician(s).

2. If you are a resident of a long-term care facility, one of the two witnesses must be a recognized member of the clergy, an attorney licensed to practice in North Dakota, or a person designated by the department of human services or the county court for that facility's county.
3. Your declaration must be substantially in the form of either Declaration A or Declaration B, but you may add personal instructions—for example, about treatments that you wish to forgo or to receive, such as dialysis or cardiopulmonary resuscitation.
4. It is your responsibility to give a photocopy of your declaration to your doctor, and he or she must then make it a part of your medical record. If your doctor is unwilling to comply with your declaration, he or she must tell you this promptly. Your declaration becomes effective once your attending physician and one other physician have determined that you have a terminal condition *and* are no longer able to make decisions about life-prolonging treatment. The declaration *does not obligate your physician to to use, withhold, or withdraw such treatment, but rather serves as strong evidence of your wishes.*

North Dakota law also lets you appoint someone to make medical decisions for you when you cannot make them yourself, based on what you would wish or on your best interests, through a durable power of attorney for health care (DPAHC). A copy of this form is shown here. Please read the document and witnessing requirements carefully before preparing to execute it.

1. If you are a resident of a long-term care facility, the nature and effect of the DPAHC must be explained to you by either a recognized member of the clergy, an attorney licensed in North Dakota, or someone designated by the department of human services or the court of your county of residence. This person must sign a statement to the effect that he or she explained the DPAHC to you.
2. If you sign the DPAHC when you are being admitted to a hospital, or as a patient in a hospital, a person designated by the hospital must explain the nature and effect of the DPAHC to you and must sign a statement confirming that he or she gave you this explanation.

Although your statutory declaration is widely recognized and may be adequate in some cases, the generic living will (Chapter 3) covers a much wider range of medical situations than those covered by the North Dakota statute. To protect yourself as fully as possible against unwanted treatment, the Society for the Right to Die advises that you execute the North Dakota declaration, the durable power of attorney for health care, and the generic living will. If you wish to refuse tube feeding, it is especially important that you use the generic living will.

DECLARATION TO PHYSICIANS

Declaration A—to withhold or withdraw life-prolonging treatment

(fill out Declaration B on reverse side to direct the use of life-prolonging treatment)

Declaration made this _____ day of _____, _____.

I, _____, being at least eighteen years of age and of sound mind, do hereby willfully and voluntarily make known my desire that my life must not be artificially prolonged under the circumstances set forth below, and do hereby declare:

1. If at any time I should have an incurable condition caused by injury, disease, or illness certified to be a terminal condition by two physicians, and where the application of life-prolonging treatment would serve only to artificially prolong the process of my dying and my attending physician determines that my death is imminent whether or not life-prolonging treatment is utilized, I direct that such treatment be withheld or withdrawn, and that I be permitted to die naturally.

   (Use this space to insert any additional, specific directions.)

2. In the absence of my ability to give directions regarding the use of such life-prolonging treatment, it is my intention that this declaration be honored by my family and physicians as the final expression of my legal right to refuse medical or surgical treatment and accept the consequences of that refusal, which is death.

3. If I have been diagnosed as pregnant and that diagnosis is known to my physician, this declaration is not effective during the course of my pregnancy.

4. I understand the full import of this declaration and I am emotionally and mentally competent to make this declaration.

5. I understand that I may revoke this declaration at any time.

   Signature _____

   _____
   City, County, and State of Residence

   The declarant has been personally known to me and I believe the declarant to be of sound mind. I am not related to the declarant by blood or marriage, nor would I be entitled to any portion of the declarant's estate upon the declarant's death. I am not the declarant's attending physician, a person who has a claim against any portion of the declarant's estate upon the declarant's death, or directly financially responsible for the declarant's medical care.

   Witness _____

   Witness _____

Statutory Citation: N. Dak. Code chapter 23-06.4

DECLARATION TO PHYSICIANS

Declaration B—to direct the use of life-prolonging treatment

(fill out Declaration A on reverse side to withhold or withdraw life-prolonging treatment)

Declaration made this _____ day of _____ , _____.

I, _____ , being at least eighteen years of age and of sound mind, do hereby willfully and voluntarily make known my desire to extend my life under the circumstances set forth below, and do hereby declare:

1. If at any time I should have an incurable condition caused by injury, disease, or illness certified to be a terminal condition by two physicians, I direct the use of life-prolonging treatment that could extend my life.

   (Use this space to insert any additional, specific instructions.)

2. In the absence of my ability to give directions regarding the use of such life-prolonging treatments, it is my intention that this declaration be honored by my family and physicians as the final expression of my legal right to direct medical or surgical treatment and accept the consequences of that directive.

3. I understand the full import of this declaration and I am emotionally and mentally competent to make this declaration.

4. I understand that I may revoke this declaration at any time.

   Signature _____

   _____
   City, County, and State of Residence

   The declarant has been personally known to me and I believe the declarant to be of sound mind. I am not related to the declarant by blood or marriage, nor would I be entitled to any portion of the declarant's estate upon the declarant's death. I am not the declarant's attending physician, a person who has a claim against any portion of the declarant's estate upon the declarant's death, or directly financially responsible for the declarant's medical care.

   Witness _____

   Witness _____

NORTH DAKOTA
STATUTORY FORM DURABLE POWER OF ATTORNEY
FOR HEALTH CARE

WARNING TO PERSON EXECUTING THIS DOCUMENT

This is an important legal document which is authorized by the general laws of this state. Before executing this document, you should know these important facts:

You must be at least eighteen years of age and a resident of the state of North Dakota for this document to be legally valid and binding.

This document gives the person you designate as your agent (the attorney in fact) the power to make health care decisions for you. Your agent must act consistently with your desires as stated in this document or otherwise made known.

Except as you otherwise specify in this document, this document gives your agent the power to consent to your doctor not giving treatment or stopping treatment necessary to keep you alive.

Notwithstanding this document, you have the right to make medical and other health care decisions for yourself so long as you can give informed consent with respect to the particular decision. In addition, no treatment may be given to you over your objection at the time, and health care necessary to keep you alive may not be stopped or withheld if you object at the time.

This document gives your agent authority to consent, to refuse to consent, or to withdraw consent to any care, treatment, service, or procedure to maintain, diagnose, or treat a physical or mental condition. This power is subject to any statement of your desires and any limitation that you include in this document. You may state in this document any types of treatment that you do not desire. In addition, a court can take away the power of your agent to make health care decisions for you if your agent authorizes anything that is illegal; acts contrary to your known desires; or where your desires are not known, does anything that is clearly contrary to your best interest.

Unless you specify a specific period, this power will exist until you revoke it. Your agent's power and authority ceases upon your death.

You have the right to revoke the authority of your agent by notifying your agent or your treating doctor, hospital, or other health care provider orally or in writing of the revocation.

Your agent has the right to examine your medical records and to consent to their disclosure unless you limit this right in this document.

This document revokes any prior durable power of attorney for health care.

You should carefully read and follow the witnessing procedure described at the end of this form. This document will not be valid unless you comply with the witnessing procedure.

If there is anything in this document that you do not understand, you should ask a lawyer to explain it to you.

Your agent may need this document immediately in case of an emergency that requires a decision concerning your health care. Either keep this document where it is immediately available to your agent and alternate agents, if any, or give each of them an executed copy of this document. You should give your doctor an executed copy of this document.

1. DESIGNATION OF HEALTH CARE AGENT. I, _____

_____

(insert your name and address)

do hereby designate and appoint: _____

_____

(insert name, address, and telephone number of one individual only as your agent to make health care decisions for you. None of the following may be designated as your agent: your treating health care provider, a nonrelative employee of your treating health care provider, an operator of a long-term care facility, or a nonrelative employee of an operator of a long-term care facility.)

as my attorney in fact (agent) to make health care decisions for me as authorized in this document. For the purposes of this document, "health care decision" means consent, refusal of consent, or withdrawal of consent to any care, treatment, service, or procedure to maintain, diagnose, or treat an individual's physical or mental condition.

2. CREATION OF DURABLE POWER OF ATTORNEY FOR HEALTH CARE. By this document I intend to create a durable power of attorney for health care.

3. GENERAL STATEMENT OF AUTHORITY GRANTED. Subject to any limitations in this document, I hereby grant to my agent full power and authority to make health care decisions for me to the same extent that I could make such decisions for myself if I had the capacity to do so. In exercising this authority, my agent shall make health care decisions that are consistent with my desires as stated in this document or otherwise made known to my agent, including my desires concerning obtaining or refusing or withdrawing life-prolonging care, treatment, services, and procedures.

(If you want to limit the authority of your agent to make health care decisions for you, you can state the limitations in paragraph 4, "Statement of Desires, Special Provisions, and Limitations," below. You can indicate your desires by including a statement of your desires in the same paragraph.)

4. STATEMENT OF DESIRES, SPECIAL PROVISIONS, AND LIMITATIONS. (Your agent must make health care decisions that are consistent with your known desires. You can, but are not required to, state your desires in the space provided below. You should consider whether you want to include a statement of your desires concerning life-prolonging care, treatment, services, and procedures. You can also include a statement of your desires concerning other matters relating to your health care. You can also make your desires known to your agent by discussing your desires with your agent or by some other means. If there are any types of treatment that you do not want to be used, you should state them in the space below. If you want to limit in any other way the authority given your agent by this document, you should state the limits in the space below. If you do not state any limits, your agent will have broad powers to make health care decisions for you, except to the extent that there are limits provided by law.)

In exercising the authority under this durable power of attorney for health care, my agent shall act consistently with my desires as stated below and is subject to the special provisions and limitations stated below:

a. Statement of desires concerning life-prolonging care, treatment, services, and procedures:

_____

_____

_____

b. Additional statement of desires, special provisions, and limitations regarding health care decisions:

_____

_____

_____

(You may attach additional pages if you need more space to complete your statement. If you attach additional pages, you must date and sign EACH of the additional pages at the same time you date and sign this document.)

If you wish to make a gift of any bodily organ you may do so pursuant to North Dakota Century Code chapter 23-06.2, the Uniform Anatomical Gift Act.

5. INSPECTION AND DISCLOSURE OF INFORMATION RELATING TO MY PHYSICAL OR MENTAL HEALTH. Subject to any limitations in this document, my agent has the power and authority to do all of the following:

a. Request, review, and receive any information, verbal or written, regarding my physical or mental health, including medical and hospital records.

b. Execute on my behalf any releases or other documents that may be required in order to obtain this information.

c. Consent to the disclosure of this information.

(If you want to limit the authority of your agent to receive and disclose information relating to your health, you must state the limitations in paragraph 4, "Statement of Desires, Special Provisions, and Limitations", above.)

6. SIGNING DOCUMENTS, WAIVERS, AND RELEASES. Where necessary to implement the health care decisions that my agent is authorized by this document to make, my agent has the power and authority to execute on my behalf all of the following:

a. Documents titled or purporting to be a "Refusal to Permit Treatment" and "Leaving Hospital Against Medical Advice."

b. Any necessary waiver or release from liability required by a hospital or physician.

7. DURATION. (Unless you specify a shorter period in the space below, this power of attorney will exist until it is revoked.)

This durable power of attorney for health care expires on _____

_____

(Fill in this space ONLY if you want the authority of your agent to end on a specific date.)

8. DESIGNATION OF ALTERNATE AGENTS. (You are not required to designate any alternate agents but you may do so. Any alternate agent you designate will be able to make the same health care decisions as the agent you designated in paragraph 1, above, in the event that agent is unable or ineligible to act as your agent. If the agent you designated is your spouse, he or she becomes ineligible to act as your agent if your marriage is dissolved.)

If the person designated as my agent in paragraph 1 is not available or becomes ineligible to act as my agent to make a health care decision for me or loses the mental capacity to make health care decisions for me, or if I revoke that person's appointment or authority to act as my agent to make health care decisions for me, then I designate and appoint the following persons to serve as my agent to make health care decisions for me as authorized in this document, such persons to serve in the order listed below:

a. First Alternate Agent: _____

_____

(Insert name, address, and telephone number of first alternate agent.)

b. Second Alternate Agent: _____

_____

(Insert name, address, and telephone number of second alternate agent.)

9. PRIOR DESIGNATIONS REVOKED. I revoke any prior durable power of attorney for health care.

DATE AND SIGNATURE OF PRINCIPAL
(YOU MUST DATE AND SIGN THIS POWER OF ATTORNEY)

I sign my name to this Statutory Form Durable Power of Attorney For Health Care on _____

(date)

at _____   _____

         (city)   (state)

_____

         (you sign here)

(THIS POWER OF ATTORNEY WILL NOT BE VALID UNLESS IT IS SIGNED BY TWO (2) QUALI-FIED WITNESSES WHO ARE PRESENT WHEN YOU SIGN OR ACKNOWLEDGE YOUR SIGNA-TURE. IF YOU HAVE ATTACHED ANY ADDITIONAL PAGES TO THIS FORM, YOU MUST DATE AND SIGN EACH OF THE ADDITIONAL PAGES AT THE SAME TIME YOU DATE AND SIGN THIS POWER OF ATTORNEY.)

STATEMENT OF WITNESSES

This document must be witnessed by two (2) qualified adult witnesses. None of the following may be used as a witness:

1. A person you designate as your agent or alternate agent;

2. A health care provider;

3. An employee of a health care provider;

4. The operator of a long-term care facility;

5. An employee of an operator of a long-term care facility;

6. Your spouse;

7. A person related to you by blood or adoption;

8. A person entitled to inherit any part of your estate upon your death; or

9. A person who has, at the time of executing this document, any claim against your estate.

I declare under penalty of perjury that the person who signed or acknowledged this document is personally known to me to be the principal, that the principal signed or acknowledged this durable power of attorney in my presence, that the principal appears to be of sound mind and under no duress, fraud, or undue influence, that I am not the person ap-pointed as attorney in fact by this document, and that I am not a health care provider; an employee of a health care pro-vider; the operator of a long-term care facility; an employee of an operator of a long-term care facility; the principal's spouse; a person related to the principal by blood or adoption; a person entitled to inherit any part of the principal's es-tate upon death; nor a person who has, at the time of executing this document, any claim against the principal's estate.

Signature: _____

Print Name: _____

Residence Address: _____

Date: _____

Signature: _____

Print Name: _____

Residence Address: _____

Date: _____

The Ohio Durable Power of Attorney for Health Care

Because Ohio does not have a specific living will form, we suggest you use the generic living will detailed in Chapter 3.

Ohio, however, recognizes the right of any competent adult (eighteen years or older) to execute a durable power of attorney for health care (DPAHC). Shown here is a copy of the Ohio DPAHC. It is especially important to note the following provisions of the Ohio DPAHC:

You may name any competent adult to be your attorney-in-fact, except a physician who is treating you, an employee of such a physician, or an employee of a health-care facility in which you are being treated. If you become incompetent, your attorney-in-fact will have the right to make any health-care decisions that you could have made, with the following *exceptions*:

1. Refusal or withdrawal of consent to health care that is needed to maintain your life, unless you are in a terminal condition, that is, a condition that is likely to result in imminent death, regardless of the nature and amount of health care provided.
2. Refusal or withdrawal of consent to treatment needed to provide you with comfort care.
3. Refusal or withdrawal of consent to artificial nutrition and hydration (food and water), unless two doctors certify that the administration of nutrition and hydration would not provide comfort to you, *and* (a) death is imminent whether or not you receive nutrition or hydration and the absence of nutrition or hydration is not likely to cause death by malnutrition or dehydration *or* (b) nutrition or hydration, if given to you, could not be assimilated by your body or would shorten your life.
4. If you are pregnant, refusal or withdrawal of consent to health care when that refusal or withdrawal of care would terminate the pregnancy, unless the pregnancy or the treatment would pose a substantial risk to your life, or unless it is determined that the fetus would not be born alive.
5. Withdrawal of consent to treatment to which you had already consented, unless it is not, or is no longer, very effective in achieving the purpose for which you agreed to its use.
6. You may add further limits on your attorney-in-fact's authority to your DPAHC.

Instructions for completing the DPAHC and witnessing requirements are included in the document. Please read them carefully.

Your DPAHC will be valid for seven years from the date of its execution, unless you specify a shorter period of time. If you lack the capacity to make informed health-care decisions for yourself on the date that your DPAHC would have expired, it will remain valid until you regain the capacity to make your own health-care decisions.

OHIO

DURABLE POWER OF ATTORNEY FOR HEALTH CARE

Notice to person executing this document

This is an important legal document. Before executing this document, you should know these facts:

This document gives the person you designate (the attorney in fact) the power to make **most** health care decisions for you if you lose the capacity to make informed health care decisions for yourself. This power is effective only when you lose the capacity to make informed health care decisions for yourself and, not withstanding this document, as long as you have the capacity to make informed health care decisions for yourself, you retain the right to make all medical and other health care decisions for yourself.

You may include specific limitations in this document on the authority of the attorney in fact to make health care decisions for you.

Subject to any specific limitations you include in this document, if you do lose the capacity to make an informed decision on a health care matter, the attorney in fact **generally** will be authorized by this document to make health care decisions for you to the same extent as you could make those decisions yourself, if you had the capacity to do so. The authority of the attorney in fact to make health care decisions for you **generally** will include the authority to give informed consent, to refuse to give informed consent, or to withdraw informed consent to any care, treatment, service, or procedure to maintain, diagnose, or treat a physical or mental condition.

However, even if the attorney in fact has general authority to make health care decisions for you under this document, the attorney in fact **never** will be authorized to do any of the following:

(1) refuse or withdraw informed consent to health care necessary to maintain your life (unless you are suffering from an illness or injury that is likely to result in imminent death, regardless of the type, nature, and amount of health care provided);

(2) refuse or withdraw informed consent to health care necessary to provide you with comfort care (except that, if he is not prohibited from doing so under (4) below, the attorney in fact could refuse or withdraw informed consent to the provision of nutrition or hydration to you);

(3) refuse or withdraw informed consent to health care for you if you are pregnant and if the refusal or withdrawal would terminate the pregnancy (unless the pregnancy or health care would pose a substantial risk to your life, or unless your attending physician and at least one other physician determine, to a reasonable degree of medical certainty, that the fetus would not be born alive);

(4) refuse or withdraw informed consent to the provision of nutrition or hydration to you, unless, prior to the refusal or withdrawal of that informed consent, your attending physician and at least one other physician record their opinions that the provision of nutrition or hydration would not provide comfort to you, and additionally that either of the following situations exists: your death is imminent whether or not nutrition or hydration is provided to you, and the nonprovision of nutrition or hydration to you is not likely to result in your death by malnutrition or dehydration; **or** if nutrition or hydration were provided to you, it could not be assimilated or would shorten your life.

(5) withdraw informed consent to any health care to which you previously consented, unless a change in your physical condition has significantly decreased the benefit of that health care to you, or unless the health care is not, or is no longer, significantly effective in achieving the purposes for which you consented to its use.

Additionally, when exercising his authority to make health care decisions for you, the attorney in fact will have to act consistently with your desires or, if your desires are unknown, to act in your best interest. You may express your desires to the attorney in fact by including them in this document or by making them known to him in another manner.

When acting pursuant to this document, the attorney in fact **generally** will have the same rights that you have to receive information about proposed health care, to review health care records, and to consent to the disclosure of health care records. You can limit that right in this document if you so choose.

Generally, you may designate any competent adult as the attorney in fact under this document. However, you **cannot** designate a physician who is treating you, an employee or agent of a physician who is treating you, or an employee or agent of a health care facility at which you are being treated as the attorney in fact under it.

Unless you specify a shorter period in this document, the document and the power it grants to the attorney in fact will be in effect for seven years from the date of its execution. However, if you lack the capacity to make informed health care decisions on the date that the document and the power it grants to the attorney in fact otherwise would expire, the document and the power it grants will continue in effect until you regain the capacity to make informed health care decisions for yourself.

You have the right to revoke the designation of the attorney in fact by giving him oral or written notice of the revocation. You have the right to revoke the authority of the attorney in fact to make health care decisions for you by giving oral or written notice of the revocation to your physician or another physician who is providing you with health care. You have the right to revoke this document and the authority granted to the attorney in fact under this document by canceling, obliterating, or destroying it with the intent to revoke it, or by doing anything else that clearly communicates your intent to revoke the document.

If you execute this document and create a valid durable power of attorney for health care with it, it will revoke any prior, valid durable power of attorney for health care that you created, unless you indicate otherwise in this document.

This document is not valid as a durable power of attorney for health care unless it either is acknowledged before a notary public or it is attested and signed by at least two adult witnesses who personally know you and who are present when you sign or acknowledge your signature. No person who is related to you by blood, marriage, or adoption, and no person who is entitled to benefit in any way from your death may be a witness. The attorney in fact, physicians, and employees or agents of a physician or a health care facility are ineligible to be witnesses.

If there is anything in this document that you do not understand, you should ask your lawyer to explain it to you.

1) I, _____, hereby appoint
    Name of principal

_____, an adult,

Name of attorney in fact

of _____ to be my

Address and telephone number

attorney in fact to make any and all health care decisions for me at any time at which I no longer have the capacity to make such decisions myself. Such decisions shall include, unless I indicate otherwise below, the decision to give, refuse or withdraw informed consent to any and all health care or treatment provided to me, including decisions to withhold or withdraw life-sustaining medical treatment.

2) In the event the person I appoint above is unable, unwilling or unavailable to act as my health care agent, I here-

by appoint _____

Name of alternate attorney in fact

of _____.

Address and telephone number

3) My attorney in fact or alternate attorney in fact shall have the same right as I would have to receive information about proposed health care, to review health care records, and to consent to the disclosure of such records. My attorney in fact or alternate attorney in fact shall have full power and authority to do and perform all that he/she determines to be necessary or proper, as I might or could do if I had the capacity. THIS POWER OF ATTORNEY BECOMES EFFECTIVE WHEN I CAN NO LONGER MAKE MY OWN MEDICAL DECISIONS AND SHALL NOT BE AFFECTED BY MY DISABILITY.

4) I have discussed my wishes with my attorney in fact and alternate attorney in fact and authorize him/her to express and carry out my specific and general instructions and desires with respect to medical treatment, including my wishes on the subject of withholding or withdrawing all forms of life-sustaining medical treatment, including tubal feeding and medication.

A. I wish to limit the authority of my attorney in fact or my alternate attorney in fact as follows: (If you do not wish to limit the authority, write: "No limit").

_____

_____

_____

B. My specific desires regarding health care and treatment are as follows: (If none, write: "None").

_____

_____

_____

_____

Principal's signature

_____

Date

ATTESTATION

We, the undersigned witnesses, hereby jointly and severally attest to the following:

1. We know the principal personally,
2. The principal signed or acknowledged his signature in the presence of ourselves as witnesses,
3. The principal appeared to be of sound mind and not under or subject to duress, fraud or undue influence,
4. We are not related to the principal by blood, marriage or adoption; not to the best of our knowledge entitled to benefit in any way from the death of the principal; not designated hereinabove as attorney in fact; not physicians; and not employees or agents of a physician or health care facility.

IN TESTIMONY WHEREOF, we hereunto set our hands as witnesses to the signature of the principal, on the _____ day of _____, 19____.

_____   _____
Name   Name

_____   _____
(Printed)   (Printed)

_____   _____
Address   Address

STATE OF OHIO   )
) SS:
COUNTY OF _____   )

    Before me, a Notary Public in and for said county and state, appeared the aforesaid

_____ who
Name of Principal

appears to be of sound mind and not under or subject to duress, fraud or undue influence, and who acknowledged the signing hereof to be his/her free act and voluntary deed.

    IN WITNESS WHEREOF, I hereunto set my hand and official seal as a Notary Public, in and for the aforesaid county and state, on the _____ day of _____, 19____.

_____
Notary Public

Oklahoma Natural Death Act

Oklahoma's Natural Death Act recognizes your right to execute a Directive to Physicians stating that you do not want your dying artificially prolonged by the use of life-sustaining procedures. Doctors must comply with your directive if you execute it—or reexecute it—after two physicians have certified that your condition is terminal. If executed earlier, it is advisory but not binding.

The Directive to Physicians shown here is in the language given in the statute, which must be "substantially" followed, permitting personalized additions. In the space provided under "personal wishes" you might want to consider listing the particular treatments to be withheld or withdrawn—for example, "I do not want antibiotics, surgery, cardiopulmonary resuscitation, a respirator." If you wish to refuse tube feeding, you *must* state that wish on the form. You might want to emphasize your desire to be kept comfortable and pain free, even though medication might shorten your life.

Your directive must be signed in the presence of two adult witnesses (age twenty-one or over), and it must be notarized. Neither of your witnesses may be

1. Related to you by blood or marriage.
2. Directly responsible for costs of your medical care.
3. Entitled to any part of your estate, by inheritance, or other claim.
4. Your attending physician or his or her employee.
5. An employee of or co-patient in the health-care facility in which you are a patient.

Properly signed and witnessed, your directive will remain in effect until or unless you revoke it. As long as you are competent, your own expressed wishes always supersede your directive.

To protect yourself as fully as possible against unwanted treatment, the Society for the Right to Die advises that you execute the Oklahoma declaration and the generic living will (Chapter 3). The generic living will may apply to situations that may not fit the Oklahoma definition of terminal.

DIRECTIVE TO PHYSICIANS

Directive made this _____ day of _____ (month, year).

I, _____, being of sound mind and twenty-one (21) years of age or older, willfully and voluntarily make known my desire that my life shall not be artificially prolonged under the circumstances set forth below, and do hereby declare:

1. If at any time I should have an incurable and irreversible condition caused by injury, disease or illness certified to be a terminal condition by two physicians, I direct that life-sustaining procedures be withheld or withdrawn and that I be permitted to die naturally, if the application of life-sustaining procedures would only serve to artificially prolong the process of my dying and my attending physician determines that my death will occur within hours or days, whether or not life-sustaining procedures are utilized;

2. I understand that I am authorizing the withdrawal of any medical procedure or intervention that will only prolong the process of dying, when I have been diagnosed as having a terminal condition (If declarant does not wish to authorize the withdrawal of any specific medical procedure or intervention, specific directions shall be specified in the directive);

(Insert your personal wishes here):

3. I understand that when I have been diagnosed as having a terminal condition, the subject of the artificial administration of food and water that will only prolong the process of dying is of particular importance. Therefore, unless I sign this paragraph, I am not authorizing the withholding of nutrition or hydration (food or water):

a. I wish not to have artificial administration of food by tube or intravenous feeding,

_____
(signed)

b. I wish not to have artificial administration of water by tube or intravenously,

_____
(signed)

4. I understand that if I have given no specific directive concerning the artificial administration of food and water, it shall be presumed that I wish to receive nutrition and hydration to a degree sufficient to sustain life;

5. In the absence of my ability to give directions regarding the use of life-sustaining procedures, it is my intention that this directive shall be honored by my family and physicians as the final expression of my legal right to refuse medical or surgical treatment including, but not limited to, the administration of any life-sustaining procedures, and accept the consequences of such refusal;

6. If I have been diagnosed as pregnant and that diagnosis is known to my physician, this directive shall have no force or effect during the course of my pregnancy;

7. I have been diagnosed and notified as having a terminal condition by _____, M.D. or D.O., whose address is _____ _____, and whose telephone number is _____. I understand that if I have not filled in the name and address of the physician, it shall be presumed that I did not have a terminal condition when I made out this directive;

8. This directive shall be in effect until it is revoked;

9. I understand the full import of this directive and I am emotionally and mentally competent to make this directive; and

10. I understand that I may revoke this directive at any time.

Signed _____

City, County and State of Residence _____

The declarant is personally known to me and I believe said declarant to be of sound mind. I am twenty-one (21) years of age or older, I am not related to the declarant by blood or marriage, nor would I be entitled to any portion of the estate of the declarant upon the death of said declarant, nor am I the attending physician of the declarant or an employee of the attending physician or a health care facility in which the declarant is a patient, or a patient in the health care facility in which the declarant is a patient, nor am I financially responsible for the medical care of the declarant, or any person who has a claim against any portion of the estate of the declarant upon the death of the declarant.

Witness _____

Witness _____

State of Oklahoma

County of _____

Before me, the undersigned authority, on this day personally appeared _____ (declarant), _____ (witness) and _____ (witness), whose names are subscribed to the foregoing instrument in their respective capacities, and, all of said persons being by me duly sworn, the declarant declared to me and to the said witnesses in my presence that said instrument is his or her "Directive to Physicians," and that the declarant has willingly and voluntarily made and executed it as the free act and deed of the declarant for the purposes therein expressed.

The foregoing instrument was acknowledged before me this _____ day of _____ 19____.

Signed _____
Notary Public in and for

_____ County, Oklahoma

My commission expires _____ day of _____, 19____.

Oregon's Rights with Respect to Terminal Illness Act

The Oregon Rights with Respect to Terminal Illness Act recognizes your right to make a Directive to Physicians, stating that you do not want your dying artificially prolonged by the use of life-sustaining procedures. The directive will become applicable whenever it is confirmed that your condition is terminal.

The directive shown here complies with the statute and must be precisely followed. It must be signed in the presence of two witnesses, neither of whom may be

1. Related to you by blood or marriage.
2. A person with a claim against your estate.
3. An heir to your estate, by your will or by law.
4. Your physician or an employee of your physician or an employee of a health facility in which you are a patient.

Note also: If you are a patient in a long-term care facility, one of the witnesses to your directive must be a person designated by the Department of Human Resources.

Properly signed and witnessed, your directive will remain in effect until or unless you revoke it. As long as you are able to make and communicate decisions, your own expressed wishes always supersede your directive.

To protect yourself as fully as possible against unwanted treatment, the Society for the Right to Die advises that you execute the Oregon declaration and the generic living will (Chapter 3). The generic living will may apply to situations that may not fit the Oregon definition of terminal.

DIRECTIVE TO PHYSICIANS

Directive made this _____ day of _____ (month, year).

I, _____, being of sound mind, willfully and voluntarily make known my desire that my life shall not be artificially prolonged under the circumstances set forth below and do hereby declare:

    1. If at any time I should have an incurable injury, disease or illness certified to be a terminal condition by two physicians, one of whom is the attending physician, and where the application of life-sustaining procedures would serve only to artificially prolong the moment of my death and where my physician determines that my death is imminent whether or not life-sustaining procedures are utilized, I direct that such procedures be withheld or withdrawn, and that I be permitted to die naturally.

    2. In the absence of my ability to give directions regarding the use of such life-sustaining procedures, it is my intention that this directive shall be honored by my family and physician(s) as the final expression of my legal right to refuse medical or surgical treatment and accept the consequences from such refusal.

    3. I understand the full import of this directive and I am emotionally and mentally competent to make this directive.

Signed _____

City, County and State of Residence_____

I hereby witness this directive and attest that:

    (1) I personally know the Declarant and believe the Declarant to be of sound mind.

    (2) To the best of my knowledge, at the time of the execution of this directive, I:

        (a) Am not related to the Declarant by blood or marriage,

        (b) Do not have any claim on the estate of the Declarant,

        (c) Am not entitled to any portion of the Declarant's estate by any will or by operation of law, and

        (d) Am not the physician attending the Declarant or a person employed by a physician attending the Declarant or a person employed by a health facility in which the Declarant is a patient.

    (3) I understand that if I have not witnessed this directive in good faith I may be responsible for any damages that arise out of giving this directive its intended effect.

Witness _____ Witness _____

This Directive complies in form with the Oregon Rights with Respect to Terminal Illness Act, Or. Rev. Stat. §§ 97.050 to -.090 (1977, amended 1979, 1983, 1985, 1987).

OREGON

POWER OF ATTORNEY FOR HEALTH CARE

I appoint _____, whose address is
_____, and whose telephone number is
_____, as my attorney-in-fact for health care decisions. I appoint
_____, whose address is _____, and
whose telephone number is _____, as my alternative attorney-in-fact for
health care decisions. I authorize my attorney-in-fact appointed by this document to make health
care decisions for me when I am incapable of making my own health care decisions. I have read the
warning below and understand the consequences of appointing a power of attorney for health care.

I direct that my attorney-in-fact comply with the following instructions or limitations:
_____
_____

In addition, I direct that my attorney-in-fact have authority to make decisions regarding the following:
___ Withholding or withdrawal of life-sustaining procedures with the understanding that death
may result.
___ Withholding or withdrawal of artificially administered hydration or nutrition or both with
the understanding that dehydration, malnutrition and death may result.

_____
(Signature of person making appointment/Date)

DECLARATION OF WITNESSES

We declare that the principal is personally known to us, that the principal signed or aknowl-
edged the principal's signature on this power of attorney for health care in our presence, that the principal appears to be of sound mind and not under duress, fraud or undue influence, that neither of us
is the person appointed as attorney-in-fact by this document or the principal's attending physician.
Witnessed By:

_____   _____
(Signature of Witness/Date)   (Printed Name of Witness)

_____   _____
(Signature of Witness/Date)   (Printed Name of Witness)

ACCEPTANCE OF APPOINTMENT OF POWER OF ATTORNEY

I accept this appointment and agree to serve as attorney-in-fact for health care decisions. I understand I have a duty to act consistently with the desires of the principal as expressed in this appointment. I understand that this document gives me authority over health care decisions for the principal only if the principal becomes incapable. I understand that I must act in good faith in exercising my authority under this power of attorney. I understand that the principal may revoke this power of attorney at any time in any manner, and that I have a duty to inform the principal's attending physician promptly upon any revocation.

_____
(Signature of Attorney-in-fact/Date)

_____
(Printed name)

_____
(Signature of Alternate Attorney-in-fact/Date)

_____
(Printed name)

WARNING TO PERSON APPOINTING A POWER OF ATTORNEY FOR HEALTH CARE

This is an important legal document. It creates a power of attorney for health care. Before signing this document, you should know these important facts:

This document gives the person you designate as your attorney-in-fact the power to make health care decisions for you, subject to any limitations, specifications or statement of your desires that you include in this document.

For this document to be effective, your attorney-in-fact must accept the appointment in writing.

The person you designate in this document has a duty to act consistently with your desires as stated in this document or otherwise made known or, if your desires are unknown, to act in a manner consistent with what the person in good faith believes to be in your best interest. The person you designate in this document does, however, have the right to withdraw from this duty at any time.

This power will continue in effect for a period of seven years unless you become unable to participate in health care decisions for yourself during that period. If this occurs, the power will continue in effect until you are able to participate in those decisions again.

You have the right to revoke the appointment of the person designated in this document at any time by notifying that person or your health care provider of the revocation orally or in writing.

Despite this document, you have the right to make medical and other health care decisions for yourself as long as you are able to participate knowledgeably in those decisions.

If there is anything in this document that you do not understand, you should ask a lawyer to explain it to you. This power of attorney will not be valid for making health care decisions unless it is signed by two qualified witnesses who are personally known to you and who are present when you sign or acknowledge your signature.

Pennsylvania Living Will and Durable Power of Attorney for Health Care

Pennsylvania does not yet have a specific living will form. (As this book goes to press, Pennsylvania is about to pass living will legislation.) We recommend that you use the generic living will outlined in Chapter 3. The Pennsylvania Durable Powers of Attorney Act authorizes consent to medical treatment, but does not specifically authorize the withdrawal or withholding of life support. Therefore, it has not been reprinted. If you want to fill out a durable power of attorney for health care, consult a local attorney. See Chapter 3 for more information about this form.

Note: Please contact the Society for the Pensylvania forms, which will be available in the future.

The Rhode Island Health Care Power of Attorney Act

Rhode Island has enacted a law that permits any competent adult to execute a durable power of attorney for health care. This document enables you to express your instructions concerning your health care and to designate an individual to carry out your desires in the event you are unable to do so. You still retain the right to consent to or refuse treatment for as long as you are able. The power of attorney will stay in effect until it is revoked. If you wish to make it effective for only a specific period of time you must indicate this in paragraph 7 of the document.

The statute creating the durable power of attorney for health care provides a form to be used and *prohibits the use of any other durable power of attorney form.* A copy of this form is shown here. You may also want to fill out the generic living will (Chapter 3), but if you do, you *may not* use the proxy provision in that form.

To protect yourself as fully as possible against unwanted treatment, the Society for the Right to Die advises that you execute both the Rhode Island durable power of attorney and the generic living will. (Again, use of the Rhode Island durable power of attorney precludes the use of any other durable power of attorney, including the provision in the living will. Just strike out the proxy designation clause in the living will.)

As this book went to press, Rhode Island passed new living will legislation which is awaiting the Governor's signature. Please contact the Society for new forms, which will be available in the future.

RHODE ISLAND
STATUTORY FORM DURABLE POWER OF ATTORNEY
FOR HEALTH CARE

Warning to Person Executing This Document

(R.I. Gen. Laws §§ 23-4.10-1 to 23-4.10-2 [1989])

This is an important legal document which is authorized by the general laws of this state. Before executing this document, you should know these important facts:

You must be at least eighteen (18) years of age and a resident of the state of Rhode Island for this document to be legally valid and binding.

This document gives the person you designate as your agent (the attorney in fact) the power to make health care decisions for you. Your agent must act consistently with your desires as stated in this document or otherwise made known.

Except as you otherwise specify in this document, this document gives your agent the power to consent to your doctor not giving treatment or stopping treatment necessary to keep you alive.

Notwithstanding this document, you have the right to make medical and other health care decisions for yourself so long as you can give informed consent with respect to the particular decision. In addition, no treatment may be given to you over your objection at the time, and health care necessary to keep you alive may not be stopped or withheld if you object at the time.

This document gives your agent authority to consent, to refuse to consent, or to withdraw consent to any care, treatment, service, or procedure to maintain, diagnose, or treat a physical or mental condition. This power is subject to any statement of your desires and any limitation that you include in this document. You may state in this document any types of treatment that you do not desire. In addition, a court can take away the power of your agent to make health care decisions for you if your agent:

(1) authorizes anything that is illegal,

(2) acts contrary to your known desires, or

(3) where your desires are not known, does anything that is clearly contrary to your best interests.

Unless you specify a specific period, this power will exist until you revoke it. Your agent's power and authority ceases upon your death.

You have the right to revoke the authority of your agent by notifying your agent or your treating doctor, hospital, or other health care provider orally or in writing of the revocation.

Your agent has the right to examine your medical records and to consent to their disclosure unless you limit this right in this document.

This document revokes any prior durable power of attorney for health care.

You should carefully read and follow the witnessing procedure described at the end of this form. This document will not be valid unless you comply with the witnessing procedure.

If there is anything in this document that you do not understand, you should ask a lawyer to explain it to you.

Your agent may need this document immediately in case of an emergency that requires a decision concerning your health care. Either keep this document where it is immediately available to your agent and alternate agents or give each of them an executed copy of this document. You may also want to give your doctor an executed copy of this document.

1. Designation of Health Care Agent.

I, _____

_____,

do hereby designate and appoint: _____

_____

as my attorney in fact (agent) to make health care decisions for me as authorized in this document. For the purposes of this document, "health care decision" means consent, refusal of consent, or withdrawal of consent to any care, treatment, service, or procedure to maintain, diagnose, or treat an individual's physical or mental condition.

2. Creation of Durable Power of Attorney for Health Care.

By this document I intend to create a durable power of attorney for health care.

3. General Statement of Authority Granted.

Subject to any limitations in this document, I hereby grant to my agent full power and authority to make health care decisions for me to the same extent that I could make such decisions for myself if I had the capacity to do so. In exercising this authority, my agent shall make health care decisions that are consistent with my desires as stated in this document or otherwise made known to my agent, including, but not limited to, my desires concerning obtaining or refusing or withdrawing life-prolonging care, treatment, services, and procedures.

4. Statement of Desires, Special Provisions, and Limitations.

In exercising the authority under this durable power of attorney for health care, my agent shall act consistently with my desires as stated below and is subject to the special provisions and limitations stated below:

(a) Statement of desires concerning life-prolonging care, treatment, services, and procedures:

(b) Additional statement of desires, special provisions, and limitations regarding health care decisions:

(You may attach additional pages if you need more space to complete your statement. If you attach additional pages, you must date and sign EACH of the additional pages at the same time you date and sign this document.) If you wish to make a gift of any bodily organ you may do so pursuant to the Uniform Anatomical Gift Act.

5. Inspection and Disclosure of Information Relating to My Physical or Mental Health.

Subject to any limitations in this document, my agent has the power and authority to do all of the following:

(a) Request, review, and receive any information, verbal or written, regarding my physical or mental health, including, but not limited to, medical and hospital records.

(b) Execute on my behalf any releases or other documents that may be required in order to obtain this information.

(c) Consent to the disclosure of this information.

(If you want to limit the authority of your agent to receive and disclose information relating to your health, you must state the limitations in paragraph 4 ["Statement of desires, special provisions, and limitations"] above.)

6. Signing Documents, Waivers, and Releases.

Where necessary to implement the health care decisions that my agent is authorized by this document to make, my agent has the power and authority to execute on my behalf all of the following:

(a) Documents titled or purporting to be a "Refusal to Permit Treatment" and "Leaving Hospital Against Medical Advice."

(b) Any necessary waiver or release from liability required by a hospital or physician.

7. Duration.

(Unless you specify a shorter period in the space below, this power of attorney will exist until it is revoked).

This durable power of attorney for health care expires on

_____

(Fill in this space ONLY if you want the authority of your agent to end on a specific date.)

8. Designation of Alternate Agents.

(You are not required to designate any alternate agents but you may do so. Any alternate agent you designate will be able to make the same health care decisions as the agent you designated in paragraph 1, above, in the event that agent is unable or ineligible to act as your agent. If the agent you designated is your spouse, he or she becomes ineligible to act as your agent if your marriage is dissolved.)

If the person designated as my agent in paragraph 1 is not available or becomes ineligible to act as my agent to make a health care decision for me or loses the mental capacity to make health care decisions for me, or if I revoke that person's appointment or authority to act as my agent to make health care decisions for me, then I designate and appoint the following persons to serve as my agent to make health care decisions for me as authorized in this document, such persons to serve in the order listed below:

A. First Alternate Agent: _____

_____

(Insert name, address, and telephone number of first alternate agent)

B. Second Alternate Agent: _____

_____

(Insert name, address, and telephone number of second alternate agent)

9. Prior Designations Revoked.

I revoke any prior durable power of attorney for health care.

Date And Signature of Principal
(YOU MUST DATE AND SIGN THIS POWER OF ATTORNEY)

I sign my name to this Statutory Form Durable Power of Attorney for Health Care on

_____ at _____ , _____
     (Date)   (City)   (State)

_____
(You sign here)

(THIS POWER OF ATTORNEY WILL NOT BE VALID UNLESS IT IS SIGNED BY TWO (2) QUALIFIED WIT-NESSES WHO ARE PRESENT WHEN YOU SIGN OR ACKNOWLEDGE YOUR SIGNATURE. IF YOU HAVE ATTACHED ANY ADDITIONAL PAGES TO THIS FORM, YOU MUST DATE AND SIGN EACH OF THE ADDI-TIONAL PAGES AT THE SAME TIME YOU DATE AND SIGN THIS POWER OF ATTORNEY.)

Statement of Witnesses
(This document must be witnessed by two (2) qualified adult witnesses. None of the following may be used as a witness:
    (1) a person you designate as your agent or alternate agent,
    (2) a health care provider,
    (3) an employee of a health care provider,
    (4) the operator of a community care facility,
    (5) an employee of an operator of a community care facility.
At least one of the witnesses must make the additional declaration set out following the place where the witnesses sign.)

I declare under penalty of perjury that the person who signed or acknowledged this document is personally known to me to be the principal, that the principal signed or acknowledged this durable power of attorney in my presence, that the principal appears to be of sound mind and under no duress, fraud, or undue influence, that I am not the person appointed as attorney in fact by this document, and that I am not a health care provider, an employee of a health care provider, the operator of a community care facility, nor an employee of an operator of a community care facility.

Signature: _____   Signature: _____

Print Name: _____   Print Name: _____

Residence Address: _____   Residence Address: _____

_____   _____

Date: _____   Date: _____

(AT LEAST ONE OF THE ABOVE WITNESSES MUST ALSO SIGN THE FOLLOWING DECLARATION.)

I further declare under penalty of perjury that I am not related to the principal by blood, marriage, or adoption, and, to the best of my knowledge, I am not entitled to any part of the estate of the principal upon the death of the principal under a will now existing or by operation of law.

Signature: _____   Signature: _____

Print Name: _____   Print Name: _____

South Carolina Death with Dignity Act

The South Carolina Death with Dignity Act recognizes the right of any person eighteen years or older to make a written directive instructing physicians to withhold or withdraw medical procedures that only prolong the dying process.

The declaration shown here complies with the form contained in the statute. (A South Carolina declaration executed before the 1988 amendment is still valid, but we recommend the new form as the preferred document to use now.*) Declarations are valid if they are "substantially" in the statutory form, and we have provided space for your personal instructions. You may wish to consider listing the particular treatments to be withheld or withdrawn, for example, cardiopulmonary resuscitation or mechanical respiration. You may also want to include the name of a proxy in the "other directions" space in your declaration—someone you trust to make the treatment decisions you would make if you were able.

Your declaration must be signed in the presence of *two* witnesses and a notary public (see "Affidavit" shown here). *Neither* of your witnesses may be knowingly:

1. Related to you by blood or marriage.
2. Directly financially responsible for your medical care.
3. Entitled to any part of your estate upon your death.
4. A beneficiary of your life insurance policy.
5. A claimant against your estate at the time you sign the declaration.
6. Your attending physician or his or her employee.

No more than one of your witnesses may be an employee of a health facility in which you are a patient. Finally, *if you are a patient in a hospital or skilled or intermediate care nursing facility* when you execute your declaration, one of your witnesses *must be* an ombudsman designated by the state ombudsman.

Properly signed and witnessed, your Declaration will remain valid until or unless you revoke it. You may name someone with the authority to revoke your declaration, but you are not required to. We suggest you write "None" in paragraph 4 of the Revocation procedures, where it says "Name of Designee," if you do not want to give anyone that power. (Revocation procedures are included in the declaration in bold face type, as required by the act.) Your declaration will take effect whenever the circumstances it describes take place.

South Carolina also has a form for a durable power of attorney for health care, which permits you to appoint someone to make medical decisions for you, including decisions about the use of life support, when you become unable to make such decisions yourself. A durable power of attorney for health care is particularly useful because it covers all medical decisions, not just those at the end of life.

The durable power of attorney must be witnessed by two individuals and notarized. Your witnesses must be at least eighteen years of age. Although anyone can serve as a witness, it is not advisable to have your agent or successor agents serve. Only one of your witnesses has to acknowledge your signature in front of the notary.

*Please note: if you executed a declaration at some earlier date, and you plan now to execute the new declaration, be sure all copies of the prior document are destroyed in order to avoid possible confusion.

SOUTH CAROLINA

DECLARATION OF A DESIRE FOR A NATURAL DEATH

State of South Carolina

County of _____

I, _____, being at least eighteen years

of age and a resident of and domiciled in the City of_____,

County of _____, State of South Carolina, make this Declaration

this _____ day of _____, 19 _____.

I wilfully and voluntarily make known my desire that no life-sustaining procedures be used to prolong my dying if my condition is terminal, and I declare:

If at any time I have a condition certified to be a terminal condition by two physicians who have personally examined me, one of whom is my attending physician, and the physicians have determined that my death will occur within a relatively short period of time without the use of life-sustaining procedures, and where the application of life-sustaining procedures would serve only to prolong the dying process, I direct that the procedures be withheld or withdrawn, and that I be permitted to die naturally with only the administration of medication or the performance of any medical procedure necessary to provide me with comfort care.

Other Directions:

In the absence of my ability to give directions regarding the use of life-sustaining procedures, it is my intention that this Declaration be honored by my family and physicians and any health facility in which I may be a patient as the final expression of my legal right to refuse medical or surgical treatment, and I accept the consequences from the refusal.

I am aware that this Declaration authorizes a physician to withhold or withdraw life-sustaining procedures. I am emotionally and mentally competent to make this Declaration.

THIS DECLARATION MAY BE REVOKED:

(1) By being defaced, torn, obliterated, or otherwise destroyed, in expression of the declarant's intent to revoke, by the declarant or by some person in the presence of and by the direction of the declarant. Revocation by destruction of one or more of multiple original Declarations revokes all of the original Declarations. The revocation of the original Declarations actually not destroyed becomes effective only upon communication to the attending physician. The attending physician shall record in the declarant's medical record the time and date when the physician received notification of the revocation;

(2) By a written revocation signed and dated by the declarant expressing his intent to revoke. The revocation becomes effective only upon communication to the attending physician. The attending physician shall record in the declarant's medical record the time and date when the physician received notification of the written revocation;

(3) By an oral expression by the declarant of his intent to revoke the Declaration. The revocation becomes effective only upon communication to the attending physician by the declarant. However, an oral revocation made by the declarant becomes effective upon communication to the attending physician by a person other than the declarant if:

(a) The person was present when the oral revocation was made;

(b) The revocation was communicated to the physician within a reasonable time;

(c) The physical or mental condition of the declarant makes it impossible for the physician to confirm through subsequent conversation with the declarant that the revocation has occurred.

The attending physician shall record in the patient's medical record the time, date, and place of the revocation and the time, date, and place, if different, of when he received notification of the revocation. To be effective as a revocation, the oral expression clearly must indicate a desire that the Declaration not be given effect or that life-sustaining procedures be administered;

(4) By a written, signed, and dated revocation or an oral revocation by a person designated by the declarant in the Declaration, expressing the designee's intent permanently or temporarily to revoke the Declaration. The revocation becomes effective only upon communication to the attending physician by the designee. The attending physician shall record in the declarant's medical record the time, date, and place of the revocation and the time, date, and place, if different, of when the physician received notification of the revocation. A designee may revoke only if the declarant is incompetent to do so. If the declarant wishes to designate a person with authority to revoke this Declaration on his behalf, the name and address of that person must be entered below:

_____   _____
Name of Designee

                                        _____
                                                Address

_____
        Declarant

AFFIDAVIT

State of _____

County of _____

We, _____ and _____,

the undersigned witnesses to the foregoing Declaration, dated the _____ day of

_____, 19 _____, being first duly sworn, declare to the undersigned authority, on the basis of our best information and belief, that the Declaration was on that date signed by the declarant as and for his DECLARATION OF A DESIRE FOR A NATURAL DEATH in our presence and we, at his request and in his presence, and in the presence of each other, subscribe our names as witnesses on that date. The declarant is personally known to us, and we believe him to be of sound mind. Each of us affirms that he is qualified as a witness to this Declaration under the provisions of the South Carolina Death With Dignity Act in that he is not related to the declarant by blood or marriage, either as a spouse, lineal ancestor, descendant of the parents of the declarant, or spouse of any of them; not directly financially responsible for the declarant's medical care; nor entitled to any portion of the declarant's estate upon his decease, whether under any will or as an heir by intestate succession; nor the beneficiary of a life insurance policy of the declarant; nor the declarant's attending physician; nor an employee of the attending physician; nor a person who has a claim against the declarant's decedent's estate as of this time. No more than one of us is an employee of a health facility in which the declarant is a patient. If the declarant is a patient in a hospital or skilled or intermediate care nursing facility at the date of execution of this Declaration at least one of us is an ombudsman designated by the State Ombudsman, Office of the Governor.

_____   _____
Witness   Witness

Subscribed before me by _____, the declarant, and sub-

scribed and sworn to before me by _____ and

_____, the witnesses, this _____day

of _____, 19 _____.

Notary Public for _____   SEAL

My commission expires: _____

_____
Signature of Notary Public

SOUTH CAROLINA

DURABLE POWER OF ATTORNEY FOR HEALTH CARE

1) I, _____,
(Name of principal)

of _____
(Address)

hereby appoint _____
(Name of attorney-in-fact)

of _____
(Address and telephone of attorney-in-fact)

as my attorney-in-fact to express and carry out my specific and general instructions and desires with respect to medical treatment.

2) In the event the person I appoint above is unable, unwilling or unavailable to act as my health care agent, I hereby appoint _____
(Name of successor attorney-in-fact)

of _____.
(Address and telephone of successor attorney-in-fact)

3) I have discussed my wishes with my attorney-in-fact and my successor attorney-in-fact, and authorize him/her to make all and any health care decisions for me, including decisions to withhold or withdraw any form of life-sustaining procedure. I expressly authorize my agent (and successor agent) to make decisions for me about tube feeding and medication. Other specific instructions:

4) This power of attorney becomes effective when I can no longer make my own medical decisions and is not affected by physical disability or mental incompetence. The determination of whether I can make my own medical decisions is to be made by my attorney-in-fact, or if he or she is unable, unwilling or unavailable to act, by my successor attorney-in-fact.

I, _____, the principal, sign my name to this instrument this _____ day of _____, 19____, and being first duly sworn, do hereby declare to the undersigned authority that I sign and execute this instrument as my durable power of attorney for health care and that I sign it willingly (or willingly direct another to sign for me), that I execute it as my free and voluntary act for the purposes therein expressed, and that I am eighteen years of age or older, of sound mind, and under no constraint or undue influence.

_____
(Principal)

We, _____ and _____, the witnesses, sign our names to this instrument, and at least one of us, being first duly sworn, does hereby declare, generally and to the undersigned authority, that the principal signs and executes this instrument as his durable power of attorney for health care and that he signs it willingly (or willingly directs another to sign for him), and that each of us, in the presence and hearing of the principal, hereby signs this durable power of attorney for health care as witness to the principal's signing, and that to the best of our knowledge the principal is eighteen years of age or older, of sound mind, and under no constraint or undue influence.

_____
(Witness)

_____
(Witness)

The State of _____

County of _____

Subscribed, sworn to, and acknowledged before me by _____,

the principal, and subscribed and sworn to before me by _____,

witness, this _____ day of _____, 19____.

(Seal)

_____
(Signed)

_____
(Official capacity of officer)

South Dakota's Declaration and Durable Power of Attorney for Health Care

South Dakota recognizes the legal right of any competent adult (eighteen years or older) to sign a written declaration providing his or her physician with instructions about life-sustaining procedures in the event of a terminal condition. According to the statute, "terminal condition" includes, among other conditions, an irreversible coma or other condition of permanent unconsciousness.

It is important that you understand the specific provisions of this statute:

1) Your declaration must be signed and dated by you (or, if you are physically unable to sign, by another person in your presence and at your express direction), in the presence of two adult witnesses and a notary public, who shall notarize the declaration.

2) The declaration must state whether or not you wish to receive artificial nutrition and hydration (food and water delivered by tube). Orally administered food and water will always be provided. Medication and medical procedures, including tube feeding, will also be provided if necessary to alleviate pain.

3) Life-sustaining procedures can only be withheld or withdrawn after your attending physician and one other physician determine that you have a terminal condition, and are no longer able to make decisions about the use of life-sustaining treatment.

4) If you make out both a declaration and a durable power of attorney for health care (a DPAHC—described below), the document that you made out more recently is the one that controls. This rule does not affect the power of your attorney-in-fact, if you name one, to implement your declaration.

5) Despite the existence of a declaration, life-sustaining treatment (including tube feeding) must be given to a pregnant woman unless the fetus could not develop to a live birth, or unless such treatment would be physically harmful to the woman or prolong severe pain that cannot be alleviated by medication.

6) It is your responsibility to give a photocopy of the completed declaration to your physician, who should make the photocopy a part of your medical record.

South Dakota law also provides for a durable power of attorney for health care (DPAHC), which lets you appoint someone, known as your "health-care agent" or "attorney-in-fact," to make medical decisions for you if you become unable to make such decisions yourself.

Your DPAHC must be either witnessed by two adults or notarized. While anyone may serve as your witness, it is not advisable to use your agent or any successor agent(s) as a witness.

Under the DPAHC statute, life-sustaining treatment (including tube feeding) must be given to a pregnant woman unless the fetus would not develop to a live birth, or unless the treatment would be physically harmful to the woman or would prolong severe pain that could not be alleviated by medication.

To protect yourself as fully as possible against unwanted treatment, the Society for the Right to Die advises that you execute: the South Dakota declaration, the durable power of attorney, and the Society's general living will. The South Dakota law covers medical conditions such as coma or advanced Alzheimer's disease, but the declaration itself does not make that clear. The general living will spells out the fact that it applies to such situations. Therefore we advise you to complete both forms in order to avoid possible confusion.

LIVING WILL DECLARATION

This is an important legal document. This document directs the medical treatment you are to receive in the event you are unable to participate in your own medical decisions and you are in a terminal condition. This document may state what kind of treatment you want or do not want to receive.

This document can control whether you live or die. Prepare this document carefully. If you use this form, read it completely. You may want to seek professional help to make sure the form does what you intend and is completed without mistakes.

This document will remain valid and in effect until and unless you revoke it. Review this document periodically to make sure it continues to reflect your wishes. You may amend or revoke this document at any time by notifying your physician and other health-care providers. You should give copies of this document to your physician and your family. This form is entirely optional. If you choose to use this form, please note that the form provides signature lines for you, the two witnesses whom you have selected and a notary public.

TO MY FAMILY, PHYSICIANS, AND ALL THOSE CONCERNED WITH MY CARE:

I, _____, willfully and voluntarily make this declaration as a directive to be followed if I am in a terminal condition and become unable to participate in decisions regarding my medical care.

With respect to any life-sustaining treatment, I direct the following:

(Initial only one of the following optional directives if you agree. If you do not agree with any of the following directives, space is provided below for you to write your own directives).

____ NO LIFE-SUSTAINING TREATMENT. I direct that no life-sustaining treatment be provided. If life-sustaining treatment is begun, terminate it.

____ TREATMENT FOR RESTORATION. Provide life-sustaining treatment only if and for so long as you believe treatment offers a reasonable possibility of restoring to me the ability to think and act for myself.

____ TREAT UNLESS PERMANENTLY UNCONSCIOUS. If you believe that I am permanently unconscious and are satisfied that this condition is irreversible, then do not provide me with life-sustaining treatment, and if life-sustaining treatment is being provided to me, terminate it. If and so long as you believe that treatment has a reasonable possibility of restoring consciousness to me, then provide life-sustaining treatment.

____ MAXIMUM TREATMENT. Preserve my life as long as possible, but do not provide treatment that is not in accordance with accepted medical standards as then in effect.

(Artificial nutrition and hydration is food and water provided by means of a nasogastric tube or tubes inserted into the stomach, intestines, or veins. If you do not wish to receive this form of treatment, you must initial the statement below which reads: "I intend to include this treatment, among the 'life-sustaining treatment' that may be withheld or withdrawn.")

With respect to artificial nutrition and hydration, I wish to make clear that

(Initial only one)

____ I <u>intend</u> to include this treatment among the "life-sustaining treatment" that may be withheld or withdrawn.

____ I <u>do not intend</u> to include this treatment among the "life-sustaining treatment" that may be withheld or withdrawn.

(If you do not agree with any of the printed directives and want to write your own, or if you want to write directives in addition to the printed provisions, or if you want to express some of your other thoughts, you can do so here.)

_____

_____

_____

_____

_____

Date: _____   _____
                                                (your signature)

_____   _____
    (your address)   (type or print your signature)

The declarant voluntarily signed this document in my presence.

Witness _____

Address _____

Witness _____

Address _____

On this the _____ day of _____, _____, the declarant, _____,

and witnesses _____, and _____, personally appeared before the undersigned officer and signed the foregoing instrument in my presence.

Dated this _____ day of _____, _____.

_____
Notary Public

My commission expires: _____.

Tennessee Right to Natural Death Act

The Tennessee Right to Natural Death Act recognizes your right to control decisions relating to your medical care, and to exercise that right by means of a living will. The form shown here should be substantially followed, but we have, therefore, provided space on the document for your personal additions. (The statute also specifies that you may include instructions on organ donation and body disposal.)

By definition, "medical care" includes any procedure for diagnosis or treatment. The statute does not permit the withholding of naturally administered food or fluids. It specifically authorizes you also to control decisions regarding the use of "sedatives and pain-killing drugs, nonartificial oral feeding, suction, hydration, and hygienic care."

Your living will must be signed in the presence of two witnesses. Neither of your witnesses may be

1. Related to you by blood or marriage.
2. Entitled to any part of your estate, by inheritance or other claim.
3. Your attending physician or his or her employee or an employee of a health facility in which you are a patient.

The statute's suggested living will form includes a place for a notary's signature. Although this requirement is not otherwise specified in the statute, we believe your best course is to have your form notarized.

Properly signed and witnessed, your living will will remain in effect until or unless you revoke it. As long as you are competent, your expressed wishes always supersede your living will.

Also shown is Tennessee's form for a durable power of attorney for health care which permits you to appoint someone to make medical decisions for you, including decisions about the use of life support, if at any time you become unable to make them yourself.

You may not name any of the following as your agent(s) on your durable power of attorney for health care: 1. Your treating health-care provider;* 2. An operator of your heath-care institution;* 3. An employee of either of the above;* 4. Your conservator (if you do wish to name your conservator as your agent, you must consult an attorney).

You can have your document witnessed by either two witnesses *or* a notary public in Tennessee. *If you choose witnesses,* make sure both of your witnesses are present when you sign and date the document. Neither of your witnesses may be: 1. The person you named as your agent; 2. A health-care provider; 3. An operator of a health-care institution; 4. An employee of either 2 or 3.

At least one of your witnesses must be a person who is neither related to you by blood, marriage, or adoption nor entitled to inherit from you under any existing will or codicil. Sign the document in the presence of your witnesses and have your witnesses sign the document and print their names and addresses. Both must swear to the first paragraph of the witnesses' statement. Only one need swear to the second. *If you choose a notary,* sign the document in the presence of a notary in Tennessee.

*If no one else is available, you may be able to name an employee of your health-care provider or institution, if he or she is related to you. You should consult an attorney in this case.

LIVING WILL

I, _____, willfully and voluntarily make known my desire that my dying shall not be artificially prolonged under the circumstances set forth below, and do hereby declare:

If at ant time I should have a terminal condition and my attending physician has determined that there can be no recovery from such condition and my death is imminent, where the application of life-prolonging procedures would serve only to artificially prolong the dying process, I direct that such procedures be withheld or withdrawn, and that I be permitted to die naturally with only the administration of medications or the performance of any medical procedure deemed necessary to provide me with comfortable care or to alleviate pain. ln the absence of my ability to give directions regarding the use of such life-prolonging procedures, it is my intention that this declaration shall be honored by my family and physician as the final expression of my legal right to refuse medical or surgical treatment and accept the consequences of such refusal.

Other instructions:

I understand the full import of this declaration and I am emotionally and mentally competent to make this declaration. In acknowledgment whereof, I do hereinafter affix my signature on this _____ day of _____, 19_____.

Declarant _____

We, the subscribing Witnesses hereto, are personally acquainted with and subscribe our names hereto at the request of the declarant, an adult, whom we believe to be of sound mind, fully aware of the action taken herein and its possible consequence.

We the undersigned witnesses further declare that we are not related to the declarant by blood or marriage; that we are not entitled to any portion of the estate of the declarant upon his/her decease under any will or codicil thereto presently existing or by operation of law then existing; that we are not the attending physician, an employee of the attending physician or a health facility in which the declarant is a patient; and that we are not a person who, at the present time, has a claim against any portion of the estate of the declarant upon his/her death.

Witness _____

Witness _____

Subscribed, sworn to and acknowledged before me by _____, the declarant, and subscribed and sworn to before me by _____ and _____, witnesses, this _____ day of _____, 19_____.

Notary Public _____

TENNESSEE

DURABLE POWER OF ATTORNEY FOR HEALTH CARE*

WARNING TO PERSON EXECUTING THIS DOCUMENT:

This is an important legal document. Before executing this document you should know these important facts.

This document gives the person you designate as your agent (the attorney-in-fact) the power to make health care decisions for you. Your agent must act consistently with your desires as stated in this document.

Except as you otherwise specify in this document, this document gives your agent the power to consent to your doctor not giving treatment or stopping treatment necessary to keep you alive.

Notwithstanding this document, you have the right to make medical and other health care decisions for yourself so long as you can give informed consent with respect to the particular decision. In addition, no treatment may be given to you over your objection, and health care necessary to keep you alive may not be stopped or withheld if you object at the time.

This document gives your agent authority to consent, to refuse to consent, or to withdraw consent to any care, treatment, service, or procedure to maintain, diagnose or treat a physical or mental condition. This power is subject to any limitations that you include in this document. You may state in this document any types of treatment that you do not desire. In addition, a court can take away the power of your agent to make health care decisions for you if your agent (1) authorizes anything that is illegal or (2) acts contrary to your desires as stated in this document.

You have the right to revoke the authority of your agent by notifying your agent or your treating physician, hospital or other health care provider orally or in writing of the revocation.

Your agent has the right to examine your medical records and to consent to their disclosure unless you limit this right in this document.

Unless you otherwise specify in this document, this document gives your agent the power after you die to (1) authorize an autopsy, (2) donate your body or parts thereof for transplant or therapeutic or educational or scientific purposes, and (3) direct the disposition of your remains.

If there is anything in this document that you do not understand, you should ask a lawyer to explain it to you.

*Drafted with the assistance of W.W. Berry, Esq., of Bass, Berry & Sims, Nashville, TN.

1) I, _____, of
(Name of principal)

_____,
(Address)

state and affirm that I have read the foregoing paragraphs concerning the legal consequences of my executing this document, and I do hereby appoint

_____
(Name of attorney-in-fact)

of _____
(Address and telephone of attorney-in-fact)

as my attorney-in-fact to have the authority hereinafter set forth in order to express and carry out my specific and general instructions and desires with respect to medical treatment.

2) In the event the person I appoint above is unable, unwilling or unavailable to act as my health care agent, I hereby appoint _____
(Name of alternate attorney-in-fact)

of _____.
(Address and telephone of alternate attorney-in-fact).

3) I have discussed my wishes with my attorney-in-fact and my alternate attorney-in-fact, and authorize him/her to make all and any health care decisions (as defined by Tennessee law) for me, including decisions to withhold or withdraw any form of life support. I expressly authorize my agent (and alternate agent) to make decisions for me about tube feeding and medication.

4) This power of attorney becomes effective when I can no longer make my own medical decisions and shall not be affected by my subsequent disability or incompetence. The determination of whether I can make my own medical decisions is to be made by my attorney-in-fact, or if he or she is unable, unwilling or unavailable to act, by my alternate attorney-in-fact.

IN WITNESS WHEREOF, I have set my hand this _____ day of _____, 19_____.

_____
(Signature of principal)

"I declare under penalty of perjury under the laws of Tennessee that the person who signed or acknowledged this document is personally known to me to be the principal, that the principal signed or acknowledged this durable power of attorney in my presence, that the principal appears to be of sound mind and under no duress, fraud, or undue influence, that I am not the person appointed as attorney-in-fact by this document, and that I am not a health care provider, an employee of a health care provider, the operator of a health care institution nor an employee of an operator of a health care institution."

_____
(First witness' signature)

_____
(First witness' name and address)

_____
(Second witness' signature)

_____
(Second witness' name and address)

"I further declare under penalty of perjury under the laws of Tennessee that I am not related to the principal by blood, marriage, or adoption, and, to the best of my knowledge, I am not entitled to any part of the estate of the principal upon the death of the principal under a will now existing or by operation of law."

_____
(Signature of first or second witness)

State of Tennessee   )
)
County of   )

On this _____ day of _____, in the year _____,

before me, _____ personally appeared
                                 (insert name of notary)

_____, personally known to me
                               (insert name of principal)

(or proved to me on the basis of satisfactory evidence) to be the person whose name is subscribed to this instrument, and acknowledged that he or she executed it. I declare under penalty of perjury that the person whose name is subscribed to this instrument appears to be of sound mind and under no duress, fraud, or undue influence.

(NOTARY SEAL)

_____
(Signature of Notary Public)

Texas Natural Death Act

Shown here is the Directive to Physicians that complies with the Texas Natural Death Act. The statute does not require you to follow precisely the form it contains, but permits you to add specific instructions of your own—including designation of a proxy to make decisions on your behalf when you are in a terminal condition, as defined in the act.

We have added a place for you to include your proxy's name and other personal instructions, if any. You might want to list particular treatment to be withheld or withdrawn if you are in a terminal condition—for example, "I do not want antibiotics, surgery, cardiac resuscitation, a respirator, artificial feeding." You might want to emphasize your desire to be kept comfortable and pain free even though medication may shorten your life.

Your directive must be signed in the presence of two witnesses, who must also sign the directive. Neither of them may be

1. Related to you by blood or marriage.
2. Entitled to any portion of your estate on your death.
3. A claimant against any portion of your estate at the time of signing.
4. Your physician or any of your physician's employees.
5. An employee in a health-care facility in which you are a patient, if the employee is providing direct patient care to you or is directly involved in the facility's financial affairs.

Properly signed and witnessed, your directive will remain in effect until or unless you revoke it. As long as you are competent, your own expressed wishes always supersede your directive.

Texas also has a durable power of attorney for health care law that permits you to appoint an agent specifically authorized to make medical treatment decisions on your behalf (Chapter 3). We view this legal device as an extremely useful complement to your Directive to Physicians. It can broaden and strengthen your control over treatment choices whenever you are unable to exercise your right of informed consent. We advise use of the durable power of attorney for health care in addition to the Directive to Physicians. Please read the durable power form carefully noting the execution and witnessing requirements.

To protect yourself as fully as possible against unwanted treatment, the Society for the Right to Die advises that you execute the Texas Directive to Physicians, the durable power of attorney for health care and the generic living will (Chapter 3). The generic living will can apply to conditions that would not fit the Texas definition of terminal.

TEXAS

DIRECTIVE TO PHYSICIANS

Directive made this _____ day of _____ (month, year).

I _____, being of sound mind, willfully and voluntarily make known my desire that my life shall not be artificially prolonged under the circumstances set forth below, and do hereby declare:

1. If at any time I should have an incurable or irreversible condition caused by injury, disease, or illness certified to be a terminal condition by two physicians, and where the application of life-sustaining procedures would serve only to artificially prolong the moment of my death and where my attending physician determines that my death is imminent or will result within a relatively short time without application of life-sustaining procedures, I direct that such procedures be withheld or withdrawn, and that I be permitted to die naturally.

2. In the absence of my ability to give directions regarding the use of life-sustaining procedures, it is my intention that this directive shall be honored by my family and physicians as the final expression of my legal right to refuse medical or surgical treatment and accept the consequences from such refusal.

Other directions:

3. If I have been diagnosed as pregnant and that diagnosis is known to my physician, this directive shall have no force or effect during the course of my pregnancy.

4. This directive shall be in effect until it is revoked.

5. I understand the full import of this directive and I am emotionally and mentally competent to make this directive.

6. I understand that I may revoke this directive at any time.

Signed _____

City, County, and State of Residence _____

I am not related to the declarant by blood or marriage; nor would I be entitled to any portion of the declarant's estate on his/her decease; nor am I the attending physician of the declarant or an employee of the attending physician; nor am I a patient in the health care facility in which the declarant is a patient, or any person who has a claim against any portion of the estate of the declarant upon his/her decease. Furthermore, if I am an employee of a health facility in which the declarant is a patient, I am not involved in providing direct patient care to the declarant nor am I directly involved in the financial affairs of the health facility.

Witness _____

Witness _____

This Directive complies with the Natural Death Act, Tex. Stat. Ann. art 4590h (1977, amended 1979, 1983, 1985, 1989).

TEXAS
DURABLE POWER OF ATTORNEY FOR HEALTH CARE

INFORMATION CONCERNING THE DURABLE POWER OF ATTORNEY FOR HEALTH CARE
THIS IS AN IMPORTANT LEGAL DOCUMENT. BEFORE SIGNING THIS DOCUMENT, YOU SHOULD KNOW THESE IMPORTANT FACTS:

Except to the extent you state otherwise, this document gives the person you name as your agent the authority to make any and all health care decisions for you in accordance with your wishes, including your religious and moral beliefs, when you are no longer capable of making them yourself. Because "health care" means any treatment, service, or procedure to maintain, diagnose, or treat your physical or mental condition, your agent has the power to make a broad range of health care decisions for you. Your agent may consent, refuse to consent, or withdraw consent to medical treatment and may make decisions about withdrawing or withholding life-sustaining treatment. Your agent may not consent to voluntary inpatient mental health services, convulsive treatment, psychosurgery, or abortion. A physician must comply with your agent's instructions or allow you to be transferred to another physician.

Your agent's authority begins when your doctor certifies that you lack the capacity to make health care decisions.

Your agent is obligated to follow your instructions when making decisions on your behalf. Unless you state otherwise, your agent has the same authority to make decisions about your health care as you would have had.

It is important that you discuss this document with your physician or other health care provider before you sign it to make sure that you understand the nature and range of decisions that may be made on your behalf. If you do not have a physician, you should talk with someone else who is knowledgeable about these issues and can answer your questions. You do not need a lawyer's assistance to complete this document, but if there is anything in this document that you do not understand, you should ask a lawyer to explain it to you.

The person you appoint as agent should be someone you know and trust. The person must be 18 years of age or older or a person under 18 years of age who has had the disabilities of minority removed. If you appoint your health or residential care provider (e.g., your physician or an employee of a home health agency, hospital, nursing home, or residential care home, other than a relative), that person has to choose between acting as your agent or as your health or residential care provider; the law does not permit a person to do both at the same time.

You should inform the person you appoint that you want the person to be your health care agent. You should discuss this document with your agent and your physician and give each a signed copy. You should indicate on the document itself the people and institutions who have signed copies. Your agent is not liable for health care decisions made in good faith on your behalf.

Even after you have signed this document, you have the right to make health care decisions for yourself as long as you are able to do so and treatment cannot be given to you or stopped over your objection. You have the right to revoke the authority granted to your agent by informing your agent or your health or residential care provider orally or in writing, or by your execution of a subsequent durable power of attorney for health care. Unless you state otherwise, your appointment of a spouse dissolves on divorce.

This document may not be changed or modified. If you want to make changes in the document, you must make an entirely new one.

You may wish to designate an alternate agent in the event that your agent is unwilling, unable, or ineligible to act as your agent. Any alternate agent you designate has the same authority to make health care decisions for you.

THIS POWER OF ATTORNEY IS NOT VALID UNLESS IT IS SIGNED IN THE PRESENCE OF TWO OR MORE QUALIFIED WITNESSES. THE FOLLOWING PERSONS MAY NOT ACT AS WITNESSES:

(1) the person you have designated as your agent;

(2) your health or residential care provider or an employee of your health or residential care provider;

(3) your spouse;

(4) your lawful heirs or beneficiaries named in your will or a deed; or

(5) creditors or persons who have a claim against you.

I have read and understood the contents of this disclosure statement.

_____   _____
          (Signature)   (Date)

DURABLE POWER OF ATTORNEY FOR HEALTH CARE

DESIGNATION OF HEALTH CARE AGENT.

I, _____ (insert your name) appoint:

Name: _____

Address: _____

_____ Phone: _____

as my agent to make any and all health care decisions for me, except to the extent I state otherwise in this document. This durable power of attorney for health care takes effect if I become unable to make my own health care decisions and this fact is certified in writing by my physician.

LIMITATIONS ON THE DECISION MAKING AUTHORITY OF MY AGENT ARE AS FOLLOWS:

_____

_____

_____

DESIGNATION OF ALTERNATE AGENT.

(You are not required to designate an alternate agent but you may do so. An alternate agent may make the same health care decisions as the designated agent if the designated agent is unable or unwilling to act as your agent. If the agent designated is your spouse, the designation is automatically revoked by law if your marriage is dissolved.)

If the person designated as my agent is unable or unwilling to make health care decisions for me, I designate the following persons to serve as my agent to make health care decisions for me as authorized by this document, who serve in the following order:

A. First Alternate Agent

Name: _____

Address: _____

_____ Phone: _____

B. Second Alternate Agent

Name: _____

Address: _____

_____ Phone: _____

The original of this document is kept at: _____

The following individuals or institutions have signed copies:

Name: _____

Address: _____

Name: _____

Address: _____

DURATION.

I understand that this power of attorney exists indefinitely from the date I execute this document unless I establish a shorter time or revoke the power of attorney. If I am unable to make health care decisions for myself when this power of attorney expires, the authority I have granted my agent continues to exist until the time I become able to make health care decisions for myself.

(IF APPLICABLE) This power of attorney ends on the following date: _____

PRIOR DESIGNATIONS REVOKED.

I revoke any prior power of attorney for health care.

ACKNOWLEDGMENT OF DISCLOSURE STATEMENT.

I have been provided with a disclosure statement explaining the effect of this document. I have read and understood that information contained in the disclosure statement.

(YOU MUST DATE AND SIGN THIS POWER OF ATTORNEY)

I sign my name to this durable power of attorney for health care on _____ day of _____ 19_____ at

_____
(City and State)

_____
(Signature)

_____
(Print Name)

STATEMENT OF WITNESSES.

I declare under penalty of perjury that the principal has identified himself or herself to me, that the principal signed or acknowledged this durable power of attorney in my presence, that I believe the principal to be of sound mind, that the principal has affirmed that the principal is aware of the nature of the document and is signing it voluntarily and free from duress, that the principal requested that I serve as witness to the principal's execution of this document, that I am not the person appointed as agent by this document, and that I am not a provider of health or residential care, an employee of a provider of health or residential care, the operator of a community care facility, or an employee of an operator of a health care facility.

I declare that I am not related to the principal by blood, marriage, or adoption and that to the best of my knowledge I am not entitled to any part of the estate of the principal on the death of the principal under a will or by operation of law.

Witness signature: _____

Print Name: _____ Date: _____

Address: _____

Witness signature: _____

Print Name: _____ Date: _____

Address: _____

Utah Personal Choice and Living Will Act

Utah recognizes the legal right of any competent adult (eighteen years of age or older) to make binding written directives instructing physicians and other providers of medical services to limit, withhold, or withdraw life-sustaining procedures in the event of a terminal illness.

Under Utah's complex act, there are three directives. It is important to note the specific provisions of each one.

1. The first document is a living will directive instructing your physician and other providers of medical services not to prolong your life artificially if you have an injury, disease, or illness certified in writing by two physicians to be a terminal illness.
2. The second document is a special power of attorney enabling you to appoint an individual to act as your agent with authority to execute a directive governing care and treatment—or withholding of treatment—should you incur an illness, disease, or injury that renders you unable to direct your care.
3. The third document (not shown) is a medical treatment plan and is designed for use *after* incurring a disease, injury, or illness (but not necessarily a "terminal" condition) or if you are contemplating an operation or medical procedure that may result in substantial impairment. The medical treatment plan provides for specific directions for care, treatment, or withholding of treatments and may be prepared by you and your physician or by your agent and physician according to your wishes.

We do not show this last document because you will not need it until you incur a specific disease, injury, or illness. Should you, for example, become ill, we advise you to contact the Senior Citizens Law Center, Utah Legal Services Inc., 124 South Fourth East, Suite 400, Salt Lake City, Utah 84111, (801) 328–8891 or (800) 622–4245 and request the medical treatment plan and accompanying instructions. You should discuss your chosen course of treatment with your physician before you and your physician sign the medical treatment plan.

Other provisions of the act which pertain to the two directives included here are as follows:

1. All directives must be signed by you or a person designated by you, dated and signed by two witnesses. The witnesses must *not* be

    a. A person who signed the directive on your behalf.
    b. Related to you by blood or marriage.
    c. Entitled to any portion of your estate.
    d. Directly financially responsible for your medical care.
    e. An agent of any health-care facility in which you are a patient at the time of executing the directive.

2. It is your responsibility to notify your physician and health-care providers of your directives. Your health-care providers must then make the directives part of your medical records.

3. Your directives may be revoked or changed at any time.
4. According to the current language of the bill, life-sustaining procedures do not include the administration of medication or sustenance or any medical procedure deemed necessary to provide comfort care or alleviate pain. *If you wish artificial nutrition and hydration withheld or withdrawn, you should specify this in your document.*
5. Your directives will have no effect during pregnancy.
6. Withholding or withdrawing life-sustaining procedures will not constitute suicide or assisted suicide.
7. The execution of a living will has no effect on the sale or issuance of health care or life insurance policies.

To protect yourself as fully as possible against unwanted treatment, the Society for the Right to Die advises that you execute the generic living will (Chapter 3) and the Utah declarations, including the special power of attorney.

Directive to Physicians and Providers of Medical Services

This directive made this _____ day of _____, _____.

1. I, _____, being of sound mind, willfully and voluntarily make known my desire that my life not be artificially prolonged by life-sustaining procedures except as I may otherwise provide in this directive.

2. I declare that if at any time I should have an injury, disease, or illness, which is certified in writing to be a terminal condition by two physicians who have personally examined me, and in the opinion of those physicians the application of life-sustaining procedures would serve only to unnaturally prolong the moment of my death and to unnaturally postpone or prolong the dying process, I direct that these procedures be withheld or withdrawn and my death be permitted to occur naturally.

3. I expressly intend this directive to be a final expression of my legal right to refuse medical or surgical treatment and to accept the consequences from this refusal which shall remain in effect notwithstanding my future inability to give current medical directions to treating physicians and other providers of medical services.

4. I understand that the term "life-sustaining procedure" does not include the administration of medication or sustenance, or the performance of any medical procedure deemed necessary to provide comfort care, or to alleviate pain, except to the extent I specify below that any of these procedures be considered life-sustaining:

5. I reserve the right to give current medical directions to physicians and other providers of medical services so long as I am able, even though these directions may conflict with the above written directive that life-sustaining procedures be withheld or withdrawn.

6. I understand the full import of this directive and declare that I am emotionally and mentally competent to make this directive.

_____
Declarant's signature

_____
City, County and State of Residence

We witnesses certify that each of us is 18 years of age or older and each personally witnessed the declarant sign or direct the signing of this directive; that we are acquainted with declarant and believe him to be of sound mind; that the declarant's desires are as expressed above; that neither of us is a person who signed the above directive on behalf of the declarant; that we are not related to the declarant by blood or marriage nor are we entitled to any portion of declarant's estate according to the laws of intestate succession of this state or under any will or codicil of declarant; that we are not directly financially responsible for declarant's medical care; and that we are not agents of any health care facility in which the declarant may be a patient at the time of signing this directive.

_____   _____
Signature of Witness   *Signature of Witness*

_____   _____
Address of Witness   *Address of Witness*

Utah

Special Power of Attorney

I,_____, of _____

_____, this _____ day of _____, _____, being of sound mind,

willfully and voluntarily appoint _____

of _____, as my agent and
attorney-in-fact, without substitution, with lawful authority to execute a directive on my behalf under Section
75-2-1105, governing the care and treatment to be administered to or withheld from me at any time after I
incur an injury, disease, or illness which renders me unable to give current directions to attending physicians
and other providers of medical services.

I understand that "life-sustaining procedures" do not include the administration of medication or sustenance, or the performance of any medical procedure deemed necessary to provide comfort care, or to alleviate
pain, unless my attorney-in-fact specifies these procedures be considered life-sustaining.

I have carefully selected my above-named agent with confidence in the belief that this person's familiarity
with my desires, beliefs, and attitudes will result in directions to attending physicians and providers of medical
services which would probably be the same as I would give if able to do so.

This power of attorney shall be and remain in effect from the time my attending physician certifies that I
have incurred a physical or mental condition rendering me unable to give current directions to attending physicians and other providers of medical services as to my care and treatment.

_____
Signature of principal

State of_____)
                : ss
County of_____)

On the _____ day of _____, _____, personally appeared before me

_____ ,
who duly acknowledged to me that he/she has read and fully understands the foregoing power of attorney,
executed the same of his/her own volition and for the purposes set forth, and that he/she was acting under no
constraint or undue influence whatsoever.

_____
(Notary Public)

    Residing at: _____

My commission expires:

_____

Vermont Terminal Care Document

The Vermont Terminal Care Document Act recognizes your right as an adult (eighteen or older) to make an advance directive stating that you do not want your dying artificially prolonged by the use of life-sustaining procedures.

The form shown here complies with the suggested document form given in the statute. You may, if you wish, add personalized directions, and we have provided space for these. You might wish to consider listing the particular treatments to be withheld or withdrawn—for example, "I do not want antibiotics, surgery, cardiac resuscitation, a respirator, artificial feeding." You might want to emphasize your desire to be kept comfortable and pain free, even though medication might shorten your life.

Your document must be signed in the presence of two witnesses. The following may *not* serve as your witnesses:

1. Your spouse.
2. Your heir.
3. Your attending physician or anyone acting under your attending physician's direction.
4. Anyone who at the time of witnessing has any claims against your estate.

Properly signed and witnessed, your Terminal Care Document will remain in effect until or unless you revoke it. It will take effect whenever the circumstances it describes takes place. Your own expressed wishes always supersede your document.

Vermont also enacted a statute authorizing powers of attorney for health care. This permits you to appoint a person the law calls an "agent" specifically authorized to make medical treatment decisions on your behalf if at any time you lack the capacity to make and communicate such decisions for yourself. These can include the decision to withhold or withdraw life-sustaining procedures.

We view this legal device as a very useful additional protection. And since the requirements regarding the power of attorney are all spelled out the form is in accordance with the statute, there is no necessity for you to consult a lawyer in order to execute the form. Please read the execution and witnessing requirements carefully.

To protect yourself as fully as possible against unwanted treatment, the Society for the Right to Die advises that you execute the generic living will (Chapter 3) and the Vermont terminal care document and durable power of attorney for health care.

TERMINAL CARE DOCUMENT

To my family, my physician, my lawyer, my clergyman. To any medical facility in whose care I happen to be. To any individual who may become responsible for my health, welfare or affairs.

Death is as much a reality as birth, growth, maturity and old age—it is the one certainty of life. If the time comes when I, _____, can no longer take part in decisions of my own future, let this statement stand as an expression of my wishes, while I am still of sound mind.

If the situation should arise in which I am in a terminal state and there is no reasonable expectation of my recovery, I direct that I be allowed to die a natural death and that my life not be prolonged by extraordinary measures. I do, however, ask that medication be mercifully administered to me to alleviate suffering even though this may shorten my remaining life.

Other directions:

This statement is made after careful consideration and is in accordance with my strong convictions and beliefs. I want the wishes and directions here expressed carried out to the extent permitted by law. Insofar as they are not legally enforceable, I hope that those to whom this will is addressed will regard themselves as morally bound by these provisions.

Signed: _____

Date: _____

Witness: _____

Witness: _____

Copies of this request have been given to: _____

_____

_____

_____

VERMONT

DURABLE POWER OF ATTORNEY FOR HEALTH CARE

INFORMATION CONCERNING THE DURABLE POWER OF ATTORNEY FOR HEALTH CARE

This is an important legal document. Before signing this document, you should know these important facts:

Except to the extent you state otherwise, this document gives the person you name as your agent the authority to make any and all health care decisions for you when you are no longer capable of making them yourself. "Health care" means any treatment, service or procedure to maintain, diagnose or treat your physical or mental condition. Your agent therefore can have the power to make a broad range of health care decisions for you. Your agent may consent, refuse to consent, or withdraw consent to medical treatment and may make decisions about withdrawing or withholding life-sustaining treatment.

You may state in this document any treatment you do not desire or treatment you want to be sure you receive. Your agent's authority will begin when your doctor certifies that you lack the capacity to make health care decisions. You may attach additional pages if you need more space to complete your statement.

Your agent will be obligated to follow your instructions when making decisions on your behalf. Unless you state otherwise, your agent will have the same authority to make decisions about your health care as you would have had.

It is important that you discuss this document with your physician or other health care providers before you sign it to make sure that you understand the nature and range of decisions which may be made on your behalf. If you do not have a physician, you should talk with someone else who is knowledgeable about these issues and can answer your questions. You do not need a lawyer's assistance to complete this document, but if there is anything in this document that you do not understand, you should ask a lawyer to explain it to you.

The person you appoint as agent should be someone you know and trust and must be at least 18 years old. If you appoint your health or residential care provider (e.g., your physician, or an employee of a home health agency, hospital, nursing home, or residential care home, other than a relative), that person will have to choose between acting as your agent or as your health or residential care provider; the law does not permit a person to do both at the same time.

You should inform the person you appoint that you want him or her to be your health care agent. You should discuss this document with your agent and your physician and give each a signed copy. You should indicate on the document itself the people and institutions who will have signed copies. Your agent will not be liable for health care decisions made in good faith on your behalf.

Even after you have signed this document, you have the right to make health care decisions for yourself as long as you are able to do so, and treatment cannot be given to you or stopped over your objection. You have the right to revoke the authority granted to your agent by informing him or her or your health care provider orally or in writing.

This document may not be changed or modified. If you want to make changes in the document you must make an entirely new one.

You may wish to designate an alternate agent in the event that your agent is unwilling, unable or ineligible to act as your agent. Any alternate agent you designate will have the same authority to make health care decisions for you.

This power of attorney will not be valid unless it is signed in the presence of two (2) or more qualified witnesses who must both be present when you sign or acknowledge your signature. The following persons may *not* act as witnesses:

- the person you have designated as your agent;
- your health or residential care provider or one of their employees;
- your spouse;
- your lawful heirs or beneficiaries named in your will or a deed;
- creditors or persons who have a claim against you.

The durable power of attorney shall be in substantially the following form:

DURABLE POWER OF ATTORNEY FOR HEALTH CARE

I, _____, hereby appoint _____

of _____ as my agent to make any and all health care decisions for me, except to the extent I state otherwise in this document. This durable power of attorney for health care shall take effect in the event I become unable to make my own health care decisions.

(a) Statement of desires, special provisions, and limitations regarding Health Care Decisions.

Here you may include any specific desires or limitations you deem appropriate, such as when or what life-sustaining measures should be withheld; directions whether to continue or discontinue artificial nutrition and hydration; or instructions to refuse any specific types of treatment that are inconsistent with your religious beliefs or unacceptable to you for any other reason.

_____

_____

_____

_____

(attach additional pages as necessary)

(b) The subject of life-sustaining treatment is of particular importance.

For your convenience in dealing with that subject, some general statements concerning the withholding or removal of life-sustaining treatment are set forth below.

If you agree with one of these statements, you may include the statement in the blank space above:

If I suffer a condition from which there is no reasonable prospect of regaining my ability to think and act for myself, I want only care directed to my comfort and dignity, and authorize my agent to decline all treatment (including artificial nutrition and hydration) the primary purpose of which is to prolong my life.

If I suffer a condition from which there is no reasonable prospect of regaining the ability to think and act for myself, I want care directed to my comfort and dignity and also want artificial nutrition and hydration if needed, but authorize my agent to decline all other treatment the primary purpose of which is to prolong my life.

I want my life sustained by any reasonable medical measures, regardless of my condition.

In the event the person I appoint above is unable, unwilling or unavailable to act as my health care agent, I hereby appoint

_____ of _____
as alternate agent.

I hereby acknowledge that I have been provided with a disclosure statement explaining the effect of this document. I have read and understand the information contained in the disclosure statement.

The original of this document will be kept at_____ and the following persons and institutions will have signed copies.

_____

_____

_____

In witness whereof, I have hereunto signed my name this _____ day of _____, 19_____.

_____
Signature

I declare that the principal appears to be of sound mind and free from duress at the time the durable power of attorney for health care is signed and that the principal has affirmed that he or she is aware of the nature of the document and is signing it freely and voluntarily.

Witness: _____ Address: _____

Witness: _____ Address: _____

Statement of ombudsman, hospital representative or other authorized person (to be signed only if the principal is in or is being admitted to a hospital, nursing home or residential care home):

I declare that I have personally explained the nature and effect of this durable power of attorney to the principal and that the principal understands the same.

Date: _____

Name: _____

Address: _____

Virginia Natural Death Act

Shown here is a copy of the declaration contained in Virginia's Natural Death Act, which permits adult Virginia residents to either instruct their physicians to withhold or withdraw life-sustaining procedures in the event of a terminal condition *or,* as an alternative, designate another person to make that decision on their behalf.

You may add additional specific directions if you wish. For instance, you might consider listing the particular treatment to be rejected—for example, cardiopulminary resuscitation or surgery. You might want to emphasize your desire to be kept comfortable and pain free, even if to do so shortens your life.

You may execute a declaration at any time, in the presence of two witnesses, *neither of whom may be related to you by blood or marriage.*

Your declaration will become effective only after your attending physician (and if you are in a coma, incompetent, or otherwise incapable of communication, a second physician) certifies, on the basis of personally examining you, that your condition is terminal.

It is your responsibility to notify your doctor of the existence of your declaration; it is your doctor's responsibility to make it part of your medical record.

As long as you are able to make medical decisions, your own expressed wishes always supersede your declaration.

To protect yourself as fully as possible against unwanted treatment, the Society for the Right to Die advises that you execute the Virginia Natural Death Act declaration and the generic living will (Chapter 3). The generic living will applies to incurable or irreversible conditions that may not fit Virginia's definition of terminal.

DECLARATION

Declaration made this _____ day of _____ (month, year)

I, _____, willfully and voluntarily make known my desire and do hereby declare:

CHOOSE ONLY ONE OF THE NEXT TWO PARAGRAPHS AND
CROSS THROUGH THE OTHER

If at any time I should have a terminal condition and I am comatose, incompetent or otherwise mentally or physically incapable of communication, I designate_____
to make a decision on my behalf as to whether life-prolonging procedures shall be withheld or withdrawn. In the event that my designee decides that such procedures should be withheld or withdrawn, I wish to be permitted to die naturally with only the administration of medication or the performance of any medical procedure deemed necessary to provide me with comfort care or to alleviate pain. (OPTION: I specifically direct that the following procedures or treatments be provided to me: _____
_____)

OR

If at any time I should have a terminal condition where the application of life-prolonging procedures would serve only to artificially prolong the dying process, I direct that such procedures be withheld or withdrawn, and that I be permitted to die naturally with only the administration of medication or the performance of any medical procedure deemed necessary to provide me with comfort care or to alleviate pain. (OPTION: I specifically direct that the following procedures or treatments be provided to me: _____
_____)

Other directions:

In the absence of my ability to give directions regarding the use of such life-prolonging procedures, it is my intention that this declaration shall be honored by my family and physician as the final expression of my legal right to refuse medical or surgical treatment and accept the consequences of such refusal.

I understand the full import of this declaration and I am emotionally and mentally competent to make this declaration.

(Signed) _____

The declarant is known to me and I believe him or her to be of sound mind.

Witness _____

Witness _____

Washington Natural Death Act

Washington's Natural Death Act recognizes your right as an adult to execute a Directive to Physicians stating that you do not want your dying artificially prolonged by the use of life-sustaining procedures. The directive will be given effect whenever your attending physician and one other doctor have verified in writing that your condition is terminal.

The form shown here complies with the suggested directive from given in the statute. The act also permits personalized additions, and we have provided space for these. You might wish to consider listing the particular treatments to be withheld or withdrawn—for example, "I do not want surgery, cardiac resuscitation, a respirator, artificial feeding." You might want to name a proxy—someone you trust to make the treatment decisions you would make if you could. You might want to emphasize your desire to be kept comfortable and pain free, even though medication might shorten your life.

Your directive must be signed in the presence of two witnesses, neither of whom may be

1. Related to you by blood or marraige.
2. Entitled to any part of your estate, by inheritance or other claim.
3. Your attending physician.
4. An employee of your attending physician or of the health facility in which you are a patient.

Properly signed and witnessed, your directive will remain in effect until or unless you revoke it. As long as you are competent, your own expressed wishes always supersede your directive.

To protect yourself as fully as possible against unwanted treatment, the Society for the Right to Die advises that you execute the generic living will (Chapter 3) and the Washington Directive. The generic living will applies to incurable and irreversible conditions that may not be covered by the Washington act.

DIRECTIVE TO PHYSICIANS

Directive made this _____ day of _____ (month, year).

I, _____, being of sound mind, wilfully and voluntarily make known my desire that my life shall not be artificially prolonged under the circumstances set forth below, and do hereby declare that:

(a) If at any time I should have an incurable injury, disease, or illness certified to be a terminal condition by two physicians, and where the application of life-sustaining procedures would serve only to artificially prolong the moment of my death and where my physician determines that my death is imminent whether or not life-sustaining procedures are utilized, I direct that such procedures be withheld or withdrawn, and that I be permitted to die naturally.

(b) In the absence of my ability to give directions regarding the use of such life-sustaining procedures, it is my intention that this directive shall be honored by my family and physician(s) as the final expression of my legal right to refuse medical or surgical treatment and I accept the consequences from such refusal.

(c) If I have been diagnosed as pregnant and that diagnosis is known to my physician, this directive shall have no force or effect during the course of my pregnancy.

(d) I understand the full import of this directive and I am emotionally and mentally competent to make this directive.

Other directions:

Signed _____

City, County, and State of Residence _____

The declarer has been personally known to me and I believe him or her to be of sound mind.

Witness _____ Witness _____

This Directive complies with the Natural Death Act, Chapter 112, Washington laws of 1979. However, additional specific directions may be included by the declarer.

West Virginia's Natural Death Act

The Natural Death Act of West Virginia recognizes your right as an adult (age eighteen or older) to make a declaration stating that you do not want your dying artificially prolonged by the use of life-sustaining procedures. The declaration will become applicable whenever your attending physician and one other doctor confirm that your condition is terminal.

The form shown here complies with the suggested declaration form given in the statute. The act also permits personalized additions, and we have provided space for these. You might wish to consider listing the particular treatments to be withheld or withdrawn—for example, "I do not want surgery, cardiac resuscitation, a respirator, artificial feeding." You might want to emphasize your desire to be kept comfortable and pain free, even though medication might shorten your life.

Your declaration must be signed in the presence of two witnesses, neither of whom may be

1. Related to you by blood or marriage.
2. Directly responsible for costs of your medical care.
3. Entitled to any part of your estate, by inheritance.
4. Your doctor, an employee of your doctor, or an employee of a health-care facility in which you are a patient.

Your witnesses must attest to the execution of your declaration in the presence of a notary public.

Properly signed and witnessed, your declaration will remain in effect until or unless you revoke it. As long as you are capable of decision making and communication, your expressed wishes supersede your declaration.

West Virginia also has a form for a medical power of attorney, which permits you to appoint someone to make medical decisions for you, including decisions about the use of life support when you become unable to make such decisions yourself. If you have someone to appoint, the medical power of attorney is particularly useful because it covers all medical decisions, not just those at the end of life.

If you decide to use both the Natural Death Act declaration and the medical power of attorney, make sure that the personal instructions each contains are the same. If the instructions are different, those in the document you executed later will control.

In West Virginia, you may not name any of the following as your agent:

1. Your treating health-care provider.
2. An operator of your health-care facility.
3. An employee of either of the above, unless the individual is a relative.

You must sign your medical power of attorney, or have it signed at your express direction, in the presence of two witnesses who are over the age of eighteen, *and* have it acknowledged before a notary public. The following people may not serve as a witness:

1. Any person who signed the durable power on your behalf.
2. Any relative of yours, by blood or marriage.

3. Anyone entitled to any portion of your estate, by will or by the laws of West Virginia
4. Anyone legally responsible for the costs of your medical care.
5. Your attending physician.
6. Your agent or alternate agent.

Your agent has a duty to act according to your personal wishes. If you have a West Virginia living will and there is any confusion about your views as expressed in the declaration or medical power of attorney, the document filled out later controls. However, it is best to be consistent.

To protect yourself as fully as possible against unwanted treatment, the Society for the Right to Die advises that you execute the generic living will (Chapter 3) and the West Virginia declaration and medical power of attorney. The generic living will applies to incurable and irreversible conditions that may not be covered in the Natural Death Act's definition of terminal.

WEST VIRGINIA

LIVING WILL

Living will made this _____ day of _____ (month, year).

I, _____ , being of sound mind, willfully and voluntarily declare that in the absence of my ability to give directions regarding the use of life-prolonging intervention, it is my desire that my dying shall not be artificially prolonged under the following circumstances:

If at any time I should be certified by two physicians who have personally examined me, one of whom is my attending physician, to have a terminal condition or to be in a persistent vegetative state, I direct that life-prolonging intervention that would serve solely to artificially prolong the dying process or maintain me in a persistent vegetative state be withheld or withdrawn, and that I be permitted to die naturally with only the administration of medication or the performance of any other medical procedure deemed necessary to keep me comfortable and alleviate pain.

SPECIAL DIRECTIVES OR LIMITATIONS ON THIS DECLARATION: (If none, write "none".)

It is my intention that this living will be honored as the final expression of my legal right to refuse medical or surgical treatment and accept the consequences resulting from such refusal.

I understand the full import of this living will.

Signed _____

Address _____

I did not sign the declarant's signature above for or at the direction of the declarant. I am at least eighteen years of age and am not related to the declarant by blood or marriage, entitled to any portion of the estate of the declarant according to the laws of intestate succession of the state of the declarant's domicile or to the best of my knowledge under any will of the declarant or codicil thereto, or directly financially responsible for declarant's medical care. I am not the declarant's attending physician or the declarant's health care representative, proxy or successor health care representative under a medical power of attorney.

Witness _____

Address _____

_____

Witness _____

Address _____

_____

STATE OF _____

COUNTY OF _____

The foregoing instrument was acknowledged before me this _____ (date) by the declarant and by the two witnesses whose signatures appear above.

My commission expires: _____

_____

Signature of Notary Public

WEST VIRGINIA

DECLARATION

Declaration made this _____ day of _____ (month, year).

I, _____, being of sound mind, willfully and voluntarily make known my desires that my dying shall not be artificially prolonged under the circumstances set forth below, and do declare:

If at any time I should have an incurable injury, disease, or illness certified to be a terminal condition by two physicians who have personally examined me, one of whom is my attending physician, and the physicians have determined that my death will occur whether or not life-sustaining procedures are utilized and where the application of life-sustaining procedures would serve only to artificially prolong the dying process, I direct that such procedures be withheld or withdrawn, and that I be permitted to die naturally with only the administration of nutrition, medication or the performance of any medical procedure deemed necessary to provide me with comfort care or to alleviate pain.

Specific instructions:

In the absence of my ability to give directions regarding the use of such life-sustaining procedures, it is my intention that this declaration be honored by my family and physician(s) as the final expression of my legal right to refuse medical or surgical treatment and accept the consequences resulting from such refusal.

I understand the full import of this declaration and I am emotionally and mentally competent to make this declaration.

Signed _____

Address _____

_____

I did not sign the declarant's signature above for or at the direction of the declarant. I am at least eighteen years of age and am not related to the declarant by blood or marriage, entitled to any portion of the estate of the declarant according to the laws of intestate succession of the state of West Virginia or to the best of my knowledge under any will of the declarant or codicil thereto, or directly financially responsible for the declarant's medical care. I am not the declarant's attending physician, an employee of the attending physician, nor an employee of the health facility in which the declarant is a patient.

Witness _____

Witness _____

AFFIDAVIT

STATE OF WEST VIRGINIA

COUNTY OF _____, to-wit:

"This day personally appeared before me, the undersigned authority, a Notary Public in and for _____ County, West Virginia, _____ (witness) and _____ (witness), who, being first duly sworn, say that they are the subscribing witnesses to the declaration of _____ (declarant), which declaration is dated the _____ day of _____, 19____; and that on the said date the said _____, the declarant, signed, sealed, published and declared the same as and for his declaration, in the presence of both these affiants; and that these affiants, at the request of said declarant, in the presence of each other, and in the presence of said declarant, all present at the same time, signed their names as attesting witnesses to said declaration.

"Affiants further say that this affidavit is made at the request of _____, declarant, and in his presence, and that _____ (declarant), at the time the declaration was executed, was in the opinion of the affiants, of sound mind and memory, and over the age of eighteen years.

_____

_____

Taken, subscribed and sworn to before me by _____ (witness) and _____ (witness) this _____ day of _____, 19____.

"My commission expires:

" _____
                               Notary Public"

WEST VIRGINIA

MEDICAL POWER OF ATTORNEY

Dated: _____, 19____.

I, _____, hereby appoint

(insert your name and address)

_____

(insert the name, address, area code and telephone number of the person you wish to designate as your representative)

as my representative to act on my behalf to give, withhold or withdraw informed consent to health care decisions in the event that I am not able to do so myself. If my representative is unable, unwilling or disqualified to serve, then I appoint _____, as my successor representative.

This appointment shall extend to (but not be limited to) decisions relating to medical treatment, surgical treatment, nursing care, medication, hospitalization, care and treatment in a nursing home or other facility, and home health care. The representative appointed by this document is specifically authorized to act on my behalf to consent to, refuse or withdraw any and all medical treatment or diagnostic procedures, if my representative determines that I, if able to do so, would consent to, refuse or withdraw such treatment or procedures. Such authority shall include, but not be limited to, the withholding or withdrawal of life-prolonging intervention when in the opinion of two physicians who have examined me, one of whom is my attending physician, such life-prolonging intervention offers no medical hope of benefit.

I appoint this representative because I believe this person understands my wishes and values and will act to carry into effect the health care decisions that I would make if I were able to do so, and because I also believe that this person will act in my best interests when my wishes are unknown. It is my intent that my family, my physician and all legal authorities be bound by the decisions that are made by the representative appointed by this document, and it is my intent that these decisions should not be the subject of review by any health care provider, or administrative or judicial agency.

It is my intent that this document be legally binding and effective. In the event that the law does not recognize this document as legally binding and effective, it is my intent that this document be taken as a formal statement of my desire concerning the method by which any health care decisions should be made on my behalf during any period when I am unable to make such decisions.

In exercising the authority under this medical power of attorney, my representative shall act consistently with my special directives or limitations as stated below.

SPECIAL DIRECTIVES OR LIMITATIONS ON THIS POWER: (If none, write "none.")

_____

_____

_____

_____

_____

_____

THIS MEDICAL POWER OF ATTORNEY SHALL BECOME EFFECTIVE ONLY UPON MY INCA-PACITY TO GIVE, WITHHOLD OR WITHDRAW INFORMED CONSENT TO MY OWN MEDICAL CARE.

These directives shall supersede any directives made in any previously executed document concerning my health care.

X_____

Signature of Principal

I did not sign the principal's signature above. I am at least eighteen years of age and am not related to the principal by blood or marriage. I am not entitled to any portion of the estate of the principal according to the laws of intestate succession of the state of the principal's domicile or to the best of my knowledge under any will of the principal or codicil thereto, or legally responsible for the costs of the principal's medical or other care. I am not the principal's attending physician, nor am I the representative or successor representative of the principal.

WITNESS: DATE:

_____   _____

WITNESS: DATE:

_____   _____

STATE OF _____,

COUNTY OF _____, to-wit:

I, _____, a Notary Public of said County, do certify that

_____, as principal, and _____

and _____, as witnesses, whose names are signed to the writing

above bearing date on the _____ day of _____, 19____, have this day acknowledged the

same before me.

Given under my hand this _____ day of _____, 19____.

My commission expires: _____

_____

Notary Public

Wisconsin Power of Attorney for Health Care

Wisconsin has a Natural Death Act that is too restrictive, so we do not distribute it. We recommend that you use the generic living will outlined in Chapter 3. Wisconsin *does* have a power of attorney for health care form, however. Wisconsin attorneys have noted that the generic living will along with the power of attorney offer you the best legal protection of your right to refuse unwanted treatment.

The durable power of attorney for health care form allows you to appoint another person (known as your "agent") to make medical decisions for you if at any time you become unable to make them yourself. We strongly advise you to do this, assuming you have someone whom you trust to make the decisions you would make if you could, and who is willing to act for you in this way.

Here are some specific instructions for the Wisconsin power of attorney for health care form:

1. Be sure to indicate your wishes regarding the "provision of nutrition or hydration" in the check-off box on the second page.
2. Be sure to have your witnesses and your agent(s) sign their statements on the last page.

Note: If you have a Wisconsin power of attorney for health care and a Wisconsin declaration to physicians, your agent's powers will be very restricted. We therefore recommend that instead of the Wisconsin declaration you use a general living will (Chapter 3) along with your power of attorney.

WISCONSIN
POWER OF ATTORNEY FOR HEALTH CARE

NOTICE TO PERSON MAKING THIS DOCUMENT

YOU HAVE THE RIGHT TO MAKE DECISIONS ABOUT YOUR HEALTH CARE. NO HEALTH CARE MAY BE GIVEN TO YOU OVER YOUR OBJECTION, AND NECESSARY HEALTH CARE MAY NOT BE STOPPED OR WITHHELD IF YOU OBJECT.

BECAUSE YOUR HEALTH CARE PROVIDERS IN SOME CASES HAVE NOT HAD THE OPPORTUNITY TO ESTABLISH A LONG-TERM RELATIONSHIP WITH YOU, THEY ARE OFTEN UNFAMILIAR WITH YOUR BELIEFS AND VALUES AND THE DETAILS OF YOUR FAMILY RELATIONSHIPS. THIS POSES A PROBLEM IF YOU BECOME PHYSICALLY OR MENTALLY UNABLE TO MAKE DECISIONS ABOUT YOUR HEALTH CARE.

IN ORDER TO AVOID THIS PROBLEM, YOU MAY SIGN THIS LEGAL DOCUMENT TO SPECIFY THE PERSON WHOM YOU WANT TO MAKE HEALTH CARE DECISIONS FOR YOU IF YOU ARE UNABLE TO MAKE THOSE DECISIONS PERSONALLY. THAT PERSON IS KNOWN AS YOUR HEALTH CARE AGENT. YOU SHOULD TAKE SOME TIME TO DISCUSS YOUR THOUGHTS AND BELIEFS ABOUT MEDICAL TREATMENT WITH THE PERSON OR PERSONS WHOM YOU HAVE SPECIFIED. YOU MAY STATE IN THIS DOCUMENT ANY TYPES OF HEALTH CARE THAT YOU DO OR DO NOT DESIRE, AND YOU MAY LIMIT THE AUTHORITY OF YOUR HEALTH CARE AGENT AS YOU WISH. IF YOUR HEALTH CARE AGENT IS UNAWARE OF YOUR DESIRES WITH RESPECT TO A PARTICULAR HEALTH CARE DECISION, HE OR SHE IS REQUIRED TO DETERMINE WHAT WOULD BE IN YOUR BEST INTERESTS IN MAKING THE DECISION.

THIS IS AN IMPORTANT LEGAL DOCUMENT. IT GIVES THE PERSON WHOM YOU SPECIFY BROAD POWERS TO MAKE HEALTH CARE DECISIONS FOR YOU. IT REVOKES ANY PRIOR POWER OF ATTORNEY FOR HEALTH CARE THAT YOU MAY HAVE MADE. IF YOU CHANGE YOUR MIND ABOUT WHETHER A PERSON SHOULD MAKE HEALTH CARE DECISIONS FOR YOU, OR ABOUT WHICH PERSON THAT SHOULD BE, YOU MAY REVOKE THIS DOCUMENT AT ANY TIME BY DESTROYING THE DOCUMENT OR DIRECTING ANOTHER PERSON TO DESTROY IT IN YOUR PRESENCE, REVOKING IT IN A WRITTEN STATEMENT WHICH YOU SIGN AND DATE OR STATING THAT IT IS REVOKED IN THE PRESENCE OF TWO WITNESSES. IF YOU REVOKE, YOU SHOULD NOTIFY THE PERSON YOU HAD SPECIFIED, YOUR HEALTH CARE PROVIDERS AND ANY OTHER PERSON TO WHOM YOU HAVE GIVEN A COPY. IF THE PERSON YOU HAVE SPECIFIED IS YOUR SPOUSE AND YOUR MARRIAGE IS ANNULLED OR YOU ARE DIVORCED AFTER SIGNING THIS DOCUMENT, THE DOCUMENT IS INVALID.

DO NOT SIGN THIS DOCUMENT UNLESS YOU CLEARLY UNDERSTAND WHAT IT MEANS.

IT IS SUGGESTED THAT YOU KEEP THE ORIGINAL OF THIS DOCUMENT ON FILE WITH YOUR PHYSICIAN.

POWER OF ATTORNEY FOR HEALTH CARE

Instrument made this _____ day of _____ (month), _____ (year).

CREATION OF POWER OF ATTORNEY FOR HEALTH CARE

I, _____ (print name)

_____ (signature)

_____ (address),

being of sound mind, intend by this document to create a power of attorney for health care. My executing this power of attorney for health care is voluntary. I expect, despite the creation of this power of attorney for health care, to be fully informed about and allowed to participate in any health care decision for me, to the extent that I am able. For the purposes of this document, "health care decision" means an informed decision in the exercise of my right to accept, maintain, discontinue or refuse any care, treatment, service or procedure to maintain, diagnose or treat my physical or mental condition.

DESIGNATION OF HEALTH CARE AGENT

If I am no longer able to make health care decisions for myself, due to my incapacity, I hereby designate

_____ (name, address and
telephone number) to be my health care agent for the purpose of making health care decisions on my behalf. If he or

she is ever unable or unwilling to do so, I hereby designate _____

_____ (name, address and telephone number) to be my alternate health care agent for the purpose of making health care decisions on my behalf. Neither the health care agent or the alternate health care agent whom I have designated is my health care provider, an employe of my health care provider or an employe of a health care facility in which I reside or am a patient or a spouse of any of those persons, or, if he or she is that health care provider or employe or spouse of that health care provider or employe, he or she is also my relative. For purposes of this document, "incapacity" exists if 2 physicians or a physician and a psychologist who have personally examined me sign a statement that specifically expresses their opinion that I have a condition that means that I am unable to receive and evaluate information effectively or to communicate decisions to such an extent that I lack the capacity to manage my health care decisions. A copy of that statement, if made, must be attached to this document.

GENERAL STATEMENT OF AUTHORITY GRANTED

Unless I have specified otherwise in this document, if I ever have incapacity I instruct my health care provider to obtain the health care decision of my health care agent for all of my health care. I have discussed my desires thoroughly with my health care agent and believe that he or she understands my philosophy regarding the health care decisions I would make if I were so able. I desire that my wishes be carried out through the authority given to my health care agent under this document.

My health care agent is instructed that if I am unable, due to my incapacity, to make a health care decision he or she shall make a health care decision for me, except that in exercising the authority given to him or her by this document my health care agent should try to discuss with me any specific proposed health care if I am able to communicate in any manner, including by blinking my eyes. If this communication cannot be made, my health care agent shall base his or her health care decision on any health care choices that I have expressed prior to the time of the decision. If I have not expressed a health care choice about the health care in question and communication cannot be made, my health care agent shall base his or her health care decision on what he or she believes to be in my best interest.

LIMITATIONS ON MENTAL HEALTH TREATMENT

My health care agent may not admit or commit me on an inpatient basis to an institution for mental diseases, an intermediate care facility for the mentally retarded, a state treatment facility or a treatment facility. My health care agent may not consent to experimental mental health research or psychosurgery, electroconvulsive treatment or other drastic mental health treatment procedures for me.

ADMISSION TO NURSING HOMES OR COMMUNITY-BASED RESIDENTIAL FACILITIES

My health care agent may admit me to a nursing home or community-based residential facility for short-term stays for recuperative care or respite care.

If I am diagnosed as mentally ill or developmentally disabled, my health care agent may not admit me to a nursing home or community-based residential facility for a purpose other than recuperative care or respite care.

If I am not diagnosed as mentally ill or developmentally disabled, and if I have checked "Yes" to the following, however, my health care agent may admit me for a purpose other than recuperative care or respite care to:

1. A nursing home – Yes ❑ No ❑
2. A community-based residential facility – Yes ❑ No ❑

If I have not checked either "Yes" or "No" to admission to a nursing home or community-based residential facility for a purpose other than recuperative care or respite care, my health care agent may only admit me for short-term stays for recuperative care or respite care.

PROVISION OF NUTRITION AND HYDRATION

If I have checked "Yes" to the following, my health care agent may have nonorally ingested nutrition and hydration withheld or withdrawn from me, unless my physician has advised that, in his or her professional judgment, this will cause me pain or will reduce my comfort. If I have checked "No" to the following, my health care agent may not have nonorally ingested nutrition and hydration withheld or withdrawn from me.

My health care agent may not have orally ingested nutrition and hydration withheld or withdrawn from me unless provision of the nutrition or hydration is medically contraindicated.

Withhold or withdraw nonorally ingested nutrition and hydration — Yes ❑ No ❑

If I have not checked either "Yes" or "No" to withholding or withdrawing nonorally ingested nutrition and hydration, my health care agent may not have nonorally ingested nutrition and hydration withdrawn from me.

HEALTH CARE DECISIONS FOR PREGNANT WOMEN

If I have checked "Yes" to the following, my health care agent may make health care decisions for me even if my agent knows I am pregnant. If I have checked "No" to the following, my health care agent may not make health care decisions for me if my health care agent knows I am pregnant.

Health care decision if I am pregnant — Yes ❑ No ❑

If I have not checked either "Yes" or "No" to permitting my health care agent to make health care decisions for me if I am known to be pregnant, my health care agent may not make health care decisions for me if my health care agent knows I am pregnant.

STATEMENT OF DESIRES, SPECIAL PROVISIONS OR LIMITATIONS

In exercising authority under this document, my health care agent shall act consistently with my following stated desires, if any, and is subject to any special provisions or limitations that I specify. The following are any specific desires, provisions or limitations that I wish to state (add more items if needed):

1)_____

2)_____

3)_____

INSPECTION AND DISCLOSURE OF INFORMATION RELATING TO MY PHYSICAL OR MENTAL HEALTH

Subject to any limitations in this document, my health care agent has the authority to do all of the following:

(a) Request, review and receive any information, verbal or written, regarding my physical or mental health, including medical and hospital records.

(b) Execute on my behalf any documents that may be required in order to obtain this information.

(c) Consent to the disclosure of this information.

SIGNING DOCUMENTS, WAIVERS AND RELEASES

Where necessary to implement the health care decisions that my health care agent is authorized by this document to make, my health care agent has the authority to execute on my behalf any of the following:

(a) Documents titled or purporting to be a "Consent to Permit Treatment," "Refusal to Permit Treatment" or "Leaving Hospital Against Medical Advice."

(b) A waiver or release from liability required by a hospital or physician.

STATEMENT OF WITNESSES

I know the principal personally and I believe him or her to be of sound mind and at least 18 years of age. I believe that his or her execution of this power of attorney for health care is voluntary. I am at least 18 years of age and am not related to the principal by blood, marriage or adoption. I am not a health care provider who is serving the principal at this time. To the best of my knowledge, I am not entitled to and do not have a claim on the principal's estate.

Witness _____ (name, address, date)

Witness _____ (name, address, date)

STATEMENT OF HEALTH CARE AGENT

I understand that _____ (name of principal) has designated me to be his or her health care agent if he or she is ever found to have incapacity and unable to make health care decisions himself or herself. _____ (name of principal) has discussed his or her desires regarding health care decisions with me.

Signed _____ Address _____

STATEMENT OF ALTERNATE HEALTH CARE AGENT

I understand that _____ (name of principal) has designated me to be his or her health care agent if he or she is ever found to have incapacity and unable to make health care decisions himself or herself and if the person designated as health care agent is unable or unwilling to make those decisions. _____ (name of principal) has discussed his or her desires regarding health care decisions with me.

Signed _____ Address _____

Failure to execute a power of attorney for health care document under chapter 155 of the Wisconsin Statutes creates no presumption about the intent of any individual with regard to his or her health care decisions.

This power of attorney for health care is executed as provided in chapter 155 of the Wisconsin Statutes.

Wyoming Act Relating to Medical Treatment to Persons Afflicted with a Terminal Condition

Wyoming's living will statute recognizes your right as an adult to make a declaration instructing your physician to withhold or withdraw life-sustaining procedures in the event you are in a terminal condition as certified by two physicians.

The form shown here complies with the suggested declaration form given in the statute. You may, if you wish, add personalized directions, and we have provided space for these. You might wish to consider listing the particular treatments to be withheld or withdrawn—for example, cardiac resuscitation or a respirator. If you are also opposed to being artifically fed in a terminal condition, add this to your list of unwanted treatment. Unfortunately, there is language in the Wyoming act that would appear to mandate the administration of nutrition and hydration. Your best course nevertheless is to specify your refusal of it if that is your preference; by doing so, you will be making clear your wishes about this form of treatment without otherwise affecting your rights under the law. Note also that the declaration includes a clause for designating another person—perhaps a family member or trusted friend—to participate in treatment decision making if you are unable to do so. You may make use of it or leave it blank.

Your declaration must be signed in the presence of *two adult witnesses, neither of whom may be related to you by blood or marriage or entitled to any part of your estate upon your death or directly financially responsible for your medical care.*

Properly signed and witnessed, your declaration will remain in effect until or unless you revoke it. As long as you are able to communicate your preferences, your own expressed wishes always supersede your declaration.

To protect yourself as fully as possible against unwanted treatment, especially as the Wyoming Act does not provide for refusal of tube feeding, we advise that you execute the generic living will (Chapter 3) and the Wyoming form.

Note: Wyoming passed a new double power of attorney for health care, which was not available as this book went to press. Please contact the Society for the Right to Die to obtain this new document.

WYOMING

DECLARATION

Declaration made this _____ day of _____(month, year).

I, _____, being of sound mind, willfully and voluntarily make known my desire that my dying shall not be artificially prolonged under the circumstances set forth below, do hereby declare:

If at any time I should have an incurable injury, disease or other illness certified to be a terminal condition by two (2) physicians who have personally examined me, one (1) of whom shall be my attending physician, and the physicians have determined that my death will occur whether or not life-sustaining procedures are utilized and where the application of life-sustaining procedures would serve only to artificially prolong the dying process, I direct that such procedures be withheld or withdrawn, and that I be permitted to die naturally with only the administration of medication or the performance of any medical procedure deemed necessary to provide me with comfort care.

Other directions:

If, in spite of this declaration, I am comatose or otherwise unable to make treatment decisions for

myself, I HEREBY designate _____ to make treatment decisions for me.*

In the absence of my ability to give directions regarding the use of life-sustaining procedures, it is my intention that this declaration shall be honored by my family and physician(s) and agent as the final expression of my legal right to refuse medical or surgical treatment and accept the consequences from this refusal. I understand the full import of this declaration and I am emotionally and mentally competent to make this declaration.

Signed _____

City, County and State of Residence _____

_____

The declarant has been personally known to me and I believe him or her to be of sound mind. I did not sign the declarant's signature above for or at the direction of the declarant. I am not related to the declarant by blood or marriage, entitled to any portion of the estate of the declarant according to the laws of intestate succession or under any will of the declarant or codicil thereto, or directly financially responsible for the declarant's medical care.

Witness _____

Witness _____

Designation of a proxy may, but need not, be included in the Declaration, according to § 35-22-102 of the Wyoming Living Will Act. If you do not wish to use this clause, it is advisable to draw a line through it.

Canada Living Will and Durable Power of Attorney for Health Care

The Canada organization, Dying with Dignity, distributes this general living will along with instructions for its use. Living wills are recognized in Canada although no province has yet legalized them. You may use the Dying with Dignity form or the Society's generic living will discussed in Chapter 3.

Dying with Dignity also distributes the Durable Power of Attorney for Health Care in Canada with instructions. It is a good idea to appoint another person to make health care decisions for you should you become incapacitated and to indicate the name of your health-care proxy in writing.

See *Resources* at the end of the book for the address of Dying with Dignity and important Canadian health-care institutions.

To My Family, My Physician, My Lawyer and All Others Whom It May Concern

Death is as much a reality as birth, growth, maturity and old age—it is the one certainty of life. If the time comes when I can no longer take part in decisions for my own future, let this statement stand as an expression of my wishes and directions, while I am still of sound mind.

If at such a time the situation should arise in which there is no reasonable expectation of my recovery from extreme physical or mental disability, I direct that I be allowed to die and not be kept alive by medications, artificial means or "heroic measures". I do, however, ask that medication be mercifully administered to me to alleviate suffering even though this may shorten my remaining life.

This statement is made after careful consideration and is in accordance with my strong convictions and beliefs. I want the wishes and directions here expressed carried out to the extent permitted by law. Insofar as they are not legally enforceable, I hope that those to whom this Will is addressed will regard themselves as morally bound by these provisions.

Signed _____ Date _____

Witness _____

Witness _____

Copies of this request have been given to _____

_____

_____

THE DURABLE POWER OF ATTORNEY FOR HEALTH CARE:

of _____
(name)
_____
(address)

directed to my family, my physician, my executor and all others whom it may concern.

1. I accept the inevitability of death. If, near the end of my life, I am no longer able to make decisions for my own future, if I am no longer able to communicate, if I am unable to care for myself, if there is no reasonable expectation of my recovery from extreme physical or mental disability or incapacity, if circumstances exist that render me incapable of rational existence, if I am afflicted with irreversible injury, disease, illness, or condition,

*

then I want my attorneys to respect my wishes listed below.

Where the application of measures of artificial life support would primarily serve to prolong the moment of my death, then let this document stand as an expression of my thoughts, intentions, wishes and directions—that I do not wish to endure any prolonged period of pain and suffering. I sign this document of my own free will and volition, while I am still of sound mind, and emotionally competent to make such decisions.

2. I believe in the philosophy of dying with dignity. If any of the situations specified in paragraph 1 should arise, I direct that I be allowed to die and not be kept alive by medications, artificial means or invasive measures of any kind.

3. Measures of extending life that are especially abhorrent to me, and which are to be withheld, withdrawn or discontinued if the circumstances stated in this Power of Attorney arise, include:

    (a)   electrical or mechanical resuscitation of my heart;
    (b)   nutritional feedings;
    (c)   artificial mechanical respiration when my brain can no longer sustain breathing;
    (d)   radiation, chemotherapy, and similar forms of treatment;
    (e)   treatment for an illness or disease which I contracted, when I was already afflicted with a terminal illness; for example, if I were dying of Alzheimer's disease or a stroke, I would not wish any form of treatment if I contracted pneumonia.

4. I request that a **"Do Not Resuscitate"** (D.N.R.) notification be with me at all times—whether I am at home, living with family or friends, in a hospital or other care facility.

5. I do ask that medication be mercifully administered to alleviate any pain, suffering or distress even though this may hasten the moment of my death.

6. I want the wishes and directions expressed in this Power of Attorney and the spirit of this document carried out to the fullest extent permitted by law. Insofar as they are not legally enforceable, I nevertheless request that those responsible for me at such time will regard themselves as morally bound by these provisions, so that they will carry out these wishes to the fullest extent possible.

7. If it will not impose an undue burden on my family, I would like to die at home rather than in an institution.

8. I have discussed my views regarding life-sustaining measures with my lawyer

**   _____
            (name)

            _____
            (address and phone number)

and with***   _____
            (name)

            _____
            (address and phone number)

to whom copies of this Power of Attorney have been delivered.

9. If any of the situations specified in this document should occur, I appoint

_____

as my attorney to carry out my thoughts and wishes, including, without limiting the generality of the foregoing, obtaining a court order, if necessary, to discontinue or forbid artificial life support measures that would primarily serve to prolong the moment of my death.

10. If I should happen to be under the care of a physician whose moral, ethical or religious beliefs are not in sympathy with my wishes as expressed in this document, I direct my attorneys to ask that physician to withdraw from my care, and to recommend another physician who agrees with my views on the prolongation of life. Similarly, my attorneys are empowered to transfer me to another hospital if such should be necessary to honour the directions in this document.

11. No participant in the making or carrying out of this Durable Power of Attorney, whether it be a health care provider, hospital administrator, spouse, a relative, friend or any other person, shall be held responsible in any way, legally, professionally or morally, for any consequences arising from the implementation of my wishes.

IN TESTIMONY WHEREOF I have to this, my Durable Power of Attorney for Health Care, subscribed my name, this

_____ day   of _____   19 , _____

SIGNED AND DECLARED by the said

_____

as and for his/her Durable Power of Attorney, in the presence of us, both present at the same time, who, at his/her request, in his/her presence, and in the presence of each other, have hereunto subscribed our names as witnesses.

X _____

Your name

(name)

(address)   (street)

Witness:

(city)   (prov.)   (postal code)

(telephone)

_____

(name)

(address)   (street)

Witness:

(city)   (prov.)   (postal code)

(telephone)

DYING WITH DIGNITY File No:

This document is prepared and distributed by **Dying with Dignity,** a Canadian Society Concerned with the Quality of Dying.

National office: 175 St. Clair Avenue West, Toronto, Ontario. M4V 1P7, (416) 921-2329

Glossary

Advance Directive. Instructions about medical-care preferences that a person puts into writing ahead of time, in case he or she should be rendered incapable of communicating those preferences when the need arises. The phrase "advance directive" is often used to mean "living will" and/or "durable power of attorney for health care."

Alzheimer's Disease. A progressive and nonreversible malfunction of the parts of the brain that control memory and reasoning. Afflicts about 4 million Americans, mostly elderly. Previously called "senility."

Amyotrophic Lateral Sclerosis (ALS). A degenerative disease characterized by progressive motor weakness and spastic limbs. Also called "Lou Gehrig's disease."

Antibiotics. Medication used to fight infections.

Artificial Nutrition and Hydration. See *Tube Feeding.*

Assisted Suicide. A suicide that is facilitated with the conscious help of another person, such as a doctor or a loved one, who has been recruited for that purpose by the person desiring to die.

Attorney-in-Fact. See *Health-Care Agent or Health-Care Proxy*

Autonomy. Broadly, the right of self-directing freedom and independence. In the context of right-to-die issues, the right to decide what is done with one's own body. Also called "self-determination."

Best Interest. A standard for health-care decision making by others on behalf of an incompetent patient, based on what they believe to be "best" for the patient, as opposed to what they know or believe the patient would have wanted. Used when there is no written record of wishes, no health-care agent and no relative, close friend, or even an acquaintance who can reliably report what the patient's wishes would be. (Contrast with *Substituted Judgment.*)

Bioethics. A field of study in which moral and ethical considerations relating to health care are explored and evaluated. A bioethicist is a person who is considered knowledgeable and authoritative in this field. Most bioethicists are also doctors, philosophers, or lawyers.

Brain Death. When all functioning of the brain, including the brain stem, has ceased permanently: a legal definition of death. Also termed "whole brain death." "Cortical brain death" refers to the cessation of all functioning in the *Cerebral Cortex.* A person who has suffered only "cortical brain death" is, legally speaking, still alive.

Brain Stem. The lower portion of the brain that controls reflexes, breathing, and other vegetative functions.

Cardiopulmonary Resuscitation (CPR). The restoration of heartbeat and breathing after it has ceased. Emergency procedures that may be used include mouth-to-mouth resuscitation, external chest compression, electric shock treatment to the heart, and the insertion of a tube into the patient's airway to assist breathing.

Case Law. Law established by court decision.

Cerebral Cortex. The most highly evolved portion of the brain, responsible for thinking and awareness.

Chemotherapy. The use of chemical agents to treat various forms of cancer.

Clear and Convincing Evidence. The highest standard of evidence in a civil court case.

Coma. A sleeplike state that can be the result of serious medical conditions, head trauma, or other bodily insults. Coma may be reversible. It is believed that a comatose patient cannot experience pain or suffering.

Comfort Care. Any kind of treatment that increases a persons physical or emotional comfort. May include visiting, touching, moistening the lips, as well as pain and other medication but not usually advanced technology.

Competent. Medically speaking, capable of making informed decisions and understanding the consequences relating to one's medical condition and treatment.

Constitutional Law. Law based on the constitution.

Declaration. A document expressing treatment preferences, such as a living will or durable power of attorney for health care. In some states, a clearly expressed and witnessed oral statement may also be accepted.

Dementia. Deterioration or loss of memory and higher intellectual function. *Alzheimer's disease* and strokes account for the vast majority of dementia cases, which are not reversible. When dementia is caused by medication or certain medical conditions, it may be reversible.

Diagnostic Tests. Tests for recognizing diseases, which include relatively noninvasive procedures such as blood tests, X rays, examination of the urine, and CAT and MRI scans. May also include invasive procedures that produce discomfort and pose significant risk.

Dialysis. The use of a machine to remove impurities from the blood of patients whose kidneys have failed. (See also *hemodialysis* and *peritoneal dialysis.*)

Do Not Resuscitate (DNR) Order. A DNR order in a patient's medical chart instructs the medical staff not to try to revive the patient if his or her breathing or heartbeat has stopped. Any competent patient may request a DNR, either verbally or by means of a living will or durable power of attorney.

Durable Power of Attorney for Health Care. A document that allows you to name another person to make decisions specifically about your health care in the event you are unable to make them yourself. More than half the states have enacted durable power of attorney statutes that directly address health-care decisions.

Durable Power of Attorney Statute. A law that authorizes the appointment of another person to make decisions for an individual if he or she becomes incompetent, usually relating to money or property matters. Called "durable" because, unlike the ordinary power of attorney, it "endures"—or goes into effect—when one becomes incompetent. All fifty states and the District of Columbia have statutes providing for some form of durable power, although they do not automatically cover health-care decisions.

Ethics Committee. A group within a health-care institution that meets to explore ethical problems and to reconcile the interests of health-care professionals and patients, and that often makes recommendations about treatment decisions such as when it might, or might not, be ethically appropriate to withdraw treatment.

Euthanasia. The bringing about of a "good death" for another, usually dying, patient. "Passive euthanasia," which is legal in virtually every state, means allowing death to occur by withholding or withdrawing life-sustaining treatment that is keeping the patient alive. "Active euthanasia" means causing death directly by some active means, such as the administration of a lethal injection. Active euthanasia is illegal in the United States and most other countries.

Extraordinary Measures. Lay term referring to life-sustaining measures that are considered "above and beyond" ordinary or appropriate care. Also called "heroic measures."

Gastrostomy Tube. A tube that delivers nutrients and water directly into a person's stomach through an incision in the abdomen.

Guardian. A court-appointed person authorized to handle another's affairs when he or she loses decision-making capacity.

Guardian Ad Litem. Someone appointed by the court to represent the interests of an incompetent patient in a legal proceeding.

Health-Care Agent or Health-Care Proxy. A person who is authorized, via a patient's living will or durable power of attorney, to make medical-care decisions on a patient's behalf, in the event that the patient becomes incapacitated. Also termed "attorney-in-fact."

Health Maintenance Organization (HMO). A medical-care organization that provides comprehensive health care services to its members for fixed, prepaid premiums. There are four basic models for HMOs—group, individual practice association, network, and staff.

Hemodialysis. Direct cleansing of the blood through tubes placed into blood vessels used when the kidneys fail to function (contrast *peritoneal dialysis*).

Hospice. A concept of care created specifically to help dying patients and their families through the final stages of terminal illness. While hospice care is most often delivered at home, inpatient care at a hospice institution may also be provided. The hospice patient receives treatment for pain control and symptom management, but not life-sustaining technology.

Immunity Clause. The provision in a living will or statute that relieves health-care providers of any liability for complying with a patient's wishes.

Incompetent. Lacking the capacity to make decisions and understand their implications. (See *competent.*)

Informed Consent. The approval a patient must give before a doctor can authorize and/or initiate a medical treatment for that patient. The physician must explain, and the patient fully understand, what the treatment is, how it will be administered, what the possible consequences of the treatment may be, what the consequences may be if the treatment is not administered, and what alternatives to the treatment are available.

Intravenous (IV) Line. A tube placed into a vein for the purpose of administering fluids, blood, or medication.

Liberty. The right to be free of governmental restraint.

Life Support. Medical interventions that can take over bodily functions and keep patients alive while curative efforts are undertaken. For hopelessly ill or dying patients, this technology may maintain the status quo by prolonging life when the body can no longer function on its own but it cannot improve the patient's underlying medical condition or offer any chances for recovery. Also termed: "life-sustaining treatment" and "life-prolonging treatment."

Living Will. A signed, dated, and witnessed document by means of which patients can tell their health-care givers in advance what life support treatments they do or do not want if they are hopelessly ill and can't speak for themselves.

Mechanical Respiration. The use of a machine, known as a respirator or ventilator, to pump air into and out of a patient's lungs and thereby assist or take over the patient's breathing function. Also termed "mechanical ventilation."

Mercy Killing. A colloquial term for active euthanasia, which assumes that the patient finds his or her existence to be intolerable.

Multiple Sclerosis (MS). A slowly degenerative disease that affects the spinal cord and brain and whose predominant symptoms are remitting but progressive weakness.

Nasogastric Tube. A pliable tube inserted through a patient's nose that delivers nutrients and water into the stomach.

Natural Death. A death that occurs as the result of allowing basic body functions to cease of their own accord, rather than maintaining them artificially by means of life support technology. In many states, the legislation pertaining to living wills is known as a "natural death act."

No Code. The phrase that refers to the status of a patient who has obtained a *Do Not Resuscitate (DNR) Order.*

Organ Donation. The transfer of a healthy vital organ from a dead person's body to the body of a live person in need of that vital organ.

Palliative Care. Medical treatments designed to relieve discomfort but that do not cure the underlying ailment—for example, placement of a colostomy in a cancerous intestine to relieve obstruction.

Parkinson's Disease. A chronic, progressive nervous disease characterized by tremor, stiffness, and abnormal gait.

Patient Representative. A person in a health-care institution who offers advice and represents the interest of the patient in any hospital conflict or dispute.

Patient Self-Determination Act. Federal legislation that requires all health-care institutions that receive Medicare or Medicaid (hospitals, nursing homes, hospices, HMOs, and home health-care services) to inform all patients on admission about their rights to receive or refuse treatment, including the right to formulate advance directives. As of December 1, 1991, institutions will have to supply written information about state law on living wills, describe their own policy toward honoring these documents, and record in each patient's medical chart whether he or she has filled out an advance directive.

Peritoneal Dialysis. The indirect cleansing of the blood through tubes placed into the abdomen, used when the kidneys fail to function.

Persistent Vegetative State (PVS). A chronic form of unconsciousness. PVS differs from coma in that the patient has sleep-wake cycles, although the PVS patient lacks any awareness even when awake. In PVS the cerebral cortex does not function but the lower portion of the brain, the brain stem that controls vegetative function, is intact. PVS is virtually never reversible.

Principal. The person who executes a document. Also called "appointer."

Resuscitation. See *Cardiopulmonary Resuscitation.*

Right to Die. The right of any individual to refuse unwanted medical treatments and to die a natural death.

Risk Manager. An employee of a medical facility whose job is to assess the liability risk that any course of action poses for the hospital.

Statutory Law. Law made by passing legislation. Forty-two states have statutory law recognizing living wills.

Substituted Judgment. The doctrine that when a patient is unable to make treatment decisions, another is permitted to stand in and substitute his or her judgment for the patient's, making the decision he or she believes the patient would have made under the circumstances. (Contrast with *best interest.*)

Suicide. The act of deliberately ending one's own life.

Surrogate Decision Maker. The person, usually next of kin, who is authorized to make decisions for an incompetent patient in the absence of a written advance directive.

Terminal Condition or Terminal Illness. Generally, a hopeless condition with no chance of recovery, but defined differently in each state.

Total Parenteral Nutrition (TPN). The most sophisticated form of tube feeding, whereby a fluid containing all the required nutrients is delivered directly into a patient's vein, thus bypassing the complex digestive processes of the stomach and intestines.

Tube Feeding. The provision by tube of prepared nutrients and fluids to a patient who is not able to swallow enough food and water to maintain adequate nutrition. Also termed "artificial feeding" and "artificial nutrition and hydration."

Resources

Concern for Dying
250 W. Fifty-seventh Street
New York, NY 10107
(merging with Society in 1991)

Dying with Dignity
175 St. Clair Avenue W.
Toronto, Ont.
Canada M4v 1P7

Hemlock Society
P. O. Box 11830
Eugene, OR 97440

Society for the Right to Die
250 W. Fifty-seventh Street
New York, NY 10107
(One set of advance directives free. Send
self-addressed stamped envelope.)

In addition, depending on where you live, you may contact your local State Department of Health, office of aging, nursing home ombudsman office, or regional AARP center.

AARP/American Association
  of Retired Persons
Special Projects Section
1909 K Street, NW
Washington, DC 20048-2837

If you run into conflicts concerning treatment refusal, you may want to find out if your area has a local health decisions group or a local medical ethics or bioethics office. Both these types of organization tend to have firsthand knowledge of the local factors at play in decision-making disputes.

The Hastings Center
255 Elm Road
Briarcliff Manor, NY 10510
(National Bioethics Center)

American Health Decisions
  (National Coalition of Citizens Groups)
c/o Oregon Health Decisions
921 SW Washington Street
Suite 713
Portland, OR 97205

Another useful resource if you run into conflicts:

American Civil Liberties Union (ACLU)
132 W. Forty-third Street
New York, NY 10036

As of December 1, 1991, all federally funded hospitals, nursing homes, hospices, health maintenance organizations, and home health service agencies will also make available information about advance directives.

Hospitals

American Hospital Association
840 N. Lakeshore Drive
Chicago, IL 60611

Physicians

American Medical Association
535 North Dearborn
Chicago, IL 60610

Nursing Homes

American Association of Homes
   for the Aging
901 E. Street, Suite 500
Washington, DC 2004

American Health Care Association
1201 L Street, NW
Washington, DC 2005

Hospices

National Hospice Organization
1901 N. Moore Street
Suite 901
Arlington, VA 22209

Home Health Agencies

American Federation of Home
   Health Agencies
1320 Fenwick Lance
Suite 100
Silver Springs, MD 20910

Health Maintenance Organizations

Group Health Association of America
1129 Twentieth Street NW, Suite 600
Washington, DC 20036
(202) 778–3200

GENERAL RESOURCES AND INFORMATION

American Bar Association
Commission on Legal Problems
   of the Elderly
1800 M Street, NW
Washington, DC 20049

Center for Medical Consumers
237 Thompson Street
New York, NY 10012

Center for Social Gerontology
117 N. First Street
Suite 204
Ann Arbor, MI 48104

ALS (Lou Gehrig's Disease)

National ALS Association
21021 Ventura Boulevard, Suite 321
Woodland Hills, CA 91364
(818) 340–7500

AIDS

National AIDS Hotline
(800) 342–2437 (English)
(800) 342–2437 (Spanish)

Gay Men Health Crisis (GMHC)
Legal Services Department
129 W. Twentieth Street,
   2nd floor
New York, NY 10011
(212) 807–6655

The AIDS ARC Switchboard
San Francisco AIDS
   Foundation
Box 6182
San Francisco, CA 94101
(415) 861–7309

Alzheimer's

Alzheimer's Association
70 E. Lake Street, Suite 600
Chicago, IL 60601
(312) 853–3060

Cancer

American Cancer Society, National
 Headquarters
1599 Clifton Road NE
Atlanta, GA 30329-4251
(404) 320–3333

Heart Disease

American Heart Association
7320 Greenville Avenue
Dallas, Texas 75231
(214) 373–6300

Multiple Sclerosis

National Multiple Sclerosis Society
205 E. Forty-second Street, 3rd floor
New York, New York 10017
(212) 986–3240

Parkinson's Disease

American Parkinson's Disease
 Association, National Office
60 Bay Street
Staten Island, NY 10301
(800) 223–2732

Living Will Registry

Society for the Right to Die
Living Will Registration Service
250 W. Fifty-seventh Street
New York, NY 10107

The Medical Directive

Harvard Medical School Health Letter
164 Longwood Avenue, 4th floor
Boston, MA 02115
($1.00 and self-addressed stamped
 envelope.)

Organ Donation

Health Resources and Services
 Administration
Division of Organ Transplantation
5600 Fishers Lane
Rockville, MD 20857

Self-Delivery (for terminally ill patients)

Hemlock Society
P. O. Box 11830
Eugene, OR 97440

Values History

The University of New Mexico
Institute of Public Law
School of Law
1117 Stanford NE
Albuquerque, NM 87131

BIOMEDICAL ETHICS ORGANIZATIONS AND HEALTH DECISION GROUPS

Northeast Region

Acadia Institute
118 West Street
Bar Harbor, ME
(207) 288–4082

American Society of Law and Medicine
520 Commonwealth Avenue
Boston, MA 02215
(617) 262–4990

Boston University School
 of Public Health
Center for Law and Health Sciences
209 Bay State Road
Boston, MA 02215
(617) 353–2910

College of the Holy Cross
Department of Religious Studies
Worcester, MA 10706
(508) 793–2011

Dartmouth Medical School
Program in Medical Ethics
Hanover, NH 0375
(603) 646–7505

Massachusetts Health Decisions
101 Tremont Street #600
Boston, MA 02108
(617) 784–1966

Vermont Ethics Network
103 South Main Street
Waterbury, VT 05676
(802) 241–2920

Mid-Atlantic Region

Albert Einstein College of Medicine
of Yeshiva University
Department of Social Medicine
1300 Morris Park Avenue
Bronx, NY 10461
(212) 430–3574

Citizens' Committee on
Biomedical Ethics, Inc.
Oakes Outreach Center
120 Morris Avenue
Summit, NJ 07901-3948
(908) 277–3858

Columbia University College of
Physicians and Surgeons
Center for the Study of Society and
Medicine
630 W. 168th Street
New York, NY 10032
(212) 305–3592

Edinboro University of Pennsylvania
Department of Philosophy
Edinboro, PA 16444
(814) 732–2604

New York Citizens' Committee
On Health Care Decisions
16 E. Ninety-sixth Street
New York, NY 10128

Pennsylvania State University
College of Medicine
Department of Humanities
Milton S. Hershey Medical Center
Hershey, PA 18020
(717) 534–8778

Society for Health and Human Values
1100 Witherspoon Building
Philadelphia, PA 19107
(215) 735–1551

Southeast Region

Bioethics Resource Group
118 Colonial Avenue
Charlotte, NC 28207
(704) 332–4421

East Carolina University School
of Medicine
Department of Medical Humanities
Greenville, NC 27858
(919) 551–2618

George Washington University
School of Medicine
Department of Health Sciences
1229 Twenty-fifth Street, NW
Washington, DC 20037
(202) 676–4269

Georgia Health Decisions
Eggleston Children's Hospital
1405 Clifton Road
Atlanta, GA 30322
(404) 325–6185

Tennessee Guild for Health Decisions
CCC-5319 Medical Center North
Vanderbilt University Medical Center
Nashville, TN 37232-2351
(615) 883–3248

University of North Carolina
at Chapel Hill School of Medicine
Department of Social
and Administrative Medicine
Chapel Hill, NC 27514
(919) 962-1136

University of South Florida
School of Medicine
Division for the Study of Human Values
in Medicine
Department of Comprehensive Medicine
13301 N. Thirtieth Street
Tampa, FL 33612
(813) 974-3294

University of Tennessee College
of Medicine
Program on Human Values and Ethics
956 Court Street
Memphis, TN 38163
(901) 528-5686

University of Virginia
Department of Religious Studies
Charlottesville, VA 22903
(804) 924-6709

University of West Virginia
Center for Health Ethics and Law
107 Crestview Drive
Morgantown, WV 26505
(304) 598-3484

Midwest Region

Case Western Reserve
University School of Medicine
Center for Biomedical Ethics
2119 Abington Road
Cleveland, OH 44106
(216) 368-2828

Medical College of Wisconsin
Bioethics Center
8701 Watertown Plank Rd.
P. O. Box 2509
Milwaukee, WI 53226
(414) 257-8498

Michigan State University
College of Human Medicine
Medical Humanities Program
East Lansing, MI 48824
(517) 355-7550

Midwest Bioethics Center
410 Archibald, Suite 106
Kansas City, MO 64111
(816) 942-1992

Minnesota Network for Institutional
Ethics Committees
2221 University Avenue SE, Suite 425
Minneapolis, MN 55414
(612) 331-5571

St. Louis University Medical Center
Center for Health Care Ethics
1438 S. Grand Boulevard
St. Louis, MO 63104
(314) 773-0646

Southern Illinois University
School of Medicine
Medical Humanities Program
801 North Rutledge
P. O. Box 3926
Springfield, IL 62708
(217) 782-4261

Stritch School of Medicine
Medical Humanities Program
Loyola University Medical Center,
Building 54, Room 114B
2160 S. First Avenue
Maywood, IL 60153
(312) 531-3433

University of Chicago
Section of General Internal Medicine
Pritzker School of Medicine
5841 S. Maryland Avenue
Chicago, IL 60637
312-962-3045

University of Illinois Health
  Sciences Center
Humanistic Studies Program
808 S. Wood Street
Chicago, IL 60612
(312) 996–7216

University of Michigan School
  of Public Health
Program in Public Health Nursing
Ann Arbor, MI 48109
(313) 764–5464

University of Minnesota
Biomedical Ethics Center
Mayo Memorial Building
420 Delaware Street SE
Minneapolis, MN 55455
(612) 625–4917

University of Wisconsin Center
  for Health Sciences
Program in Medical Ethics
470 N. Charter Street
Madison, WI 53706
(608) 263–3414

Wisconsin Health Decisions
Lawrence University Program
  in Bioethics
Box 599
Appleton, WI 54912
(414) 832–6647

Southwest Region

Arizona Health Decisions
Box 4401
Prescott, AZ 86302
(606) 778–4850

Baylor College of Medicine
Center for Ethics, Medicine
  and Public Issues
One Baylor Plaza
Houston, TX 77030
(713) 799–6290

Ecumenical Center for Religion
  and Health
4507 Medical Drive
San Antonio, TX 78229
(512) 696–9966

New Mexico Health Decisions
501 Carlyle Boulevard
Albuquerque, NM 87106
(505) 255–6717

University of Arizona College
  of Medicine
Division of Social Perspectives in
  Medicine
1505 N. Campbell Avenue
Tucson, AZ 85724
(602) 626–6506

University of Nevada School of Medicine
Program in Medical Ethics
Reno, NV 89557
(702) 784–6001

University of Texas Medical School
  at Galveston
Medical Humanities Program
Institute for the Medical Humanities
301 University Boulevard
Galveston, TX 77550
(409) 761–2376

Western Region

California Health Decisions
505 S. Main Street, Suite 400
Orange, CA 92668
(714) 647–4920

Colorado Speaks Out On Health
Campus Box 133 UCD
P. O. Box 173364
Denver, CO 80217-3364
(303) 556–4837

Nebraska Health Decisions
Lincoln Medical Center Association
4600 Valley Road
Lincoln, NE 68510
(402) 483–4537

Northwest Institute of Ethics and the Life
  Sciences
1416 East Thomas Street
Seattle, WA 98112
(206) 322–2165

Oregon Health Decisions
921 SW Washington, Suite 723
Portland, OR 97205
(503) 241–0744

Rose Medical Center
Center for Applied Biomedical Ethics
4567 E. Ninth Avenue
Denver, CO 80220
(303) 320–2101

Sisters of St. Joseph of Orange
  Health System
Center for Bioethics
404 South Batavia Street
Orange, CA 92668
(714) 997–7690

University of California Los Angeles
  School of Medicine
Program in Medicine, Law and
  Human Values
2859 Slichter Hall
Los Angeles, CA 90024
(213) 825–4976

University of California San Francisco
  School of Medicine
Health Policy Program in Bioethics
1362 Third Avenue
San Francisco, CA 94143
(415) 476–3093

Canada

Clinical Research Institute of Montreal
Center of Bioethics
110 Pine Avenue W.
Montreal, Quebec H2W 1R7
(514) 842–1481

McGill University Faculty of Medicine
Humanities and Social Studies in
  Medicine
3655 Drummond Street
Montreal, Quebec H3G 1Y6
(514) 392–4226

University of Calgary Faculty
  of Medicine
Medical Bioethics Program
3330 Hospital Drive, NW
Calgary, Alberta T2N 4N1
(403) 284–6541

STATE DEPARTMENTS OF HEALTH

Alabama Department of Public Health
(205) 242–5052

Alaska Department of Health and Social
  Services
(907) 465–3030

Arizona Department of Health
  Services
(602) 542–1024

Arkansas Department of Health
(501) 661–2111

California Department of Health Services
(916) 445–1248

Colorado Department of Health
(303) 331–4600

Connecticut Department of Health
Services
(203) 739–4701

Delaware Division of Public Health
(302) 739–4701

District of Columbia Department of
Human Services
(202) 673–7700

Florida Health and Rehabilitative
Services
(904) 488–2381

Georgia Department of Human
Resources
(404) 894–7505

Hawaii Department of Health
(808) 548–6505

Idaho Department of Health and Welfare
(208) 334–5700

Illinois Department of Public Health
(217) 782–4977

Indiana State Board of Health
(317) 633–8400

Iowa Department of Health
(515) 281–5605

Kansas Department of Health and
Enviroinment
(913) 296–1343

Kentucky Department of Health
(502) 564–3970

Louisiana Department of Health and
Hospitals
(504) 568–5050

Maine Department of Human Services
(207) 289–2736

Maryland Department of Health and
Mental Hygiene
(301) 225–6500

Massachusetts Department of Public
Health
(617) 335–8024

Michigan Department of Public Health
(517) 335–8024

Minnesota Department of Health
(612) 623–5460

Mississippi Department of Health
(601) 354–6646

Missouri Department of Health
(314) 751–6001

Montana Health Services Division
(406) 444–2037

Nebraska Department of Health
(402) 471–2133

Nevada Department of Human Resources
(702) 885–4740

New Hampshire Department of Health
and Welfare
(603) 271–4505

New Jersey Department of Health
(609) 275–8714

New Mexico Department of Health and
Environment
(505) 984–2000

New York Department of Health
(518) 474–2011

North Carolina Division of Health
  Services
(919) 733–3446

North Dakota Department of Health
(701) 224–2372

Ohio Department of Health
(614) 466–2253

Oklahoma Health Division
(503) 229–5032

Pennsylvania Department of Health
(717) 783–2500

Rhode Island Department of Health
(401) 277–2231

South Carolina Health and
  Environmental Control
(803) 734–4880

Tennessee Department of Health and
  Environment
(615) 741–3111

Texas Department of Health
(512) 458–7375

Utah Department of Health
(801) 538–6111

Vermont Department of Health
(802) 863–7280

Virginia Department of Health
(804) 786–3561

Washington Department of Health
(206) 586–5846

West Virginia Health and Human
  Resources Department
(304) 348–2400

Wisconsin Health and Social Services
  Department
(608) 266–1511

Wyoming Health and Social Services
  Department
(307) 777–7121

Living Will Legislation in the United States

All appropriate documents and guidelines are available from the Society.

Enacted Laws: Alabama, Alaska, Arizona, Arkansas, California, Colorado, Connecticut, Delaware, Florida, Georgia, Hawaii, Idaho, Illinois, Indiana, Iowa, Kansas, Kentucky, Louisiana, Maine, Maryland, Minnesota, Mississippi, Missouri, Montana, Nevada, New Hampshire, New Mexico, North Carolina, North Dakota, Oklahoma, Oregon, South Carolina, South Dakota, Tennessee, Texas, Utah, Vermont, Virginia, Washington, West Virginia, Wisconsin, Wyoming and the District of Columbia.

1991 Bills: Massachusetts, Michigan, Nebraska, New Jersey, New York, Ohio, Pennsylvania and Rhode Island.

State Law Governing
Durable Power of Attorney • Health Care Agents
• Proxy Appointments •

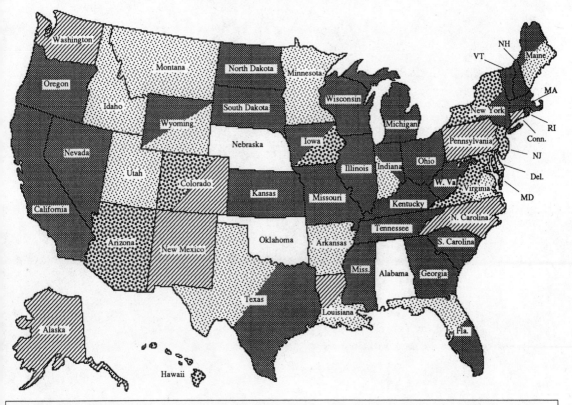

Documents are available from the Society for states that clearly recognize an agent's power to have life support withheld or withdrawn.

Jurisdictions with Durable Power of Attorney statutes that permit agents to make medical decisions, specifically including decisions to withdraw or withhold life support (**the District of Columbia and 28 states: California, Florida, Georgia, Illinois, Iowa, Indiana, Kansas, Kentucky, Maine, Massachusetts, Michigan, Mississippi, Missouri, Nevada, New Hampshire, New York, North Dakota, Ohio, Oregon, Rhode Island, South Carolina, South Dakota, Tennessee, Texas, Vermont, West Virginia, Wisconsin and Wyoming**). The agent can act when the patient loses the ability to make his or her own medical decisions.

States with Durable Power of Attorney statutes that positively authorize consent to medical treatment, but do not specifically authorize the withdrawal or withholding of life support (**8 states: Alaska, Colorado, Connecticut, Louisiana, New Mexico, North Carolina, Pennsylvania and Washington**).

States with Durable Power of Attorney statutes that, through court decisions, Attorney Generals' Opinions or other statutes, have been interpreted to permit agents to make medical decisions, including those to withhold or withdraw life support (**8 states: Arizona, Colorado, Hawaii, Iowa, Maryland, New Jersey, New York and Virginia**).

States that authorize proxy appointments through their "living will" or "natural death" acts (**13 states: Arkansas, Delaware, Florida, Idaho, Indiana, Louisiana, Maine, Minnesota, Montana, Texas, Utah, Virginia and Wyoming**). Proxies are permitted to make decisions authorized by the act when the patient is in a medical condition covered by the act (usually "terminal" as defined in the act).

States with general Durable Power of Attorney statutes that make no mention of medical decisions. (An Oklahoma Attorney General's Opinion states that the general Durable Power of Attorney **cannot** provide the authority to delegate health care decisionmaking.)

About the Authors

Evan R. Collins, Jr. has been a member of the board of the Society for the Right to Die since 1978, and its president since 1983. He has four children and one grandchild. Previously a partner in Kidder, Peabody & Co., Inc., he is currently vice president and resident officer with Prudential Securities in Westport, Connecticut. He believes that the U.S. Bill of Rights guarantees the nation's citizens freedom from intervention in their personal decisions, and that the control of medical treatment and the process of dying is the quintessential example of those rights in action. As an amateur race car driver he is especially aware that life and death issues are intimately present, every day of our lives.

Doron Weber is the former communications director of the Society for the Right to Die and a frequent media spokesperson for the rights of patients to control treatment decisions. He has appeared on national and international television, lectured at colleges, hospitals and community centers, and has debated the right to die issue on radio across the country. He has written widely on health and policy issues, and is the co-author of *Safe Blood: Purifying the Nation's Blood Supply in the Age of AIDS* (Free Press, 1990). His articles have appeared in the *Baltimore Evening-Sun, Barron's, Longevity,* and the *Village Voice,* among others.

Fenella Rouse is president of Concern for Dying and executive director of the Society for the Right to Die, and has worked for the Society as an attorney since 1983. She is known as a speaker and writer on behalf of patients' rights at the end of life, and has lectured nation-wide at conferences on these issues, including the National Health Policy Forum, the American Society of Law and Medicine, and the American Hospital Association.